W9-CFI-936

KITCHEN
Memories

Alexandra Greeley is the author of several cookbooks—including *Good Enough to Eat; Asian Grills; Asian Soups, Stews & Curries; Mexico;* and several cookbooks on Vietnamese and Thai cooking—and was a coauthor of the 2005 *Vegetarian Times Complete Cookbook.*

A CAPITAL LIFESTYLES BOOK—
OTHER BOOKS IN THE SERIES INCLUDE:

The Asian Diet: Get Slim and Stay Slim the Asian Way
by Diana My Tran

The Family Table: Where Great Food, Friends and Family Gather Together
by Christy Rost

The Kitchen Answer Book: Answers to All of Your Kitchen and Cooking Questions
by Hank Rubin

Nosthimia! The Greek American Family Cookbook
by Georgia Sarianides

Sabroso! The Spanish-American Family Cookbook
by Noemi Christina Taylor

Savvy Eating for the Whole Family: Whole Foods, Whole Family, Whole Life
by Margaret McCullers Kocsis, MD

Tea & Etiquette: Taking Tea for Business and Pleasure
by Dorothea Johnson

Upper Crusts: Fabulous Ways to Use Bread
by Sheilah Kaufman

Save 25% when you order any of these and other fine Capital titles from our website: www.capital-books.com.

KITCHEN
Memories

A LEGACY OF FAMILY RECIPES FROM AROUND THE WORLD

Anne Snape Parsons
Alexandra Greeley

Capital Lifestyles Series

CAPITAL
BOOKS, INC.
Sterling, Virginia

Copyright © 2007 by Anne Snape Parsons and Alexandra Greeley

All rights reserved. No part of this book may be reproduced or utilized in any form or by any means, electronic or mechanical, including photocopying, recording, or by any information storage and retrieval system, without permission in writing from the publisher. Inquiries should be addressed to:

Capital Books, Inc.
P.O. Box 605
Herndon, Virginia 20172-0605

ISBN 13: 978-1-933102-45-0 (alk. paper)

Library of Congress Cataloging-in-Publication Data
Parsons, Anne Snape.
Kitchen memories : a legacy of family recipes from around the world / Anne Snape Parsons, Alexandra Greeley.
p. cm. — (Capital series)
ISBN 978-1-933102-45-0 (alk. paper)
1. Cookery, International. 2. Food habits. I. Greeley, Alexandra. II. Title. III. Series.

TX725.A1P337 2007
641.59—dc22

2007010989

Printed in the United States of America on acid-free paper that meets the American National Standards Institute Z39-48 Standard.

First Edition

10 9 8 7 6 5 4 3 2 1

We dedicate this book to all our children—
Douglas, Heather, Jennifer, and Albert;
Michael, Kathy, Christopher, Nicci, and Susan;
and to all our grandchildren—
Tucker, Mikayla, Jackson, John, Spencer, and Grant . . .
and to all the generations to come—
so they never forget family times.

*Tucker, Douglas, and
Heather Arcos.*
Sharon Little

*Albert Chou and
Jennifer Parsons.*

*Susan Greeley and
Lakota.*

*John, Nicci, Grant, Spencer, and
Christopher Greeley.*

*Mikayla, Kathy, Jackson, and
Michael Greeley.* Paige Brown

CONTENTS

FOREWORD

*W*hen I studied food at New York University, I did so through the lens of Performance Studies, an excellent discipline for examining feasts because its focus on theater lends itself to investigating the entire food event rather than just the food itself. Indeed, a holiday feast—and certainly a family gathering—is a charged performance with the table as center stage, actors, scripts, climax, a backstage, and props.

Tragically, with the arrival of TV dinners, drive-through meals eaten in the back of SUVs, and frenetic schedules that keep families apart at meal time, not only are these performances at risk but also the many age-old recipes passed down for generations around which these events revolve. I applaud this book for being among the first to chronicle so many of these recipes and traditions so that they might not be forgotten just when we need them most.

One of my favorite aspects to a feast or a family meal is that choice and abundance are key. As with any rite of passage, the host must be generous, and the objective must be that the meal etches itself in memory: the most expensive food, numerous courses, the best utensils, the nicest costumes are all on display. In medieval times, European nobility used to color food gold with saffron to demonstrate the power of the host and to show respect towards the guest.

The actors are also part of the performance: when a guest enters the dining area, he crosses a charged threshold. The importance of his role can be determined by where he is seated—near the host, above or below "the salt," at the head of the table or at the end, at the children's table or with the grownups. No matter where you sit, any actor must come with a stimulating script. Whether it is the retelling of old stories or witty response to a moment in time, when you attend an event that only happens once a year, you better bring it!

Perhaps the most fascinating aspect to any gathering of friends and family for me is what happens backstage: secret ingredients, timing the arrival of different dishes, presentation, competition between parents and children on how they perform traditions, comments made on the down-low about the taste of the food.

But none of this would happen without the food and the recipes that mold it. While the decorations and conversation can bring pleasure, it is the food that creates the single emotion that is the goal of every great recipe: epiphany, marvel, ravishment, magnificence. In this century, with the industrialization of the food supply, disappearance of the family farm, fast food, and the loss of the table as the center of all human interaction, it is more important than ever to read this book and re-enact the traditions that have meaning to you.

I applaud Anne and Alexandra for reminding us to slow down and remember the wise words of the Slow Food Manifesto: "A firm defense of quiet material pleasure is the only way to oppose the universal folly of Fast Life."

Ciao,
Patrick Martins
Founder of Slow Food USA
Co-founder Heritage Foods

PREFACE: ANNE SNAPE PARSONS

The pleasure of the table belongs to all ages, to all conditions, to all countries, and to all areas; it mingles with all other pleasures, and remains at last to console us for their departure.
—Jean Anthelme Brillat-Savarin (1755–1826)

*N*othing is as comforting as a freshly baked scone slathered with fresh raspberry jam and daubed with thick clotted cream. My taste buds salivate as they anticipate the first bite of that thick, moist wedge of sublimity. No wonder, then, that as a wee lass growing up in Bothwell-park Rows, Scotland, I loved to watch my rotund Aunt Aggie bake scones at the long wooden table while her brood of thirteen children swarmed through the scullery (kitchen). She didn't have any fancy gadgets, just a big bowl, a rolling pin, a sharp knife, and a large spoon and fork.

Among all this chaos, Auntie would bake and hum and lift the tray of scones above the heads of these scalawags as she twirled around and stuck it in the oven. As the enticing smell of the scones seeped out from the oven and filled the kitchen, I'd close my eyes, inhale, and feel giddy. For me, that aroma is a trigger that takes me back to a time when I was young and unfettered and loved to run barefoot through the grass. It takes me to a time when the craft of baking and cooking was at its best—family recipes worked by hand with local, seasonal ingredients.

There is simply no comparison between locally grown produce and mass-produced imports. Granny and Daddy carefully raised and tended all their own vegetables—beetroot, carrots, turnips, potatoes, leeks, cauliflower, cabbage, and peas. Everything in the garden was laid out in neat, tidy rows. When Granny peeled a cooked beetroot straight from the pot and handed me some slices, I would eagerly devour those pieces of nirvana.

To me, every culture has its roots in the soil, and locally produced food determines the characteristics of its cuisine. Although I emigrated from Scotland in my twenties, to this day when I see someone trim the dough around a pie or smell scones baking in the oven, like Proust's scent of madeleines, I feel a tremendous nostalgia for "auld lang syne."

In these days of homogeny, fast foods, and the demise of home cooking, I worry that family recipes and cooking secrets will forever disappear. After speaking with my friend, Alexandra Greeley, we decided to collaborate on a cookbook that is a compilation of family recipes handed down from one generation to the next. We spoke to hundreds of people who shared their most valued recipes, the ones that they want to pass on to their children and grandchildren. In doing this, we found that talking about family recipes usually triggers happy childhood memories of mealtimes, family members, or special moments.

After all, whether it is a Queen Anne table, a fold-up stand, a Persian rug, a picnic bench, or whatever works as a dining area, all that matters is the camaraderie and fun that ensues when friends and family gather to eat. I'm sure many of you notice that guests often congregate around the kitchen—could it be a primordial instinct that draws them to the source of the food? It is not unusual for our eclectic dinner guests to spend hours sitting around the kitchen table talking, debating, and sharing various points of view. I consider it a celebration of our cultural diversity.

My husband, Jimmy, and I are convinced that serving traditional family meals, from many parts of the world, is a great way to teach our children about their ancestral roots, and the holidays that distinguish cultures and religions. Since food is a fundamental factor in most celebrations, the dinner table is the ideal place to excite the senses, to savor traditional cuisines, and to cultivate a culinary taste for other cultures that affects and enhances the texture of our lives.

This book opens the door to a world full of exhilarating colors, tastes, and textures, where we hang up our coat of limited cuisine and enter a room in which the sights, aromas, and sounds of cooking stimulate our taste buds and awaken us to a celebration of other cultures. But, more importantly, we hope that this book will invite all our children—and your children and grandchildren—to take the time to preserve their family's favorite recipes and food memories.

Anne Snape Parsons

PREFACE: ALEXANDRA GREELEY

*W*hile visiting the Malaysian island of Penang some years ago, I toured the island with a local woman who was talking about the culture and history of her hometown. When I spotted a fast-food outlet near a popular beach area, I asked about it. It seemed very out of place, I thought. Her answer made a profound impression and may well have changed the course of my cooking and food life. She lamented the arrival of such modern Western food fads and fast-food alternatives because her children and their friends wanted to eat only hamburgers, pizzas, and french fries. She worried that within a few years, none of the younger generation—not even her children—would remember or even prepare any of the old-fashioned traditional dishes of her country. Family recipes and cooking secrets would disappear forever, she said.

As I traveled around Asia, I found the same story elsewhere—the loss of traditional recipes, and even more distressing, the loss of food memories and traditional cooking techniques. The lure of American fast foods is seductive for the young locals who want to copy everything they see on television, and that includes eating pizzas and hamburgers instead of chicken satay and rich coconut curries. One chef on the Indonesian island of Bali told me that the advent of television had probably changed the lives of the islanders more than anything else he could imagine: where once the locals used biodegradable and disposable banana leaves as an all-purpose kitchen device and eating utensil/plate, they had turned to foil and Styrofoam and now found their landscapes littered.

Even Asians who emigrate to the United States quickly abandon their old culinary ways to become assimilated in their new society. While aunties and grannies continue to cook traditional dishes in their new homes, the younger generations flee to fast-food eateries and eschew their native cuisine. One Malaysian lady, living in the suburbs of Washington, D.C., remarked that two of her three sons would no longer eat Malaysian food, preferring instead hot dogs and spaghetti. Is it possible that in several generations, so many Asians will have forgotten their native foods?

But such culinary changes are not limited to Asia, nor probably even to the United States. Can it be that modern life with its snappy appliances and easy-do convenience foods will end noble culinary traditions? To help prevent such gastronomic losses, organizations such as Slow Food, dedicated in part to the premise that our culinary heritage should be honored and preserved, are finding growing support. The Slow Food movement has certainly galvanized me, and in part, inspired this book, a gathering of generations of family recipes. May my children—and your children—remember the pleasures of the traditional table and of foods carefully and lovingly prepared . . . from scratch.

Alexandra Greeley

ACKNOWLEDGMENTS

WITH MUCH APPRECIATION TO . . .

A book like this comes together only when individuals reflect on their own histories and food stories, and then willingly share their thoughts and recipes. This cookbook is a tribute to our precious families, and to all our eclectic friends—old and new—who shared their memories, their recipes, and allowed us into the private kitchens of their lives.

Nina Alexiou
Clara Andonian
Rosemary Antsey
Douglas James Arcos
Heather McCready Arcos
Chef Chuck Arnold (Meridian 42 Restaurant)
Norma Auer
Dr. Sambhu Banik
Russell Bates
Harold and Marty Batsel
Giovanna Biagi
Alison Bigelow
Helen Bigelow
Ruth Bown
Paige Brown
Deborah Burns

Albert Chou
Brian Chou
Bora Chu
Alice Leather Cleland
Ronald Cleland
Janet Colegrove
Donna Countryman
Yolande Crozier
Nongkran Daks
Serena di Liberto
Annie Dingwall
Bryan Ellis (Meridian 42 Restaurant)
Bunty Fernon
Patricia Fernon
Dah Fwu Fine
Kwang-Yen Hsu Fine

Helen Flenley
Elmira Friedman
Christopher Greeley, MD
Michael Greeley
Susan Greeley
Patricia Grimshaw
Jon Gudbrandsson
Rennie Hackmann
Mary Hager
Chef Evan Hayes (Meridian 42 Restaurant)
Nancy Alice Holmes
Sosie Hublitz
Jane Buckley Kaddouri
Malika Kaddouri
Ajit Kalra
Lan Kaufman
Alan Kiernan
Vivian Lawson
Dr. Neou Leakhena
Sofia Lee
Jennifer Lewis
Tammy Lewis
Serena di Liberto
Sharon Little
Carla Hall Lyons
Joyce Cleland MacLeod
Catherine McOrmond
George and Isabel McPhee
Gosia Malicka
Marisa Manus
Nittaya Maphungphong
Humberto Martinez
Sumenesh Merawi
Martine Monette
Karla Montano
Richard (Dick) Murphy
Jill Neilson
Lindsay Neilson
Regina Wojtecki Bianchi O'Connor

Chef Hiroyuki Ohashi
Chef Kaz Okochi
Alice Olteanu
Lea O'Quinn
Ezzat Parsa
Jennifer Parsons
Tahmineh Parsons
Bob Pokelwaldt
Don Pokelwaldt
Gloria Pokelwaldt
Norm Pokelwaldt
Bunny Polmer
Montha C. Prom
David Quang
Brigitte Rasmussen
Yoko Murase Ray
Richard (Dick) Rodine
Nikki Rose
Minhaj Saiyid
Chef Sudhir Seth
Tooran Shadman
Chef Grant Sharp (Meridian 42 Restaurant)
Jill Sheffer
David and Doreen Smith
James C. Smith
Jean Curnow Smith
Thomas and May Smith
Fred Speno
Nick Srisawat
Mary Sweeney
Judy Turpin
Seth Underwood
Victor Vazquez
Petch Vailikit
Kuei-Fang Wang
John White
Elizabeth (Peggy) Williams
Peg Williams
Yoko Zoll

For all the big and little details and for all the good advice, good cheer, and helping hands, a special thanks to:

Jim Parsons, who gave unending support, encouragement, advice, and insight—and for tasting everything we put in front of him;

Patrick Martins, formerly of Slow Food USA and now of Heritage Foods, who wrote the foreword;

Douglas James Arcos, who copied and edited all the photos, and designed and manages the cookbook website— www.familyfoodmemories.com;

Susan Greeley for her tasting comments and cheerfully eating leftovers;

Michael Greeley and Christopher and Nicci Greeley, for their patience and support;

Mary Hager, for her sage advice;

Bill and Sandra Brew, Rue Capri, Brian Chou, Mary Hager, Nancy Holmes, Margo Moser, Jennifer Parsons, and Judy Turpin for their recipe testing and proofreading;

To the women of the Outer Banks of North Carolina who tested and re-tested so many of these recipes . . . Norma Auer, Marty Batsel, Janet Colegrove, Donna Countryman, Rennie Hackmann, Catherine McOrmond, Jill Neilson, and Jill Sheffer.

Please Note:

Anne Snape Parsons and Alexandra Greeley decided to divvy up the chapters, the recipe testing, the introduction writing, and the research, primarily by the countries and cuisines they know best. While both authors share recipes for some of the chapters, by and large, each was responsible for the following:

Anne Snape Parsons

Austria-Germany, Bolivia, Canada, England, France, Iran, Ireland, Italy, Morocco, Poland, Scandinavia, Scotland, Spain, Wales

Alexandra Greeley

Argentina, Armenia, Cambodia, China, Greece, India, Japan, Mexico, Thailand, USA, Vietnam

INTRODUCTION

FROM CAVE TO KITCHEN

*F*or many thousands of years, our species ate raw food. Historians believe sometime between 1,400,000 BC (in Africa) and 500,000 BC (in Asia) humans discovered fire, and cooking was born. So, what came next—did people then create cultural celebrations to coincide with the seasons, or did they use feasts to honor their gods?

This book is not intended to be encyclopedic or a historic treatise. It is written to rescue, share, and increase our repertoire of treasured family recipes and to ensure that traditional methods of cooking are not lost.

Let's begin with the piece of meat that accidentally fell into the embers of a fire, got good and roasted, and, voilà, a new form of cuisine was born. At least, that's how some cultural anthropologists explain the genesis of cooking. Other cultural anthropologists counter with such theories as a hut burning down with pigs inside and the inhabitants sampling the roasted meat.

Curiously enough, archaeologists contend that cooking did not evolve any further until cooking pots were invented. Yet, artifacts from archaeological excavations in the Ukraine and Moravia indicate that in 13,000 BC, leather skins were used for cooking, and, circa 7000 BC, the peoples of the Tehuacan Valley of Central America were using stone cooking pots.

Of course, cultural anthropological evidence shows that as cultures developed, so did their ingenuity in using leaves, bamboo, and animal shells for cooking. Many of these methods are still in use today in such areas as Indonesia, where they use bamboo sections stuffed with food; in India, where fish is cooked in banana leaves; and around the globe, where there is the ever-present campfire with food on a stick. Prior to pottery, bronze, and then iron, the most-used container that was both waterproof and heatproof—if suspended over a fire—was an animal's stomach, and it is still used today as a casing for haggis.

Food historians believe that ancient hunters and gatherers used caves for storage and refrigeration, and, by the third millennium BC, Egyptians and Mesopotamians used fermentation, and ancients developed various methods of pickling.[1] With climatic changes, around 12,000 BC, came conditions that supported fast-growing plants, so Neolithic tribes moved their settlements closer to areas where plants grew. Villages sprang up and sustained the hunter-gatherers, and as villagers became more knowledgeable about planting, they became farmers.

ENTERTAINING, MENU PLANNING, AND RECIPES

Feasts, or banquets, became the standard method of entertaining important guests, so the quality and presentation of the food reflected on the host. During the Roman Empire, slaves were plentiful and cooks had more sous-chefs than they could put to work. According to Roman historians, Marcus Gavius Apicius wrote two cookbooks in the first century AD. The first, *De condituris*, concentrated only on sauces. These recipes were later absorbed into the second book, *De re coquinaria*, known as one of the earliest complete cookbooks. Pliny the Younger, first century AD (63–113), a Roman senator, lawyer, and author, credited Apicius with force-feeding geese with figs to enlarge their livers, indicating that *foie gras* originated in Italy and not France.

Even taking a brief look at 6000 years of recorded history, one cannot deny the pivotal part that spices and sugar play in the economics, politics, and celebrations of modern civilization. Many people think of spices as something to perk up their suppers, but spices were formerly treasured as medicines, perfumes, ointments, and embalming preservatives. Historical records indicate that onions and garlic were fed to 100,000 laborers in the construction of the Great Pyramid of Cheops (2600–2100 BC). Although the ancient Asians gave the West such spices as pepper, ginger, turmeric, and mace, beginning as early as the thirteenth century,

---

[1] Encyclopaedia Brittanica, 15th Ed., Vol. 19, "Food Processing."

when Marco Polo first saw the commercial potential in Hangzhou—where Persians and Arabs haggled over prices—the subtle use of such herbs and spices as dill, fennel, mustard seed, saffron, sage, and cumin can be traced to the Middle East, where these ingredients remain a feature of many dishes.

In the meantime, throughout Europe, small herb gardens flourished. During his reign, Charlemagne, king of the Franks (742–814 AD), encouraged systematic plantings of such herbs as anise, fennel, and fenugreek in the imperial gardens. Religious feasts, based on spices, formerly celebrated by the Goths,[2] were later adapted by the Christian Church. Spiced drinks became an important part of monastery medicine, and throughout the Dark Ages, Benedictine monastery gardens cultivated numerous spices and herbs. The medieval German nun, St. Hildegard (1098–1179 AD) of Bingen, famed for her prophecies and visions, recorded much of the medieval botanical knowledge relating to the curative powers of natural objects for healing and wrote treatises about medicinal uses of plants, animals, and trees.

While feasting had been part of social entertaining in Roman and Greek colonies for centuries, the feast became an important political statement in medieval Europe (approximately 1100–1500 AD). When sugar and spices arrived at British ports from the Middle East, they were transported to royal and wealthy households. Although highly valued and expensive, medieval Europeans—at least those who could afford it—used spices to conceal the noxious smells of decomposing food, to enhance the flavors of rather dull cuisine, and to make their dishes more palatable. Naturally, the lady of the manor, or castle, kept the larder key and controlled the small amounts of sugar and spice allotted to the cook.

It was also this same lady, with assistants of course, who planned the menus, gathered the garden produce, arranged the placement of guests at the table, and worked closely with the cook to create dishes that titillated the palates of important guests.

According to Reay Tannahill, who wrote in her book *Food in History*: "If the last medieval cuisine of the West was directly indebted to any one source, it was to the Arabs, the cultural middlemen of the post-Classical world. From their synthesis of Roman, Persian and desert-

---

[2] Originally from Scandinavia, the Goths were an East Germanic tribe, some of whom migrated southward and conquered parts of the Roman Empire.

nomad foods, Europe's cooks borrowed many, perhaps most of the techniques and materials."

Medieval cooks used many of the foods currently in use today. They created meat pies filled with venison, beef, and pork; soups with wine and almonds; wild game and fowl accompanied by rich sauces; and fruit and sugar sculptures. Food sculpture such as the Helmeted Cock riding a suckling steed, the Cockentrice, half-pig and half-capon, and other eccentric viands graced the tables of the nobility. Most of the history of this medieval food is garnered from court catering records and the bookkeeping records of noble homes and monasteries.

In China between 960 and 1279 AD, during the Song Dynasty, regional cuisines emerged in three regions around the Yangtze River delta. While the Asian upper classes moved from sitting on the floor to chairs and continued to eat polished rice, their European counterparts developed more appetizing fare and the presentation of it. As trade increased, the merchant class grew and the middle classes' desire for more exciting foods increased. Too, as explorers mapped out new worlds, the demand for foreign foods gained momentum.

When Richard II came to the British throne in 1377 AD, his court was very sophisticated and shared many contemporary ideas in fashion and entertaining with his counterparts in the European capitals. Maggie Black writes in her book, *The Medieval Cookbook*: "At the royal table, dishes were tinted a regal gold with saffron, or might be striped or chequered in varied colors . . . The chronicler Hollingshead alleged that Richard had two thousand cooks. This is fanciful but his cuisine certainly became a byword for luxury." Not surprisingly, one of Richard's cooks wrote the first known English cookery book, "The Form of Cury" (cookery). In it there's a recipe for Afronchemoyle, a haggis: "Nym Eyren with al the wyte & myse bred & scheps talwe, get as dyse grynd pepr & safron & caste thereto & do hit in the schepys trype. Set it wel & dress it forth." Translation: Take eggs, with the white and the yolk together, and mix with breadcrumbs and finely diced sheep's fat. Season with pepper and saffron. Stuff a sheep's tripe with the mixture, sewing securely. Steam or boil and drain before serving." In any event, many of the top people in King Richard's court adopted the new conventions that included exaggerated styles and colors of clothing, and an increased interest in the developing culinary cuisine.

Not surprisingly, many in the nobility wanted to invest in the lucrative mercantile trade of exotic seasonings. To that end, banquets were held to elicit financial support from wealthy, or politically influential, allies willing to invest in the commodity market. To thwart the notion that the feast was a political fundraiser, the noble lady would choose a particular date, usually one that coincided with a Saint's Day, to entertain.

FAMILY RECIPES AND CULTURAL TRADITIONS

Jimmy Smith, a Scottish coal miner, always reminded his five children that "We're a' Jock Tamson's bairns"—we're all the creator's children. Certainly this truth is self-evident. Even though we spring from many latitudes and longitudes on the planet, all humans must eat . . . but what and how we eat defines our culture.

In many cultures, traditional dietary practices safeguarded our ancestors from many diseases, such as trichinosis. Until recently, staple foods such as rice in Asia, wheat, barley, and potatoes in Western Europe, kasha in Central Europe and Russia, and whole grains in the Middle East, coupled with local fresh meats and vegetables, served as the core of traditional diets. As we move further away from our roots and eat more mass-produced and imported foods, the balance of our life totters on the edge of inharmonious living with the rise in food-borne illnesses and the introduction of new pathogens such as E. coli. Yet, farming cultures are still integral to all societies, and the seasons still play a large part in our choice of foods. Perhaps for the cuisine of the future, we should draw upon the roots of our past, provided enough sustainable land remains to cultivate.

Supposedly, the human odyssey from eating raw food to savoring gourmet cuisine has come full circle. This journey is described succinctly in Meg Dods' cookbook, *The Scots Kitchen*, of 1826. She was the landlady of the Cleikum Inn, in St. Ronan's, near Peebles, Scotland. In describing the evolvement of man as a "cooking animal," Nabab, a member of the Cleikum Dining Club, says, "in whatever situation he is found, it may be assumed as an axiom, that his progress in civilization has kept exact pace with the degree of refinement he may have attained in the science of gastronomy. From the hairy man of the woods, digging his roots with his claws, to the refined banquet of the Greek, or the sumptuous entertainment of the Roman; from the ferocious hunter, gnawing the half-broiled bloody collop, torn from the still-reeking carcass, to the modern gourmet, apportioning his ingredients and blending his essences, the chain is complete."

But a mutant link has been added to the chain. From around the globe, processed foods are delivered to us in frozen packages that are quickly nuked in the microwave. However, globalization, for all its flaws, makes it possible to share the culinary heritage of other cultures, indeed to obtain the products and ingredients needed to re-create their recipes and celebrate their holidays.

Has our culinary heritage drifted off with the twilight skies? Surely not. Are we finally hearing the call of our atavistic roots that awaken each of us to our extraordinary heritage? We hope so.

As the light of spring returns to chase away the darkness of winter, as the cycle of life continues with the earth's regeneration and fertility, as summer unfolds and autumn reveals her bounty, isn't it time to resuscitate grandma's recipes? How else might we celebrate the favorite recipes and cooking traditions of friends and neighbors, whether next door or across the seas? Too, what better way to keep connected to our families—past, present, and future—than to preserve and share our culinary heritage with members of the global family?

Anne Snape Parsons

Argentina

- ♦ ARGENTINEAN BARBECUE (ASADO)

- ♦ RUSSIAN SALAD (ENSALADA RUSA)

- ♦ MEAT PIE (PASTEL DE PAPAS)

- ♦ BREAD PUDDING

*T*hink "tango" and you think Argentina. Think "beef" and chances are you will name Texas, Nebraska, or Kansas. But statistics show that as of this writing, Argentina's population numbers only about thirty-six million, yet the country is the second largest beef consumer in the world, second only to the United States.

Because of its vast fertile plains, known as the *pampas*, Argentina grows enough feed not only for its plentiful cattle but also for Argentinean cooks, who use the wheat and corn as staples. Shaped by the influx of Europeans settling in the country at the end of the nineteenth century and later, the cuisine is more European than indigenous native, with pastas, baked goods, vegetable dishes, and seafood as the foundation for local mealtimes.

Yet without question, beef—grilled or roasted over an open fire—forms the cornerstone of the cuisine. In fact, one of the most popular ways to entertain family and friends is to hold an *asado*, or a beef-roast barbecue; some restaurants even tap into this national passion by offering a whole roasted beef, including the hide. Other restaurants may offer an all-you-can-eat *asado*, featuring grilled beef, of course, but possibly also pork, lamb, and chicken.

Otherwise, beef turns up in many other forms, including *bife a caballo*, or "beef on horseback"; *parrillada*, a mixed grill of blood sausages, ribs, and other meat; *churrasco*, grilled steak; and *milanesa*, breaded and deep-fried steak. Beef—*chorizos* and other meats and fish—is everywhere, inspiring this popular saying written anonymously, "A vegetarian in Argentina is like a duck out of water."

Argentineans traditionally eat four meals a day, starting with a light breakfast of rolls and coffee. Lunches include a meat dish with vegetables or salad, or possibly pasta or pizza or *empanadas*; the afternoon snack at cafés consists of coffee and small dishes. And in the evening, the largest meal of the day usually includes beef.

As far as desserts, it seems that most people have a giant sweet tooth, for cooks have created delicious cookies, such as the *mil hojas*; puddings; cakes; and that ultimately wonderful sauce/spread, *dulce de leche*, or caramelized milk.

Gaucho resting at an estancia.
Anne Parsons

Argentinean Barbecue
ASADO

A native of Buenos Aires, Marisa Manus talks about the beef tradition in her country, remembering that at one time during her mother's youth, field hands would start their early day by drinking *mate* (a strong tealike beverage often served in a *bombilla* gourd with a metal straw), and for lunch, would have *asado* with red wine.

"That's what kept them strong. I remember when I would come home from school for lunch, all the construction workers were eating *asado*, and I would get very hungry," she says.

Carlos Manus barbecuing meat the Argentinean way. Justin Stegall

Mealtimes were important to her family because food was an important part of family life. "Once a week we ate rice with chicken, or noodles with meat stew. My mother was a very good cook," she says.

As for grilled meat—the cornerstone of Argentinean cooking—the men traditionally do the barbecuing, although women know how to barbecue. Her husband, Carlos Manus, has passed on the tradition and taught their son how to prepare the following, cooked with *chorizos* and served with the traditional *chimichurri* sauce usually made with garlic, herbs, and olive oil.

She suggests buying the cuts of meat from an Argentinean butcher and using short ribs, or select *vacio*—that is, flank steak. Typically, the cook covers the meat with kosher or granular salt at least two hours before cooking to prevent shrinkage. As with any barbecue, let the coals burn to the white-ash stage, and cook the meat to desired doneness. The *asado* is served with a green salad and the *ensalada rusa*.

Russian Salad
ENSALADA RUSA

Delicious with barbecued meats or on its own, this potato salad calls for more than just potatoes—Marisa Manus says she uses either canned, frozen, or fresh peas, carrots, and corn for this dish.

Salad
4 large potatoes
1 cup peas
1 cup diced carrots
1 cup corn kernels
4 hard-boiled eggs, peeled and
   diced

Golf Sauce (Salsa Golf)
1 cup mayonnaise
1 to 2 tablespoons ketchup
1 teaspoon Dijon mustard
pinch salt

Barbecue ready to serve with the potato salad. Justin Stegall

Boil and skin the potatoes, drain, and when cool enough to handle, cube them uniformly. Cook the peas, carrots, and corn in lightly salted water until tender; drain. Put the potato cubes, peas, carrots, and corn into a large mixing bowl. Add the eggs.

Mix the *Salsa Golf* by combining the mayonnaise, ketchup, mustard, and salt, and stirring well. Pour onto the salad, and toss gently before serving.

Serves 6 to 8.

Meat Pie

PASTEL DE PAPAS

Empanadas *eaten as an appetizer or an entrée.*
Anne Parsons

Marisa Manus remembers that her mother served this to her family often, but today it's become an old-fashioned dish not often served, except occasionally at restaurants in Buenos Aires. To simplify making this dish, buy ready-made mashed potatoes from the market; you will need enough to cover the meat with one inch of potatoes. If you want to make *empanadas*, use this meat mixture as a delicious filling. For a more intense tomato flavor, use two to three tomatoes.

2 tablespoons vegetable oil
2 large onions, diced
1 green pepper, diced
1 tomato, diced
1 pound 90-percent fat-free ground beef
2 hard-boiled eggs, chopped
1 cup pitted black olives
1/2 cup raisins
1 teaspoon dried oregano
salt to taste
freshly ground black pepper to taste
about 3 cups mashed potatoes, or more as needed

Preheat the oven to 350°F. Spray a 9x13-inch baking dish with nonstick spray.

Heat the oil in a large skillet over medium heat. Add the onions, and cook about 5 minutes, or until they turn golden. Add the green pepper and tomato, and cook until softened. Add the meat, breaking it apart, and sauté the mixture until the meat cooks through. Stir in the eggs, olives, raisins, oregano, salt, and pepper. Spoon the mixture into the prepared baking dish. Spread the mashed potatoes over top.

Bake for about 15 minutes, or until the potatoes start to brown. Serve hot.

Serves 8.

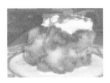 *Bread Pudding*

A family favorite, this dessert is one that Marisa Manus learned from her mother, and she still serves it to her family. "It is incredible," she says. You can add raisins to the soaking mixture, and serve the pudding with heavy cream or the Argentinean favorite, *dulce de leche*, a caramelized sweet-milk product.

4 cups whole milk
1 1/2 cups granulated sugar
3 eggs, lightly beaten with 1 teaspoon vanilla extract
8 slices of soft, white buttermilk bread, such as Wonder bread

Combine the milk, 1 cup sugar, and 3 beaten eggs in a large baking pan. Soak the bread in the mixture for 30 minutes.

Preheat the oven to 500°F.

Friends enjoying beef at an estancia. Anne Parsons

Heat the remaining 1/2 cup sugar in a saucepan over medium-low heat with about 1/4 cup water, stirring constantly, until the sugar melts and the mixture begins to darken and caramelize. Pour the sugar mixture into a heatproof and waterproof tube pan, such as an angel-food cake pan, or other 2-quart, heatproof baking dish. Stir the bread-egg mixture well, and pour it into the prepared pan. Set the tube pan into a larger pan, and add about 1 inch water.

Bake for 30 minutes, or until the top is browned and puffy. Cool. Refrigerate until cold, and serve cold.

Serves 6.

Armenia

- Small Pastries with Cheese and Parsley (Beurek)

- Armenian Meat Pizza (Lahmejun)

- Stuffed Meatballs (Harpoot Kufta)

- Armenian Bread (Lavash)

A land of mountains, rushing rivers, and fertile valleys, the Republic of Armenia has on its borders Georgia in the north, Azerbaijan on the east, Iran in the south, and Turkey on the west. Armenia is similar to New Mexico in size and topography. Because Armenia was at the crossroads of the main trade routes of Asia, Mesopotamia, and the Mediterranean, there were constant battles with invaders such as the Ottomans, Mongols, and Persians. However, Armenians were able to preserve an ethnic identity that perhaps is slightly embroidered with threads from those invading cultures.

Armenians claim that apricots and peaches originated in their country. It is not surprising, then, that there is an incredible variety of fresh fruits and vegetables, and that menus in most restaurants reflect only seasonal produce. For that reason, a visit to a *shuka* (fresh food market) is in order. Here you will discover fresh meat, fish, cheeses, spices, herbs, and produce. In the fields, Armenian farmers still grow wild rice and wheat as they have done for millennia.

In the home, Armenians welcome guests with open arms and a loaded dining table, filled with course after course of splendid food. Custom or courtesy dictates that guests should accept and eat at least one helping, or possibly two, but then may decline further offers so long as they have at least tasted everything once. Of course, people acknowledge that the best food comes from home cooks, who spend time and energy preparing and seasoning their specialties. They start with the freshest seasonal ingredients or naturally preserved ones for cold-weather eating, and then the cooks produce a cuisine that has been influenced by the numerous cultures that have invaded and inhabited the country. In general, one might describe the cuisine as bearing similarities to Middle Eastern cooking as lamb and eggplants, squash, and peppers are prevalent. But the discerning gastronome might also detect European and Indian influences.

Armenian women in traditional clothing at Slow Food's Terra Madre 2006. Anne Parsons

Fortunately, all the conquests and migrations have left the cuisine intact with recipes handed down from one generation to the next. And wherever a community of Armenians exists, you might hope to receive an invitation to at least drop in for coffee, at which time you will be honored with cookies and sweet pastries.

Small Pastries
with Cheese and Parsley
BEUREK

A professional cook and resident of the Outer Banks, in North Carolina, Sosie Hublitz comes by her love for cooking naturally: she grew up in a traditional, close-knit Armenian community in upstate New York. Hublitz tells Anne Parsons, "The Armenian way of eating is more like grazing. At family get-togethers, tables groan under the weight of all the food choices."

Hublitz's grandparents, Meerjohn and Antara Gergosian, immigrated to the United States from Govedoon, Armenia. They entered the United States through Ellis Island, in New York, and were relocated to a small town, called Massena, in upstate New York, where they and others in the Armenian community were employed by ALCOA. Hublitz's relatives still live there, and it remains an Armenian community to this day.

The following recipes are old family ones from the Gergosians, who still serve them at every gathering. Small pastries resembling turnovers, *beurek*, or *borek*, are often served as appetizers. Hublitz admits that nowadays it's so much easier to use phyllo dough, readily available in the frozen foods section of most supermarkets, than to make this dough from scratch. To use it, follow the package directions.

Sosie Hublitz's grandparents, Meerjohn and Antara Gergosian.
Hublitz's family album

Filling
4 tablespoons cottage cheese
6 ounces feta, Greek, or goat cheese, crumbled

10 ounces mozzarella cheese, grated
3 large eggs, well-beaten
1/2 cup minced parsley
2 tablespoons all-purpose flour
2 tablespoons vegetable oil

Dough
1 pound phyllo dough, thawed
1/2 pound (2 sticks) melted unsalted butter or margarine, plus extra for
   brushing pan

Preheat the oven to 350°F. Brush a 12x17-inch baking sheet with the melted butter.

Combine all the filling ingredients together in a bowl, and mix well.

Sheet by sheet, layer half the dough into the pan, brushing every other layer with the butter and folding in or trimming the edges as needed. Spread all the filling over the layers, and then continue layering and buttering in the same way until all the dough is used up. Brush the top layer with butter. Cut into 3-inch squares.

Bake about 30 minutes, or until golden brown. Cut through the squares once more, and serve hot.

Note: Always, always cover the dough that you are not immediately using with plastic wrap or a damp kitchen towel. If the phyllo dries out, it will become brittle to the touch, and you'll never be able to work with it. Don't worry if the pastry tears. Just brush butter on it, and layer on another sheet.

Makes 12 pieces.

Armenian Meat Pizza

LAHMEJUN

S osie Hublitz says that "to become part of an Armenian family, newlyweds cannot be gastronomically challenged." She goes on to explain that an integral part of any celebration or gathering is a table overflowing with an array of cold *meza* (appetizers), long loaves of *lavash*, condiments, fresh roasted vegetables, and slow-cooked meats, all followed by melt-in-your-mouth delicate pastries. Because Hublitz recognizes that any family event or celebration can be lots of work, she advises making the dough and filling for this dish the day before, and then assembling it before the guests arrive.

Dough
1 package (1 tablespoon) active dry yeast
1/2 cup warm water
1 teaspoon granulated sugar
5 cups all-purpose flour
1 tablespoon olive oil
1 teaspoon salt

Filling
1 pound ground beef or lamb, cooked until browned and drained
6 medium-sized fresh tomatoes, peeled and diced
1 cup tomato paste
1 bunch parsley, minced
1 green bell pepper, minced
3 cloves garlic, minced
1 teaspoon salt
1 teaspoon ground allspice
1/2 teaspoon crushed red pepper
1/2 teaspoon freshly ground black pepper

Sprinkle the yeast in a small bowl, and add the warm water and the sugar; stir well. Let stand for 2 to 3 minutes, and stir to dissolve completely. Set aside until the mixture doubles.

Meanwhile, combine the flour, oil, salt, 1 1/2 cups water, and shortening in a large bowl. Stir in the yeast mixture until well blended. Knead about 10 minutes, or until the dough is smooth and pliable; add more water as needed. Put the dough into a large bowl, cover, and let it rise in a warm place for 2 to 3 hours, or until doubled in bulk.

Combine the meat with all the other ingredients, mixing well.

Preheat the oven to 375°F. Grease the baking sheets lightly.

Shape the dough into about 24 balls. On a lightly floured surface, roll each ball into a 3- or 3 1/2-inch circle. Place on the baking sheets. Cover the entire surface of each circle with a thin layer of the meat mixture, spreading it to about 1/4 inch from the edge.

Bake for 25 to 30 minutes. Serve hot.

Serves 24.

Liz Andonian Nader brushing butter on unbaked bourma.
Harry Naltchayin

Stuffed Meatballs
HARPOOT KUFTA

A daughter of survivors of the Armenian crisis, Clara Andonian spent much time with her grandparents while her parents struggled to make a living in their new homeland, the United States. Because the grandparents doted on Clara, the oldest of seven, she never had to cook. But she remembers watching her mother cook and often asked about measurements and recipe guidelines. Her mother always answered "cook '*achgi chop*,' or 'by the eye.'" And, she would add, "You know what the taste should be." As it turned out, her father owned Arthur's restaurant in Georgetown, Washington, D.C., and Andonian herself became well known locally as one of the "Gourmet Angels," a group of Armenian ladies who were hired to cook for special occasions.

Her mother often made the following recipe, a family favorite, but without her mother's written recipe, Andonian has used as a guideline the recipe from *Treasured Armenian Recipes*, compiled by the Detroit Women's Chapter of the Armenian General Benevolent Union. She has added her own touches, using ground allspice in place of ground cinnamon. She adds that some women prefer to use ground cumin, and a cook may use her own special seasoning, depending on the family's town of origin.

You can make the filling a day ahead. If not, begin it early in the day you plan to serve the dish as the filling needs to chill. If you have any leftover filling, shape it into patties, and cook it in the broth. Do not store any leftover *kufta* in the broth; to reheat, simmer them in the broth or in water. Be sure to use fatty meat; meat that is too lean will not hold together. As for the outer layer, Andonian says that you can "knead" the ingredients in the bowl of an upright mixer, preferably one with a dough hook.

You can vary the size of the meatballs—making them as large as golf balls or as small as walnuts or marbles. This dish makes a meal in itself. Top the meatballs with yogurt and serve them with a salad, and rice or chicken *beurek*, if you like. It is also time-consuming, and Andonian notes that the women in her church work together as a crew to assemble large amounts of the dish. In the old days, several women would gather twice a week to make such dishes cooperatively.

Filling
1 tablespoon vegetable oil
1 pound ground lamb
8 large onions, sliced
1/2 green bell pepper, chopped
4 tablespoons chopped parsley
1/2 teaspoon minced mint leaves
1 teaspoon minced basil
1 teaspoon ground allspice
1 teaspoon salt
1 teaspoon freshly ground black pepper
1 or more soup bones for the broth

Keyma
1 pound ground lamb
1 cup very finely ground bulgur
1 small onion, minced
1/2 tablespoon chopped parsley
salt to taste
freshly ground black pepper to taste

A cooking demonstration by a chef at Slow Food's Salone del Gusto. Anne Parsons

To make the filling, heat the oil in a large skillet over medium heat, and sauté the meat, stirring occasionally, until it is heated through. Add the onions, and reduce the heat to low. Cook for about 30 minutes, stirring often. Add the green pepper and parsley, and cook 10 minutes more. Add the remaining ingredients, and cook 5 minutes more. Chill the filling until cold.

Put the bones in a large stockpot, cover with lightly salted water, and bring to a boil over medium-high heat. Cook for about 30 minutes, skimming off the scum. Set aside.

Meanwhile, to make the *keyma*, mix the meat, bulgur, onion, parsley, salt, and pepper, and, using your hands, knead the mixture like a dough for 20 minutes, adding a little water from time to time to make the mixture pliable if needed.

Shape the chilled meat into balls the desired size, and set aside. Dip your hands in cold water, and shape the outer balls to the desired size. Make a dent in the middle with your thumb, and press around to form a hollow, making the sides as thin as possible. Place a filling meatball in the hollow, and seal the outer ball closed, smoothing the edges together to seal shut. Roll the *kufta* slightly between the palms. Repeat until all the ingredients are used up. Set aside.

Bring the broth to a boil. Reduce the heat to medium, add the *kuftas*, a few at a time, and cook until they float to the surface. Using a slotted spoon, carefully remove them from the boiling liquid, and repeat until the remaining ingredients are used up. Serve immediately.

Note: Traditional cooks will make the beef broth from scratch using bones, but if you are in a hurry, substitute the modern equivalent: commercially prepared beef broth, or even chicken broth.

Serves 4 to 6.

Armenian Bread

LAVASH

Clara Andonian has a painting in her home of traditional Armenian women gathered in a large hall, or kitchen, equipped with a wood-burning brick oven dug into the ground. The painting depicts clusters of women in various stages of bread baking—kneading the dough, rolling it out, baking it, and stacking it into piles for storage.

Andonian uses her mother's recipe for this bread, a staple of the Armenian diet. She makes it in batches and stores leftovers stacked and wrapped in plastic bags, ready for the next meal. She says her mother used two rolling pins: a standard one and one that resembled a dowel. The latter she used for wrapping the rolled-out dough around and placing the dough on the baking sheet. The rolled-out dough should be very thin, thinner than a pizza dough. To freshen each dried sheet of bread, she sprinkles it lightly with water to soften.

Clara Andonian sits with her painting of traditional Armenian women in various stages of bread making.
Alexandra Greeley

1 1/2 cups warm water
1 package (1 tablespoon) active dry yeast
2 tablespoons granulated sugar
1 tablespoon salt
about 6 cups all-purpose flour
4 tablespoons butter or 1/2 cup solid shortening
1 cup warm whole milk

1/4 teaspoon baking soda
2 tablespoons plain yogurt, optional

Mix together 1/2 cup water, the yeast, and sugar, and set aside until the mixture foams. Combine the yeast mixture with the remaining ingredients, starting with 3 cups flour. Stir in more flour until the mixture is no longer sticky. Dust a surface with flour, and knead the dough for about 10 minutes, or until it has an "earlobe" consistency. Put the dough in a lightly greased bowl, cover it with a damp towel, and set aside in a warm area for about 1 hour.

Punch the dough down on a lightly floured surface, and roll it out into a log shape. Cut the dough into 16 tangerine-sized balls, place them on a cookie sheet, and cover with lightly oiled wax paper; let rest for 15 minutes.

Preheat the oven to 500°F.

Roll out each ball to 1/16- to 1/8-inch-thick oval shape on a lightly floured surface. Place the ovals on cookie sheets or a pizza stone, and prick them randomly with a fork.

Bake for 7 to 10 minutes, or until the loaves are beginning to show brown spots and becoming crispy.

Makes about 12 loaves.

Austria/Germany

- ◆ POKELWALDT'S TRADITIONAL EUROPEAN SAUSAGES

- ◆ NUT STRUDEL (NUSSBEIGEL)

- ◆ DOUGHNUTS FOR FASTING NIGHT (FASTNACHT KEUCHELES)

- ◆ PRUNE DUMPLINGS (ZWETCHEN DAMPFNUDELN)

*W*hat makes Austria so appealing? For many people, the von Trapp Family story portrayed in *The Sound of Music*, revives the timeless, comforting qualities of family bound together by love and loyalty. Of course, it didn't hurt that breathtaking images of the Alps created the perfect backdrop for the von Trapp story. For centuries, artists have shown and described the Austrian Alps with their craggy vistas as the most romantic of natural scenery. Others profess that the Austrian landscape of majestic mountains, meadows, and forests defines the character of Austrians and recalls the history of a proud, warm, and hospitable people who speak German, yet who are not German.

With Italy, Switzerland, Germany, the Czech Republic, Hungary, and Germany, bordering Austria, the repertoire of regional dishes reflects the influence of those countries, but with a laconic absence of fussy details. Compare the regional dishes, where canny cooks measure every ingredient and waste absolutely nothing, to the rich fare of Vienna, the capital of Austria and home to the former Habsburg royal family; the contrast in cuisine is huge. Because the royal chefs served many of the international monarchic dishes, Viennese food is well known for such fare as weiner schnitzel, *fiaker* goulash, apple strudel, and the renowned Sacher Torte. But, whatever your taste—regional or royal—you can be assured that Austrian cuisine has the comforting qualities of home-cooked food.

Crossing the Alps into Germany, you'll find this country is not just about BMWs, VWs, Mercs, and stainless-steel appliances. Germany is a land of forests, lakes, and winding rivers, not forgetting, of course, the well-traveled magical romantic road in Bavaria. Connecting many small towns and villages, such as Rothenburg and Dinkelsbuhl, you'll discover that these gorgeous medieval villages haven't changed much in many centuries. Along the road, you will find that the German cuisine has taken a turn for the better. While you can still order waist-enlarging wursts, to-die-for dumplings, sturdy breads, and tantalizing tortes, chefs here are raiding the world's larders to whet the appetites

The dramatic Austrian Alps.
Beate Wildner

of a growing health-conscious nation. Once upon a time, the motto was "meat is the best vegetable"; nowadays, vegetables are often the centerpiece of the meal with meat as an accompaniment. Not to fear, however, beer is still a major component of any meal.

Pokelwaldt's Traditional European Sausages

The Pokelwaldts show off the results of their labor.
The Pokelwaldt family

The Brothers Pokelwaldt, Norm, Don, and Bob, are second-generation Americans whose forebears are from Germany. Naturally, a staple in their mother's kitchen was sausages—delicious herb, hot, and spicy sausages. When they moved to North Carolina's Outer Banks from the northern states, they couldn't find good sausages so they decided to make them. These sausages are now an inherent part of their large family's treasured recipes, which their children and grandchildren now appreciate.

First off, they select the very best ingredients. Bob suggests finding a good butcher in your neighborhood. For hanging the sausages, he purchases 3/4-inch dowels at the local hardware store, and for the casings, he prefers to use the 38–42 mm size. Because Bob prefers less fat, while Norm likes some fat, and Don likes more, they grind the meat on a 3/8-inch plate, then take 20 percent of the fatty trimmings and grind it on a 3/16-inch plate. Although they used to mix the meat and seasonings by hand, they now have a hand mixer.

When asked if they ever encounter any problems, Bob said that it's important not to make the meat too lean because it becomes dry, nor too fat, which is repulsive, and not to soak the casings too long, otherwise they stick and it's difficult to stuff them. For these brothers, life is like sausage making—they take pleasure in their creations, and then they savor the result with children, grandchildren, and friends.

25 pounds boneless pork butts, trimmed of fat
5 cups ice water
5 cups soy protein concentrate or non-fat dry milk

3/4 cup kosher salt, or medium-coarse sea salt

2 1/2 tablespoons sugar

3 1/2 tablespoons coarsely ground black pepper

6 cloves garlic

2 1/2 tablespoons marjoram

5 teaspoons instant cure (saltpeter)

casings for sausages

All the meat should be kept in a waterproof container in the refrigerator until ready to use. Prior to grinding, remove all the sinews and blood clots.

To make it easier to add the spices to the meat, put the soy protein, salt, sugar, pepper, garlic, and marjoram in 1 cup of the ice water and mix. Now mix with the meat and cure, using the hand mixer. Before stuffing, let the mixture sit in the refrigerator for 45 minutes to 1 hour.

Soak the casings in water for 30 minutes.

Put the meat through the sausage stuffer so it will slide into the casings. Rinse off the stuffed casings, then hang the sausages to dry.

Put the sausages in the smoker and keep them there until the internal temperature reaches approximately 160°F. They should take about 20 minutes of smoking—too much is overpowering. Remove and hang on dowels, then rinse with a hose and let dry.

The sausages can then be grilled or fried. They are also excellent as an hors d'oeuvre. Otherwise, refrigerate them or freeze them, but remember to cook them before serving.

Note: Smoking does not cook the sausages but only gives them flavor. Also note that the cure is saltpeter (sodium nitrate) that controls botulism during the smoking and storage process. All equipment, cure, and casings can be found online at various sites, such as www.sausagemaker.com.

Produces about 25 pounds of sausage in link.

Nut Strudel
NUSSBEIGEL

Mary Duffy Sweeney treasures this recipe from her grandmother, Klara Schaush, who was born August 10, 1874, in Kittsee, Austria (near the Hungarian border). On January 18, 1892, Klara married Andreas Leszkovich. When he arrived at Ellis Island in 1893, his name changed to Laskowitz. A couple of years later, Klara came through Ellis Island with her son, Simon, met her husband in Wisconsin, and then finally settled in St. Louis, Missouri. Although some of her children died in infancy, six children survived. Sweeney recalls, "Grandma spoke very broken English and often reverted to German. My mother, the youngest child, tells me that my first words were in German."

Loaves
2 cups whole milk mixed with 2 cups lukewarm water
1 1/3 cups plus 1 teaspoon granulated sugar
1 1/2 teaspoons salt
1/4 pound (1 stick) butter
2 packages (2 tablespoons) active dry yeast
10 cups all-purpose flour, sifted
4 egg whites

Filling for Nussbeigel:
3 cups granulated sugar
1 1/2 cups water
2 pounds shelled English walnuts, ground
1/2 box raisins
dash of nutmeg

Preheat the oven to 350°F. Generously grease 2 baking sheets.

Scald the milk, and add the sugar, salt, and butter; stir, and let cool.

Dissolve the yeast in 1/2 cup lukewarm water with 1 teaspoon sugar; let foam.

Mix the milk mixture with 2 cups sifted flour; add the yeast mixture, then add the remaining flour with a wooden spoon. (The dough will be sticky).

Grease a large bowl. Place the dough in a bowl, and turn once so the top of the dough is also greased. Let the dough rise until double in bulk, about 50 minutes.

Meanwhile prepare the filling by cooking the sugar and 1 1/2 cups water together in a saucepan over medium heat until it spins a thread when dropped from a spoon. Add the ground nuts, raisins, and nutmeg.

Laskowitz family, circa 1901.
Sweeney family album

Grease your hands. Push the dough down, then separate it into 8 sections. Flour a board generously, and knead the dough slightly. Roll out each section into a rectangle, about 1/2 inch thick. Spread the nut mixture evenly over the dough, and roll it. Put the seam end on the bottom.

Place on the prepared cookie sheets, allowing enough space between rolls to double in size. Once raised, brush the tops with unbeaten egg whites.

Bake until golden brown (turning trays once in oven for even baking), about 40 minutes.

Makes 8 strudel loaves.

Doughnuts for Fasting Night
FASTNACHT KEUCHELES

Gloria Pokelwaldt recalls, "Gram came over on 'da boat' as she would say, in 1914, and she spoke very little English. Christina Kirisits traveled from Austria by herself with three of her children, and had three more after she arrived in Buffalo. My father was one of the American born. Likewise, I was born in Buffalo, and my parents built their one and only home in North Tonawanda, NY, in 1950. Grandma cooked every day and had particular recipes for special holidays. For example, Shrove Tuesday is a day of celebration of sorts, because the next forty days we fast. In those days—the '40s through the '60s or so—Catholics over the age of seven (I think) were only allowed one full meal a day and two others not to equal the full meal. My Gram adhered strictly to that and so did my parents. My brothers and I were not made to follow that line as strictly, but NO ONE ate meat on Friday EVER, thus the prune recipe was a meal often served then. All of the daily fasting rules are 'man made,' and they are no longer in force since Vatican II. Catholics are still supposed to observe Fast and Abstinence during Lent, but over the age of sixty-five it's not a law!"

Fastnacht translates as "eve of the beginning of the fast" and is the Tuesday eve before Ash Wednesday. Although Pokelwaldt's grandmother spent every Saturday making this dish, Pokelwaldt recalls: "One memory of Gram was her standing at the kitchen table, which was metal covered with white enamel with a black stripe around the edge. She always wore a flowered cotton 'house dress' covered with a large full apron. Gram was a large woman, probably standing 5 feet 7 inches or 5 feet 8 inches tall. Her hair was completely gray and was always pulled back in a bun. Often she had it covered with a cotton scarf that she called a *babushka*."

1 package (1 tablespoon) active dry yeast
1/4 cup granulated sugar
2 cups whole milk, scalded and cooled to lukewarm temperature
5 cups all-purpose flour

1 large egg
2 teaspoons salt
1 tablespoon shortening, melted
2 tablespoons unsalted butter, melted
3 cups vegetable oil for cooking
confectioners' sugar for sprinkling

Gloria with her grandmother and Aunt Christine, circa 1948. Pokelwaldt family album

Combine the yeast and 1/2 tablespoon of sugar with 1/2 cup of milk in a bowl, and let sit for 10 minutes, or until the yeast foams.

Meanwhile, put the flour in a mixing bowl, and make a well in the center. Pour the yeast mixture into the center of the bowl and mix well with the flour.

Add the remaining milk, egg, remaining sugar, salt, and melted shortening and butter. Knead the mixture, adding flour as necessary to make a soft dough. Cover the bowl, and let rise in a warm place until double in bulk, about 1 to 2 hours. Turn onto a lightly floured board and roll to 1/2-inch thickness. Cut into diamond, or triangle, shapes and cover with a damp towel.

Heat vegetable oil to hot temperature. Place a few *keucheles* at a time into the hot oil, raised side down. When golden, turn and cook the second side until also golden. Place on brown paper or paper towels, and, while still warm, sprinkle with granulated or confectioners' sugar.

Makes 36 keucheles.

Prune Dumplings

ZWETCHEN DAMPFNUDELN

Gloria Pokelwaldt says her Gram "would mix the dough for her noodles in an enormous bowl (I was six or seven so it seemed huge to me!), and then dump the mixture in the middle of the table, which was covered with cotton kitchen towels and flour. There was flour flying all over the place. After rolling out the dough and cutting it into strips she would hang the noodles on strings strung all over the kitchen. She also used the same kind of dough for her 'Friday' prune dumplings that they ate during Lent. It was a wonderful meatless meal."

When asked if the prunes were pitted, Pokelwaldt responded, "Oh, no, they added to the taste, there was always a bowl handy for the pits." If you prefer not to "spit the pit," you may replace the pit with a small lump of sugar, before cooking of course!

After testing recipes for keucheles and dampfnudeln, Jill Neilson does a taste test.
Anne Parsons

2 cups all-purpose flour
2 pieces solid shortening, each the size of an egg
3/4 teaspoon salt
2 tablespoons sugar
2 large eggs
24 prunes, unpitted and washed
4 tablespoons unsalted butter
1/2 cup plain dry breadcrumbs
granulated sugar for sprinkling

Put the flour into a large mixing bowl and, using two knives, cut in the solid shortening. Add the salt, sugar, eggs, and enough water to make a dough. Knead until smooth—don't make it too soft.

Roll the dough to 1/4-inch thickness on a lightly floured surface, and cut into squares. Put 1 prune in the center of each square, fold the dough over the prune, and press and crimp the edges.

Bring a large pot of water to a boil over medium heat, and gently slide the dumplings into the water. Boil the dumplings for about 15 minutes, or until done. Pick out dumplings with a skimming ladle as they surface.

Heat the butter in a large skillet over medium heat, and fry the breadcrumbs until crisp. Roll the dumplings in this mixture, coating them completely. Sprinkle with sugar, if desired, and serve hot.

Makes 24 dumplings.

Bolivia

- BOLIVIAN CORN CASSEROLE (HUMITA)

- QUINOA CASSEROLE (HUNINTA DE QUINUA)

*B*olivia, dominated by the great mountain range of the majestic Andes, embraces a staggering array of landscapes and climates that include tropical rain forests, vast savannas, and fertile valleys.

Famous since Spanish colonial days for its mineral wealth, modern

View of Potosi, Bolivia.
Vicky Vega

Bolivia was once a part of the ancient Incan empire. After the Spaniards defeated the Incas in the sixteenth century, Bolivia's predominantly Indian population was reduced to slavery. Yet, the remoteness of the Andes helped protect the Bolivian Indians from the European diseases that decimated other South American Indians.

Like the range of climates and landscapes, Bolivian cuisine sets a diverse table of foods. In the high, cold climate, spicy hot peppers dominate many dishes of potatoes, corn, grain, and meats. The lowland regions of this land-locked country abound in vegetables, fruits, and freshwater fish. Overall, the flavors that Spanish traders and merchants brought to the table centuries ago prevail today to tease the taste buds.

Furthermore, the inherited and adopted culinary skills remain in the best eating places—the Bolivian kitchens where food is cooked for families and friends.

Bolivian Corn Casserole
HUMITA

Karla Montano and her sister, Vivian Lawson, own and operate a restaurant called Luna Maya, in Virginia Beach, Virginia. Although Montano has always been the passionate, creative cook in her family, she believes cooking for large family gatherings requires easy-to-make, simple recipes that taste fabulous. Therefore, the old family standbys are always appreciated. *Humita* is a traditional Bolivian dish consisting of fresh corn and cheese. To be truly authentic, it should be steamed inside a corn husk. However, there are many variations, depending on the region and the cook.

Casserole straight from tester Marty Batsel's oven. Mike Batsel

Montano says that using fresh corn provides a better flavor, but when corn is out of season and you are pressed for time, frozen corn kernels are an acceptable substitute. Masa mix—a corn flour product for making tortillas, tamales, and other products—is readily available in many supermarkets: check where flour products are displayed. The filling calls for a crumbly cheese such as the Mexican *queso fresco* or the Italian *ricotta salata*. If neither of these is available, try the mozzarella, grated. For a richer filling, increase the amount of cheese. For an effect resembling crème brûlée, sprinkle sugar over the top layer and let the heat melt it into the mixture.

1/2 cup granulated sugar
1/2 cup masa mix
1/4 cup cornbread mix
2 teaspoons salt
1 teaspoon mild ground red pepper, such as New Mexico Red or paprika
1/2 teaspoon ground cinnamon

1 teaspoon chipotle powder, or other chili powder
1/2 teaspoon ground cumin
1 (2-pound) bag frozen corn kernels, thawed and drained
1/4 pound (1 stick) butter, melted
1 pound grated crumbly cheese, such as *queso fresco*

Preheat the oven to 400°F. Butter a 3-quart ovenproof baking dish.

Mix the sugar, masa mix, cornbread mix, salt, ground red pepper, cinnamon, chipotle powder, and ground cumin together in a large bowl.

Put the corn kernels in a food processor, and process until finely chopped. Mix the corn with the dry ingredients. Stir in the butter until fully incorporated.

Spoon half the mixture into the baking dish. Spread three-quarters of the cheese filling over the mixture. Spoon the remaining mixture over the cheese. Top with the remaining grated cheese.

Bake about 45 minutes, or until the top is golden brown. Serve hot.
Serves 8.

Quinoa Casserole
Huninta de Quinua

Bolivian tamales, like the recipe for *humitas* in this chapter, can be wrapped in cornhusks or baked in a casserole. Karla Montano says for large family gatherings it is much easier on the cook to make casseroles. That way, rather than spending time wrapping tamales, the cook can enjoy time with the guests.

3 cups uncooked quinoa
10 cups chicken stock
2 tablespoons salted or unsalted butter
3 tablespoons olive oil
8 cloves garlic, minced
1 large onion, diced
1 carrot, diced
1 large stalk celery, diced
1 red bell pepper, diced
12 chicken thighs, cut into pieces
2 quarts chopped tomatoes
1 tablespoon ground cumin
3 tablespoons ground Bolivian yellow pepper, New Mexico Red, or other
  mild ground red pepper
1 tablespoon salt
3 hard-boiled eggs, chopped, optional
1 small jar green olives, optional
4 ounces jalapeño, Chihuahua, mozzarella, or Muenster cheese, grated

Put the quinoa, 7 cups stock, butter, 1 tablespoon olive oil, and 3 cloves minced garlic into a large saucepan, stirring to distribute the quinoa evenly. Bring the mixture to a boil over medium heat, cover, and reduce the heat to low. Continue cooking until the quinoa has popped open, about 10 minutes. Remove from the heat, and set aside before fluffing the quinoa with a fork.

Meanwhile, heat the remaining 2 tablespoons oil in a large skillet over medium heat, and sauté the garlic, onion, carrot, celery, and red bell pepper for 1 minute. Add the chicken pieces, chopped tomatoes, and the remaining 3 cups stock. Reduce the heat to medium-low, and cook the mixture, uncovered, until the chicken is tender, about 30 minutes. Stir in the cumin, yellow pepper, and salt.

Preheat the oven to 400°F.

To assemble the casserole, layer the quinoa and the chicken mixture. Put the eggs and olives on top, if using. Top with grated cheese.

Bake the casserole until the cheese melts and the mixture is bubbly, about 30 minutes. Serve hot.

Serves 10.

Selling Bolivian spices at Slow Food's Terra Madre.
Anne Parsons

Cambodia

- SALTY FISH AND PORK PASTE SALAD (PRAHOC KREUNG)

- SIDEBAR: BANANA LEAVES

- CHICKEN AMOK

- COCONUT PORK WITH RICE CAKES OR PLAIN SHRIMP CHIPS

- SWEET AND SOUR PORK CURRY (KOR CHRUEK)

- JACKFRUIT CAKE

- PARADISE FRESH FRUIT CUSTARD

*D*ecades after the horrific killing fields decimated the population of this Southeast Asian country, Cambodia has reemerged, and if reports are correct, is once again a thriving Buddhist stronghold peopled with gentle folk and graced with dramatic landscapes of lush splendor. And at the center of interest: the famed, ancient Buddhist temple, Angkor Wat.

Its hushed beauty and serenity seem to parallel the gentle subtleties and simplicity of Cambodian cooking: without complex seasonings, Cambodian foods are basic, flavorful, and wholesome. Rice is a staple—Cambodians revere rice, explains one Cambodian—and basic seasonings include lemongrass, citrus leaves, garlic, galangal, cumin, turmeric, salt, pepper, and coconut milk. A key, and beloved, flavoring is *prahok*, a fermented fish paste that is similar in flavor and usage to the Thai and Vietnamese fish sauce. Chili use in cooking is limited, and as a result, Cambodian food is generally mild, though cooks may decide to offer sliced chilies as a table condiment. As Cambodian cook, Bora Chu, notes, one variety of Cambodian chili is so hot that its name, *mateh khamang*, means "enemy."

Traditionally, breakfasts consist of rice porridge topped with dried fish or meat, or possibly barbecued pork, salty egg, and pickles. Lunches and dinners are very similar and consist of rice, a soup, a grilled or fried meat or fish, maybe a stir-fry, and fresh vegetables. Snacks and street foods include grilled bananas. While rural Cambodians enjoy a simple cuisine, city folk, with more goods at hand, have many more choices, yet perhaps not at the same level of sophistication as when the French lived in Phnom Penh.

But exiles from and travelers to Cambodia, perhaps remembering the cuisine of its colonial days, will find that truly elegant Cambodian court cooking is a cuisine of the past. In an interview with the Asia Society, Longtiene De Monteiro, who wrote the classic Cambodian cookbook *The Elephant Walk Cookbook*, says the older generations who knew and practiced the art of old-fashioned, refined Cambodian cooking, "are too old or were killed by the Khmer Rouge." Another Cambodian lady with a distinguished pedigree, Mrs. Montha C. Prom, concurs. It's a world and a cuisine that have vanished, she has said, adding that while Cambodians are trying to piece together some remnants from the past, the techniques and recipes from before the revolution are gone forever.

Angkor Wat temple in Siem Riep. Christopher Greeley, MD

The loss of a culinary heritage . . .

Salty Fish and Pork Paste Salad
PRAHOC KREUNG

Dr. Neou Leakhena, a pediatrician at the Angkor Hospital for Children in Siem Riep, Cambodia, has enjoyed this dish since she was a child. She would sometimes watch her mother prepare it from scratch and serve it to the family. The blend of flavors is unique to Cambodian cooking, and Dr. Leakhena hopes that traditional Cambodian dishes will continue to be passed down to future generations.

Prahoc is a pungent fermented fish paste that is used in dishes such as *pleah sach ko*, a sweet and sour Cambodian salad with lightly cooked beef. When *prahoc* is combined with pork and other herbs, the result is this tasty fermented dish to be eaten with fresh vegetables.

2 stalks lemongrass, chopped, to equal 1 cup
10 dried chilies
5 cloves garlic, chopped
1/2 teaspoon crushed saffron threads
about 1/2 pound ground pork with fat
4 tablespoons *prahoc*, or to taste
2 large eggs, beaten
3 shallots, thinly sliced
banana leaves for wrapping
2 ounces yard-long beans
2 ounces thinly sliced cabbage
4 ounces sliced cucumbers
2 ounces thinly sliced green or white Thai eggplant

Preheat the oven to 350°F.

Chop up the lemongrass, chilies, and garlic, and grind all the ingredients together using a mortar and pestle or a blender with enough water to process. Mix the pork with the salty fish mixture until pasty in a large bowl.

Add the beaten egg and shallots to the ground pork mixture, and stir well. Stir in the lemongrass mixture, and mix well.

To make the packets, cut 6 strips of banana leaves into 4x6-inch pieces, spoon the pork mixture onto the center, and fold the leaf over the filling, using toothpicks to close the packet. Repeat with the remaining mixture for a total of 6 packets.

Bake until the banana leaves are slightly browned, about 30 minutes. Serve with the fresh, cut-up vegetables, such as yard-long beans, cabbage, cucumbers, and eggplant.
Serves 2.

Dr. Leakhena's prahoc *salad.*
Dr. Leakhena

♦ Banana Leaves ♦

Instead of foil, many Asians wrap their foods prior to cooking in the large, pliable, and aromatic leaves of the banana plant—these impart a delicate flavor to whatever is cooked inside, making the dish even more appealing and appetizing. To the inexperienced,  however, wrapping food up in banana leaves can be tricky, especially since most available in the West are frozen. Even after thawing and warming, they remain brittle and can tear or shred easily. Before use, cut away the tough central spine and trim the leaves into usable sections with a pair of scissors. To soften them, dip the leaves briefly into hot water. To make things simple, you can just use the easiest folding method: lay the piece of banana leaf out flat and place the food in the center of the leaf. Fold one side of the leaf to the center, and fold the other side over the first fold. Use toothpicks or short bamboo skewers to "stitch" the ends shuts. Aluminum foil can replace banana leaves; to prevent a banana leaf packet from leaking, overwrap it with foil.

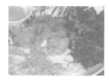

Chicken Amok

Our cooking resembles Thai food, says Cambodian Montha C. Prom, a native of Phnom Penh. Associated with the former Cambodian royal family, she and her husband Assompion Som and three children were among the fortunate refugees who escaped the killing fields into Thailand. She remembers her childhood, a golden dreamy time of affluence when she enjoyed the ease of court life. All that changed when the communists and Pol Pot came to power. She, her husband, and children now live in the suburbs of Washington, D.C., where he works as a taxi driver and she as a cook in a nursing home. They are active in their Cambodian community's social activities. Although Mrs. Montha never cooked as a child—"I hate cooking," she says—she remembers some of the special dishes served in her home. This is one of them. In former times, the cook would wrap this chicken mixture in banana leaves before cooking.

Seasoning Paste
Kroeung
1 teaspoon paprika, or 5 dried red chilies, seeded
1 (1-inch-long) piece fresh or frozen turmeric
1/2 cup chopped lemongrass
1 head garlic, separated and cloves peeled
1 large shallot, peeled and chopped
4 thick slices fresh or frozen galangal, chopped
1/4 cup coconut milk

Chicken Filling
1 1/2 pounds boneless, skinless chicken breast, thinly sliced
1 cup thick coconut milk
4 to 5 lime leaves, very thinly sliced
1 tablespoon granulated sugar
2 tablespoons *prahoc*

5 tablespoons fish sauce
1 pound baby spinach, well rinsed

To make the *kroeung*, combine the ingredients in a blender, and puree until the mixture forms a paste. Add just enough water to help process.

Put the chicken slices in a large nonreactive (glass or stainless steel) baking dish or bowl. Pour the paste over the chicken, and set aside to marinate for about 1 hour. Meanwhile, combine the 1 cup coconut milk, sliced lime leaves, sugar, *prahoc*, and fish sauce, and set aside.

Preheat the oven to 350°F. Dip the baby spinach in boiling water for 4 to 5 seconds, or until slightly wilted. Spray the bottom of a large baking dish with cooking spray. Lay the spinach leaves on the bottom, and spoon the chicken mixture on top. Cover the chicken with the coconut milk mixture, and top with foil or banana leaves.

Bake for 45 to 50 minutes, or until firm in the center. Remove from the oven, and serve with rice.

Serves 4 to 6.

Mrs. Montha C. Prom at home.
Alexandra Greeley

Coconut Pork with Rice Cakes or Plain Shrimp Chips

Native Cambodians, Bora Chu and her husband were lucky survivors of the Pol Pot regime, having fled Cambodia. They now live in Northern Virginia, leading a quiet life in their new country. But Bora Chu still cooks her native dishes and remembers that as a child, her mother taught her to cook by taste, aroma, and what she observed, not by measurements—for example, she learned that if a curry bubbles, it may need more salt. For this recipe and other dishes, she had to slice the lime leaves into thread-thin slivers. This may seem easy, but it requires stacking them one on top of another, about six leaves total, and using a very sharp paring knife to cut slivers lengthwise from the leaves. And she was tasked with preparing the peanuts, each hand-cut into slivers rather than chopped into small pieces. She admits she would try to convince a cousin or sister to help her out.

Serve this appetizer spread with rice cakes, plain shrimp chips, or toasted slices of French bread. You can buy already prepared fried rice cakes in an Asian market, but you can make some at home: soak 1 cup of sticky rice in water to cover for 6 hours or overnight. Then steam the rice in a wire or bamboo basket set over hot water until the rice is tender. Form a 3-inch round circle from a long metal tie used for tying up plastic bags. Moistening your fingers, take a scoop of about 2 teaspoons of the steamed rice and pat it into the circle, flattening the rice to fit into the circle in a single, thin layer. Set these circles aside to dry out— in Cambodia in the old days, says Bora Chu, the women would place the rice circles on banana leaves and let them dry in the sun. Once dry, the circles can be deep-fried until golden and crispy.

Not only can you find and use already prepared rice cakes, you can also purchase already fried sliced shallots and sliced garlic; if you use the commercial fried garlic, you will still need to refry it to bring out the flavor. For a richer flavor, use frozen coconut milk. For city-dwelling Cambodians, the color of the coconut pork must be golden. But country dwellers use ground chilies and dried shrimp instead, giving this dish an entirely different flavor and color.

Serve this with a side of sliced or whole fresh chilies marinated in tamarind juice stirred with a few tablespoons of fish sauce.

4 tablespoons vegetable oil
1 cup sliced garlic
1 cup sliced shallots
1 1/2 pounds ground pork
1/2 to 3/4 cup palm sugar
1/4 to 1/2 cup fish sauce
2 tablespoons ground turmeric
1 teaspoon salt
1/2 cup thread-thin lime leaves
2 cups coconut milk
1 1/2 cups finely sliced toasted peanuts

Bora Chu's pork dish.
Alexandra Greeley

Heat the oil in a large skillet or wok over medium-high heat. Fry the garlic until golden, and drain on paper towels. Fry the shallots until golden, and drain on paper towels. With about 1/2 cup oil remaining in the pan, sauté the pork until well done. Add palm sugar, fish sauce, turmeric, and salt; adjust seasonings.

Reduce the heat to medium. Add half of the lime leaves, and stir in with the coconut milk and peanuts. Stir in the fried garlic and shallots, and bring the mixture to a boil. Pour the mixture into a serving dish, and garnish with remaining lime leaves. To serve, spread some mixture on to rice cakes or shrimp chips.

Serves 5 to 6.

Sweet and Sour Pork Curry
KOR CHRUEK

This pork dish combines the best features of a soup, but is so full of meat it might be considered a stew. Because this feeds so many and is such a beloved dish, Bora Chu remembers that in the old days, the women (men never did the cooking) made pots of it and left it out at room temperature, reheating it just before serving time. She notes that women would add little china or pottery cups to the cook pot to help tenderize the meat, something that modern cooks don't know about.

Cambodian Bora Chu making her sweet and sour pork curry.
Alexandra Greeley

Serve this with steamed long-grain rice or sticky rice. You may use only cubed pork meat rather than a combination of cubed meat and bone-in meat, but if so, cook it for only 1 1/2 hours. Regardless of which you select, the amount of meat should total 5 pounds. Bora Chu notes that young Cambodian women prefer to use lean pork, but she adds that it does not have nearly the flavor as the skin-on meat. You may use fresh bamboo shoots, but these will need special precooking, so canned bamboo shoots are an easier choice. Using coconut soda, an Asian soft drink, helps to tenderize the meat and give it a sweetish flavor, but you may wish to use less palm sugar. The coconut soda is available at Asian markets.

1/4 cup vegetable oil
2 pounds pork leg, bone in

3 pounds cubed pork, skin on
4 to 5 cups coconut soda or coconut juice
1/2 cup mushroom or dark soy sauce
1/2 cup soy sauce
1/2 cup fish sauce
1/2 cup palm sugar, or to taste
freshly ground black pepper to taste
2 (16-ounce) cans bamboo shoots, drained and rinsed
1 dozen hard-boiled eggs, shelled

Heat the vegetable oil in a stockpot over medium-high heat, and fry the meat, a few pieces at a time, stirring, for about 20 minutes, or until the meat is browned and crisped.

Add the soy sauces, fish sauce, palm sugar, and black pepper, and mix well. Add 3 cups water, and bring to a boil over medium-high heat. Cook for 30 minutes.

Add the coconut soda or juice and enough water to cover; add the bamboo shoots and eggs, reduce the heat to medium-low, and cook for 2 to 3 more hours, or until the pork is tender.

Serves 10.

Jackfruit Cake

The perfect ending to a Cambodian meal, this "cake" also has a banana variation calling for special small Asian bananas. Not a cake by Western standards, this recipe makes compact bundles of sweetened sticky rice stirred with coconut milk, sugar, and fruit, then wrapped in banana leaves and steamed for a final cooking, Banana leaves are sold frozen at Asian markets; thaw them briefly before using. Popular during Cambodian New Year, it also makes a memorable treat any time of year!

Buddhist monks.
Christopher Greeley, MD

2 cups coconut milk
2 pounds sticky or glutinous rice, soaked overnight
1/2 cup granulated sugar
2 (14-ounce) cans jackfruit, drained and cut into strips
salt to taste
sheets of banana leaves

Pour the coconut milk into a large wok, and heat over low heat. Stir in the soaked sticky rice, the sugar, and salt, and cook until the rice grains absorb the coconut milk. Stir in the jackfruit, and set aside to cool.

To make cakes, cut along the spine of the banana leaf 6-inch long strips. Fold each strip in half, and round the opposite ends and trim them to make a semicircle. Spoon about 1/4 cup of rice and jackfruit mixture down one side of strip, leaving about 1 inch free at each end. Fold up tightly into a cigar-shaped roll, and fold each end over, securing it with toothpicks, to make a packet. Set aside, and repeat with remaining rice and banana leaf strips. Steam packets over boiling water until rice is thoroughly tender. Serve hot.

Serves 20.

Banana Cake Variation

2 cups coconut milk
2 pounds sticky or glutinous rice, soaked overnight
1/2 cup granulated sugar
1 (15.5-ounce) can black-eyed peas, drained
10 baby bananas, peeled and sliced in half lengthwise
salt to taste

Cook the rice with the coconut milk as above, but instead of adding jackfruit to the mixture, add the black-eyed peas. To make cakes, place one banana half in banana leaf, and mound rice mixture around it. Fold as above.

Paradise Fresh Fruit Custard

"My family ate this dessert often," remembers Mrs. Montha, "and I still love it to this day." Of course, in Cambodia, fresh jackfruit was readily available as were the seeds, which needed to be boiled, skinned, and shredded before use. Canned jackfruit is readily available, but since jackfruit seeds may be hard to find—Mrs. Montha says they are sometimes available canned in Asian markets—you may use all jackfruit instead. In the olden days, cooks would form bowls from banana leaves; today, heatproof glass bowls are handy to use. You can steam this pudding, if you prefer, instead of baking it. Mrs. Montha always steams it.

In a Cambodian marketplace.
Christopher Greeley, MD

Mrs. Montha says that even to this day she uses freshly grated coconut milk for the pudding because she believes the flavor is superior to that of the canned milk. "My son always gets upset when I make this dessert because I ask him to do the grating," she says, displaying her wooden grating tool that resembles a small stool with wire teeth on the end. Some cooks prefer to use the whole egg and not just the yolk. If you use canned coconut milk, she says, it is important to use the thick milk, or cream, on top.

1 dozen jumbo egg yolks
1 cup sugar
1 cup thick coconut milk
1/2 cup shredded jackfruit

1/3 cup shredded jackfruit seeds, optional
1/4 teaspoon salt

Preheat the oven to 375°F.

Combine the yolks, sugar, and coconut milk, beating to mix well. Layer the jackfruit and seeds, if using, on the bottom of a 2- or 3-quart baking dish. Pour the egg mixture over the jackfruit. Put the baking dish inside a large dish or pan, and fill the outer pan with water halfway up the baking dish.

Bake 40 to 45 minutes, or until the custard firms and the top turns golden. Cool slightly before eating.

Serves 4 to 6.

Canada

- ♦ Salmon with Sweet Corn Relish
- ♦ Corn Fritters
- ♦ Canadian Ham with Maple Syrup Sauce
- ♦ Madame Lafleur's Laurentides Pie

*P*ickled beaver, fried woodchuck, stuffed whale breast, and moose meat soup. Not exactly your cup of tea? Not to worry, because the natural process of culinary mutation has allowed these original First People of Canada recipes to evolve into such cookery delights as venison rib roast, stuffed baked lake trout, and grilled salmon.

Officially a bilingual country of French- and English-speaking people, Canada is a nation of diverse cultures, climates, and landscapes. From coast to coast, Canada's natural environment is one of the most beautiful in the world; one where you are easily smitten by the sublime splendor and serenity in this land of charming islands, pristine coastlines, rugged mountains, and dazzling waterfalls and lakes.

In its early history, Canadian cuisine consisted mainly of whatever food was readily available and prepared as circumstances allowed. Now, with so many indigenous peoples and immigrants, the basis of Canadian cuisine encompasses, by and large, traditional dishes from the British, European, and First Nation cultures.

From the indigenous peoples come such foods as pemmican (dried meat mixture), buffalo meat, wild turnips, and wild rice (Canada annually produces approximately two million kilograms of wild rice from unpolluted lakes in Prince Edward Island, Saskatchewan, and Ontario). Newfoundland and the Maritime provinces of Prince Edward Island, Nova Scotia, and New Brunswick are famous for cod tongues, mussels, lobster, scallops, smoked mackerel, oysters, and eels. In French-speaking Quebec, a gastronome's heaven, offerings include Brome Lake duck and Matane shrimps. Moving further west, note Ontario's world-famous pork and bacon, the variety of fish from the pristine lakes of Manitoba, and the buffalo meat and beef from Alberta. On the west coast, British Columbia is famous for its salmon, but did you know about their amazing oysters, Manila clams, and salt-spring island lamb? And, did you know that in 1811, John McIntosh of Ontario found some abandoned trees that he transplanted and eventually produced the delicious McIntosh apple?

Canadian flag with the Rocky Mountains in the background.
Gary Scott

Born of immigrants and indigenous peoples from distinct cultures, Canadian cuisine ranks high in the annals of gastronomy.

 *Salmon with Sweet Corn Relish*

Every Sunday afternoon, the children and grandchildren of David and Doreen Smith gather at their home on Vancouver Island, British Columbia, for dinner. Their philosophy toward family cooking is "keep it simple and use the freshest meats, fish, and vegetables you can find." David remarks, "Congeniality, good conversation, and wholesome food bring us together. But, more than that, we are passing on a family legacy that cements family relationships and connects one generation to the next."

Doreen said she didn't have to raid her grandma's recipe box because they stick to the dishes grandma used to make—no fuss meals that have been favorites with her family for generations.

David's freezer is often filled with salmon since it is so plentiful in his neck of the island. Doreen usually doubles this recipe for family dinners. Make sure that your skillet is very hot before searing the fish.

1/2 cup rice vinegar
4 tablespoons granulated sugar
1 cup fresh or frozen corn kernels
1/2 cup finely diced yellow squash
1/2 cup finely diced zucchini
1/2 cup finely chopped Vidalia onion
1/2 cup finely chopped canned tomatoes, drained
3 tablespoons extra virgin olive oil
1 tablespoon balsamic vinegar
1/4 teaspoon salt
1/4 teaspoon white pepper
6 (8-ounce) center-cut salmon fillets, skin removed
salt to taste
freshly ground black pepper to taste

Preheat the oven to 450°F.

Combine the vinegar and sugar in a saucepan. Cook over medium-

low heat until the sugar is dissolved. Stir in the corn, zucchini, onion, tomatoes, 2 tablespoons of the olive oil, vinegar, salt, and pepper. Cook for 5 minutes. Cool and set aside.

Heat a heavy skillet over high heat for 5 minutes.

Rub both sides of the salmon fillets with olive oil, and season with salt and pepper. Place the salmon fillets in the pan, and cook over medium heat for 2 minutes, until brown. Turn the fillets, and place the pan in the oven for 6 minutes, or until the salmon is cooked rare.

Salmon for supper. David Smith

Spoon some relish on a plate and place a salmon fillet on top.

Serves 6.

 *Corn Fritters*

The Menzels have lived in Pemberton, British Columbia, since the early 1900s. Their nephew's daughter, Alice Olteanu, inherited this recipe from her great Aunt Phemie; she claims it is a family favorite because it is so versatile. Sometimes she serves the fritters, drizzled with maple syrup, to her children for breakfast. She does advise keeping fritters covered and away from husbands and kids because they'll want to snack on them, especially when the fritters are topped with applesauce.

Corn ready for shucking.
Alice Olteanu

2 cups all-purpose flour
2 teaspoons baking powder
1 teaspoon salt
1 tablespoon granulated sugar
2 large eggs
4 tablespoons (1/2 stick) butter, melted
1/2 cup whole milk
2 (15-ounce) cans sweet corn, or about 4 cups fresh kernels
vegetable oil for deep-fat frying

Sift together the flour, baking powder, salt, and sugar. Add the eggs, butter, milk, and corn, and stir together.

Heat the oil in a large, deep saucepan over medium heat until the oil shimmers. Carefully put tablespoonfuls of the mixture into the hot oil, and deep-fry for 3 minutes; alternatively, sauté the batter in hot butter in a skillet over medium heat. Drain well.

Makes 25 fritters.

Canadian Ham
with Maple Syrup Sauce

Although Canadian artist Patricia Grimshaw, of Napanee, Ontario, does not love baking, she does enjoy cooking. She says her grandmother and mother were fine family cooks, and she saved their bedraggled recipes to pass on to her children and grandchildren.

Hams galore at Slow Food's Salone del Gusto.
Anne Parsons

1 (4-pound) ham, uncooked
whole cloves
4 to 5 tablespoons brown sugar

Wash the ham, and soak it for several hours in water; drain.

Preheat the oven to 375°F.

Wrap the ham in aluminum foil and bake for 20 minutes per pound. Twenty minutes before the cooking is finished, remove the foil, and carefully slice the skin off the ham. Score the fat in diamond shapes, stud with cloves, and dredge with brown sugar. Return to the oven for 20 minutes, and, when the fat has browned, remove, and serve hot.

Serves 8.

Maple Syrup Sauce

Grimshaw tells us that Canada is the top-ranking syrup producer in the world, and syrup appears in many forms on local tables, from this superb syrup sauce to maple cream cookies. She explains it is important to use good balsamic vinegar and suggests serving the syrup in a gravy boat, so each guest may pour individual amounts.

1/2 cup pure Canadian maple syrup
1/4 cup horseradish sauce
2 tablespoons mustard
1/2 cup plus 2 tablespoons balsamic vinegar
6 tablespoons extra virgin olive oil
2 cloves garlic, finely crushed

Mix all the ingredients together thoroughly, and heat in a small sauce-pan until warm.

Serves 8.

Madame Lafleur's Laurentides Pie

Martine Monette of Quebec tells us the provenance for this pie was during the colonization of Eastern Canada when it was made with deer, partridge, rabbit, or moose. Her grandmother, Madame Lafleur, handed it down to Lise Bouthillier, Martine's mum, who, in turn, passed it to her. Martine explains, "This recipe is a Laurentides' recipe that is generations old and comes from the region of a thousand lakes, north of Montreal. The southern part of the region, where most food is made from fresh quality products, has large crop farms, milk farms, and apple orchards. Maman always made this meal for us in the autumn and winter."

Sifting through the recipes.
Anne Parsons

Note: It's important for the dough to be compact, so it doesn't rise too much while cooking. Serve with a rich brown or fruity sauce.

Dough
2 cups all-purpose flour
2 teaspoons baking soda
1/2 teaspoon salt
3 tablespoons vegetable oil

Mix the flour, baking soda, and salt. Add the oil and enough water to make a stiff dough. Mix well and roll the dough until it is 1/4-inch thick. Cut the dough into 2x6-inch strips.

2 pounds pork, cubed
2 large white onions, sliced
2 pounds white potatoes, peeled and sliced
2 cups beef broth
salt to taste
freshly ground black pepper to taste

In a heavy-bottomed pot, arrange in layers the onions, beef, pork, and potatoes. Cover with the beef broth, salt, and pepper. Arrange the dough strips in a lattice effect on top of layers.

Cover the pot, and cook over medium-low heat for 4 hours; adding more broth as needed to keep it from drying out. Make sure it does not boil over.

Serves 8.

China

*S*ummarizing briefly the profoundly sophisticated arts of the Chinese kitchen, Chinese cooking evolved along mainly geographic boundaries: wheat-eaters live in the north, rice-eaters in the south, fish-eaters in the east, and chili pepper-eaters in the west. Furthermore, this ancient cuisine has been shaped by several universal principles: frugality (every edible animal or plant part is used); seasonality (foods are eaten fresh and seasonally whenever possible); and sensuality (a proper Chinese meal is balanced for contrasting tastes, colors, aromas, and textures). The Chinese cook relies on numerous cooking techniques—commonly stir-frying, boiling, braising, and steaming—but the skilled person has a repertoire of at least forty ways to cook a dish.

The Chinese also have developed what is likely the world's oldest cuisine; one food historian talks about a second-century BC Chinese script that contains nine thousand characters pertaining to food and cooking techniques. And, writes Guan, for a central China TV show on the history of Chinese cooking, "Emperor Fuxi taught people to fish, hunt, grow crops and to cook twenty centuries before Christ. However, cooking could not be considered an art until the Chou Dynasty (1122–249 BC)."

According to many Sinophiles, the Cultural Revolution nearly terminated a majestic cooking tradition. As one Chinese observer noted about Mainland policy, "During the Cultural Revolution, they [the leaders] associated good living with political impropriety. That's the first time ever that eating out had become a political crime." But the preservers of China's culinary history—cookbook authors; scholars; artists;

poets; Chinese chefs who took up new posts in Hong Kong, Taiwan, and elsewhere; and families who fled to new homes overseas or who survived the long years in China—have ensured that traditional techniques and recipes live on and continue to please generations of Chinese and Westerners alike.

But modern times and Western ideas are making their impact on this ancient giant dragon. Change is inevitable, and for the gourmand, change is not always for the best. This is especially true in a place like Hong Kong, which has earned its reputation as the training ground for top-notch chefs (since most chefs who could, fled the mainland fifty-odd years ago) and as the showcase for the best of Asian, particularly Chinese, cooking.

Chinese festival food.
Kwang-Yen Hsu Fine

William Mark, a leading culinary spokesman in Hong Kong and man about the kitchen, once commented that today's Chinese chefs and their modern cuisine have become pretentious, with such dishes as "sashimi of Australian lobster sprinkled with gold flakes. That is Chinese cooking today," he said. "My heart aches when I think of this. That's the trend . . . Chefs are not interested in traditional cuisine."

Revolutionists—sometimes it seems that we do not learn very much from history's lessons.

Meat and Vegetable Buns
BAO TZE

D ah Fwu Fine, a longtime friend of the Parsons, has spent many years researching and documenting a family history that spans a thousand years and includes recent events such as the Chinese civil war prior to and after World War II, the Japanese occupation of China, the Cultural Revolution, and the Economic Reform in China today. Not surprisingly, his work-in-progress is entitled, *One Thousand Years of Family Tradition.*

Born in Koolonyu, a tiny island in the southeastern coast of China, Fine, a tall, quiet-spoken, retired engineer, who now lives on the Outer Banks of North Carolina, remembers an important annual event called "Tomb Sweeping Day," during which the family cleans the ancestors' tombs. He recalls it as a fun time because the family spent the afternoon working, then eating and socializing. At the last event he attended in 1947, when he was thirteen years old, Fine and other family members traveled to a remote area to visit one of his ancestor's tombs. They hiked twelve *li* (about six miles) along the mountainous trail to the tomb of his great-great-great grandfather, who had migrated to the southern part of China from Jeikiang province some three hundred years before. Their picnic food included a whole chicken, some duck, pork, steamed meat and vegetable buns, and fruit. Although he no longer celebrates this holiday, Fine says his family remains steeped in decades of memories and family traditions that include old photos and his grandmother's recipes.

Unlike their dumpling counterparts, *jaozi*, these dumplings are steamed rather than boiled and do not require a dipping sauce at the table to bring out their full flavor. For the best results, use a Chinese bamboo steamer that fits onto a stand in the bottom of a large wok.

Filling
1 pound ground pork
1 pound napa, or Chinese, cabbage, chopped
3 tablespoons chopped scallions

6 dried Chinese mushrooms, soaked in water and chopped
3 tablespoons sesame oil
3 tablespoons vegetable oil
2 tablespoons rice wine
5 tablespoons soy sauce
1 teaspoon minced ginger
1 teaspoon salt
1 teaspoon sugar
1 egg white

Buns
1 packet (1 tablespoon) active dry yeast
2 to 3 cups warm water, or enough to make a
    soft dough
7 to 8 cups all-purpose flour
2 tablespoons granulated sugar
1/2 teaspoon salt
3 tablespoons vegetable oil

Bao tze *dumpling.*
Brian Chou

To make the filling, combine the pork, cabbage, scallions, mushrooms, sesame oil, vegetable oil, rice wine, soy sauce, ginger, salt, sugar, and egg white, mixing well. Set aside.

To make the buns, combine the yeast with the water, stirring well. Put the flour in a second large bowl, and stir in the yeast. Add the sugar, salt, and oil, and knead into a soft dough. Remove the dough, lightly flour the bowl, put the dough in the bowl, and cover it. Let the dough rise for about 1 hour in a warm place.

Flour a work surface. Punch down the dough, and knead again on the floured surface. Roll the dough into a long sausage shape. Cut the dough into 1-inch lengths, flatten the pieces, and roll into the shape of a saucer.

Put 1 tablespoon of filling in the center of each flattened piece of dough, fluting the edges, pulling up the sides to form a bundle enclosing the filling. Seal by twisting and pinching the dough with thumb and forefinger.

Using a bamboo steamer, set the buns inside, without crowding, and steam them over boiling water for 15 minutes. Repeat the steaming process with extra buns, as needed. Serve hot.

Serves 8.

Eight Precious Rice

BA BO FUN

A native of Hunan province in China, Kwang-Yen Hsu, an architect and award-winning professional photographer, escaped with her family in 1948 when the Communists were taking over the country. Known to her Outer Banks' friends as Yen, she and her family were constantly on the run; each time they fled they were barely ahead of the advancing enemy forces. She will never forget the burning buildings, charred bodies, and the chaotic mass of humanity during this exodus. Yen vividly remembers taking shelter with her family, during air raids, in a huge cave by the banks of the Yangtze River, where cruise ships now sail. Yen, recollecting this time period, believes that "we kids survived simply because of our immense family bond." Yen quotes her husband, Dah Fwu, "I believe the family bond is an integral and indivisible part of life. Also, I believe triumph is not so much to defeat the enemy, achieve fame, or accumulate a fortune, it is being able to suffer through the worst of humanity and still survive, believing in the best of humanity." Yen feels one way for the family to bond is through the universal language of food—that families who eat together will cherish those special times." And, to remember those past relatives, Yen preserves her family's recipes—this is just one from her ancient chest of memories.

Fine says this dessert is traditionally served at holidays when family members and friends gather together. Sticky Asian "glutinous" or "sweet" rice, either long- or short-grain, is opaque and very glutinous, which is why the grains clump together after steaming. The rice is sold in Asian markets and is essential for the success of the recipe. Dried red dates, or *jujubes*, are a Chinese ingredient sold at Asian markets. They need to be soaked and pitted before use.

1 1/2 cups uncooked glutinous rice, rinsed
2 teaspoons vegetable oil plus extra for coating
2 tablespoons plus 2 teaspoons granulated sugar
1/2 cup lotus seeds, cooked 20 minutes and drained
1/2 cup dried red dates, steamed until softened

1/2 cup unsalted roasted peanuts
1/2 cup walnut halves
1/2 cup lychee pulp
1/2 cup seedless raisins, mix of golden and dark
1/2 cup red bean paste
1 tablespoon cornstarch
1/4 cup orange zest

*Portrait of her parents' wedding,
1936.* Kwang-Yen Hsu Fine

Place the rice in a deep pot. Add cold water to about three-quarters of an inch above the rice. Bring the water to a boil over high heat, and cook for about 4 minutes. Reduce the heat to low, cover the pot, and cook for about 15 minutes.

Remove the rice to a large bowl, and add 2 teaspoons of vegetable oil and 2 tablespoons of the sugar. Mix together well.

Coat an 8-inch-round bowl with vegetable oil. Lay out in a pattern the seeds, red dates, peanuts, walnut halves, lychee pulp, and raisins. Cover the ingredients with half the rice.

Spread the red bean paste over the rice, and top it with the remaining rice. Sprinkle 2 teaspoons sugar over the rice.

Put the bowl on a rack in a steamer, cover, and cook over boiling water for about 1 1/2 hours. Remove the bowl from the steamer, and invert it onto a serving platter. Combine the cornstarch, 3 tablespoons water, the remaining 2 teaspoons sugar, and the orange zest. Sprinkle this mixture over the rice, and serve hot.

Serves 8.

Grandma Wang's Superb Seaweed Noodles

Kuei-Fang Wang, born and raised in Nanjing, was the fourth child in a family of seven children (many decades before the government enacted the "one child" law). As the oldest daughter, she learned at a very young age to care for her brothers and sister, to help her mother run the household, and to assist in cooking the daily meals. The three surviving younger siblings still reside in Nanjing, but Grandma Wang came to the United States just a few years ago to spend time with her children and grandchildren. Growing up, her greatest joy was working in the kitchen where she showed unique talent for creating amazingly delicious dishes from fresh produce and little else. Her grandson, Albert Chou, lives in Cary, North Carolina, and believes his grandmother makes the best "Chinese Spaghetti" on the continent. Because she speaks only Mandarin, Chou follows her around as she cooks, takes notes, and translates her recipes into English. Since she never measures anything, Chou computes every ingredient. Chou, who earned a public health graduate degree from Emory University, believes that seaweed is an excellent source of trace minerals in our diet, essential for fighting stress and fatigue.

Grandma Wang prepares to cook. Albert Chou

Brian Chou, another grandson living in Virginia, suggests preparing this dish several hours in advance to give the seaweed time to marinate and absorb flavors.

8 ounces seaweed sheets (*kombu*)
1/2 tablespoon salt
1 tablespoon minced ginger
1/2 tablespoon minced scallions
1/2 tablespoon minced hot chilies
1/2 tablespoon salt
1/2 cup soy sauce
2 tablespoons fresh lime juice
1/2 teaspoon minced garlic
1/4 cup chopped fresh cilantro
1 tablespoon hot sesame oil
red chili strips, for garnish

Thoroughly wash the seaweed, and cut the sheets into 10-inch-long strips. Put the salt and 4 cups water into a large saucepan, and bring to a boil. Add the seaweed, and cook 20 minutes. Drain.

Put the seaweed into a large bowl, and toss with the ginger, scallions, chilies, salt, soy sauce, lime juice, garlic, cilantro, and sesame oil. Garnish with thinly sliced red chili strips, and serve.

Serves 6.

Candied Potatoes, Chinese-Style

Although rarely available in a Chinese-American restaurant, the classic Northern Chinese dessert of toffee apples—also known as "drawn thread toffee apples"—or toffee bananas appears often in restaurants in Beijing and elsewhere in China and Hong Kong. But during Mao's era, such delicacies disappeared, and for celebratory dishes, Chinese cooks had to substitute inexpensive and plentiful potatoes for apples. Sofia Lee of Xian remembers how her mother used to prepare this dish for her as a special birthday treat; her mother taught her how to make the candied potatoes, a dish Ms. Lee still enjoys as it brings back memories of her childhood. As she says, "When I was a little girl, life was hard. We were not able to get too many vegetables. When we had a special day, this was the special dish. Sugar was precious; we said it made life sweeter because our diet was so bitter. For the majority of Chinese, this is still a kind of memory. Now when we eat this, maybe our children don't understand, but we now appreciate life."

On Yangtze River, Sofia Lee cooks for authors. Anne Parsons

4 cups plus 1 tablespoon vegetable oil
4 large potatoes, peeled and cut into chunks
pinch salt
1 cup sugar
1/4 cup warm water

Heat the 4 cups oil in a large, heavy-bottom wok. Deep-fry the potatoes on all sides until golden, remove from the oil, and put on a serving platter. Sprinkle lightly with salt.

Drain the oil from the wok, and heat the remaining 1 tablespoon oil over medium heat. Add the sugar and water, and cook over medium heat, stirring constantly, until the sugar melts and browns slightly and forms a syrup. Add the potatoes to the sugar, stir, and coat well. Remove from the heat, and plunge the potatoes into cold water 1 or 2 at a time; this forms a caramelized crust on the potatoes.

Serves 6.

◆ Birthday Noodles ◆

When Sofia Lee was a child in Xian, China, her mother always fixed her these special noodles for her birthday. Sofia's mother taught her how to make them, and now Sofia prepares them for her son.

She writes, "Mix enough water with an amount of flour and 1 teaspoon salt to form a dough. Make the dough in the morning so that it can rest for at least four hours. When you are ready to eat, bring a large pot of salted water to a boil. Roll the dough out to 1/8 inch thick on a lightly floured surface. Roll the flattened dough up jellyroll style to form a plump log-shaped roll, and slice it thinly. Place the noodles in boiling water, drain, and boil a second time. Serve them topped with cooked greens, such as Chinese broccoli."

Birthday noodles
Brian Chou

England

- Bangers and Mash with Onion Gravy

- Bread and Butter Pudding

- Roast Beef with Horseradish Sauce and Yorkshire Pudding

- Fish with Yogurt and Saffron

- English Sticky Toffee Pudding

*W*herever you travel in England, you come face to face with England's heritage. Breathtaking views, historical characters, castles, ancient cathedrals, secluded beaches, and wild moors all add up to an amazing wonderland that inspired poets like Wordsworth and painters like Turner.

From the noble houses, gastronomic passions erupted into sustained extravagance with food painting and sculpture for fantastic feasts. Here, fowl such as peacocks and swans were de-feathered, roasted, and then reassembled to look alive. Augmented by wild game, fish, and ordinary fowl, the courtly table groaned under the excess of the chefs' culinary masterpieces. Meanwhile, the common folk grew their own vegetables, raised and butchered their animals, caught fish, and survived on a diet of plain, but superb, peasant fare.

English cottage with thatched roof in Somerset. Anne Parsons

Nowadays, although roast beef is England's national dish, a variety of ethnic foods are readily available all over the country. Many foodies of the older generation fret that traditional cooking will be lost in the melting pot of cuisines. Not to worry, there is an awakening of interest in regional cooking and in preserving a proper English culinary heritage.

Bangers and Mash with Onion Gravy

Cry God, for Harry, England, and St. George.
—William Shakespeare, *Henry V*

Russell Bates, of London, England, is very interested in promoting St. George's Day—a day to celebrate St. George, a martyr who protected the poor and defenseless—through traditional dishes the English and his family have cooked for generations. Take sausages, for example; Bates explains, "Bangers are sausages in England and supposedly derive their name from the tendency of the impoverished product during the last war to explode during cooking, due to the amount of water in them. Sausages with mashed potatoes and gravy are another of the great unregarded common dishes of English households still widely eaten and a delight in winter after a long trudge on a cold gray day."

Bangers and mash, bangers and mash. Jason Pittock

Bates advises using your local butcher, if you're lucky to have one—"the sort with sawdust on their floors, who still make sausages themselves and hang the links up in great hanks above their window display." He also says, "Although recently it has become a fashion to make weird and wonderful varieties, such as lamb and apple or whatever, for this you want good old-fashioned 'herby' pork sausages with a bit of sage in them, the big fat ones of which you get about eight in a pound's weight. Even raw, they smell wonderful."

Sausages
18 pork sausages

Bates advises not cooking sausages in a skillet or even barbecuing them because "they stick and split, and end up blackened on the outside and raw on the inside." Rather, he suggests roasting them in a greased dish in a 350°F oven for about 45 minutes.

Mash

"About half an hour after the sausages go in, start the potatoes for the mash. Peel a good number of potatoes (more than you think), place them in a pan full of cold, salted water, and put them on to boil. Generally they will take about 20 minutes to cook. Check them near the end; they are done when you can push a fork through them. Drain the boiling water from the potatoes (hold the lid on and tip the pan, but run some cold water down the sink if you have plastic drains). Add a knob of butter, a splash of milk or cream, and mash the potatoes thoroughly. (You need a potato-masher for this, a sort of iron-mongery grid on the end of a handle. Do **not** put the potatoes into a food processor because it will turn your mash into potato glue.) Mix the mashed potatoes up thoroughly until they are smooth, and cover the pot so they keep warm. (If you are a bit ahead of schedule or like your mash piping hot, put it into the oven with the sausages.) Meanwhile, you should also have been making your onion gravy."

Gravy

"Peel and roughly chop a couple of onions—you want quite a good quantity of onions. Drain some fat from your sausages in the oven, and then fry your onions in it in a skillet on the top of the stove. Stew the onions gently for a fair time so that they gradually brown a bit—the gravy will need a bit of color. (If the sausages have produced any sticky meat goo, scrape it up and add that to the fried onions, too.) Stir a big teaspoonful of ordinary flour into the greasy onion mix, and then add some water and stir the mixture until it thickens. Adjust the liquid content until you have the right consistency for your gravy and bring it back to a simmer. Don't worry if it doesn't look very good yet—at this stage the gravy is probably rather light and insipid, so the next thing to do is to correct its color and flavor. This is your chance to be creative with any odds and ends you have in your larder [pantry]. Add a small amount of tomato, some mustard, and a bit of marmite or soy to produce a richer color, and adjust the seasoning. Add a few herbs (a very few) if you feel like it, and if you have any beer, a bit of that is even better. Tinker with your gravy until you are reasonably happy with its appearance and flavor, then set it back on the stove, and allow it to simmer a little while longer.

"All things being equal, everything is now ready, and canny cooks will already have been warming the dinner plates. Put a big dollop of the mashed potatoes on each plate, lay several sausages beside the mash, pour some of the onion gravy over it, serve, and eat."

Serves 6.

Bread and Butter Pudding

Russell Bates loves this classic dessert that has been in his family as far back as he can remember. As he tells it, "It is an old English favorite. A shallow, glass baking dish really helps. Grease the baking dish with a little butter. Cut and butter a number of slices of white bread. (Do not remove the crusts.) Lay the slices in a layer in the bottom of the dish. Sprinkle over a little brown sugar, a little powdered cinnamon if liked, and some mixed dried fruit—currants, sultanas [raisins], and chopped candied peel. Add another layer of slices of bread and butter and more sugar and dried fruit. Finish with a layer of bread slices. (Do not put dried fruit on top, because it dries and burns.) Grate some nutmeg over the top. Beat 1 egg into about 1 3/4 cups milk. Pour over the pudding, and press it down a little, so that the milk comes nearly, but not up to, the top layer. Bake in a medium-to-low oven for about 1 hour, or until the top is browned. Serve."

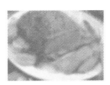

Roast Beef with Horseradish Sauce and Yorkshire Pudding

Jean Curnow Smith grew up just outside of Whitby in the Northeast of England. Curnow recalls, "Although we were near the seaside, my favourite times were spent on the farm in the Yorkshire Dales with my granny and great Aunt Margaret. I used to watch Auntie, after she cooked or baked something that she had tweaked, sit down at her well-scrubbed kitchen table and write in her jotter the updated recipe. She and granny took great pride in their table, and it was always loaded with good Yorkshire dishes when visitors popped by, which was often."

Yorkshire sheep on their way home. Anne Parsons

Curnow cherished that book, but tells us, "In one of my flittings (moves), the book got lost. Fortunately, there were many recipes I knew by heart, some I got from my dad before he died, and the rest I've tried to make by feel and taste."

Not long after Curnow shared her story, she was misdiagnosed for an ailment that turned out to be encephalitis—it damaged both of Jean's frontal lobes. Her husband and caretaker, Jim Smith, continues to use his wife's recipes that he has preserved for daughter Jale and granddaughters, Amanda and Sydney.

For this recipe, Smith suggests using joints of beef such as topside or sirloin, and if they are large, leaving them on the bone. He also mentions his roast beef is served slightly underdone—actually, rare, and that he serves the meat with flagons of ale—and plenty of horseradish sauce, the classic seasoning for roast beef.

Horseradish Sauce
4 tablespoons white wine vinegar

2 tablespoons balsamic vinegar
2 tablespoons stone-ground mustard
4 teaspoons granulated sugar
salt to taste
freshly ground black pepper to taste
6 tablespoons plain horseradish
6 tablespoons sour cream

Beef

1 (6- to 7-pound) sirloin or standing rib roast, trimmed
flour for sprinkling
2 ounces lard, melted

To make the sauce, stir the vinegars, mustard, sugar, salt, and pepper into the horseradish, and beat in the sour cream. Let sit for 4 hours before serving.

Preheat the oven to 425°F.

Wipe the meat with paper towels to remove any excess blood, and sprinkle it with flour. Put the meat into a roasting pan and cover it with the melted lard. Set the roasting pan on the middle shelf of the oven.

Roast for 30 minutes, basting frequently, and reduce the temperature to 350°F. Finish roasting at 20 to 25 minutes per pound, plus an extra 20 minutes. Let the roast stand 10 minutes before slicing.

Yorkshire Pudding

Smith says that when Jean's granny made "Yorkshire Pud," she'd put the mixture under the meat to catch the drippings. Of course, that's when meat was cooked at a very high heat. Smith advises beating the batter well; he says it causes air bubbles that encourage the batter to rise. If necessary, the batter may be made an hour before and set aside until the roast has cooked. It's important, however, to remember to beat the batter just before putting it in the oven. Smith also mentions that the pudding can be made in individual patty pans and, if they look magnificent as they pop up and stick out their chests, demanding to be eaten, then you know you've made a great "pud."

3/4 cup all-purpose flour
1/2 teaspoon salt
1 large egg

1 cup whole milk
1 tablespoon meat drippings

Preheat the oven to 400°F.

Sift the flour and salt into a bowl, and make a well in the center. Add the egg and gradually mix it in. Add half the milk slowly to keep the mixture smooth. Beat the mixture for 8 minutes, or put in a blender and process for 30 seconds. Slowly stir in the remainder of the milk.

Put some drippings into patty pans, and put in the oven until smoking hot. Pour the batter into the pans.

Bake for 15 to 20 minutes. Do not open the oven door during baking or the Yorkshire pudding may not rise properly. Serve hot.

Serves 6.

Fish with Yogurt and Saffron

"Yes, I know," says Minhaj Saiyid, whose law chambers are at the Inns of Court in London, "that most Americans on their first visit to England expect that, with the exception of fish and chips, all food here is tasteless." Saiyid has an inborn love of cooking and entertaining, especially for his three children, Adam, Anna, and Ben, and his multicultural friends. His passion for cooking began when his father taught him the art of making a delicious curry and stressed the importance of adding each spice separately and letting it release its essence before adding the next one. With all his culinary creations, Saiyid still loves to experiment in the kitchen, especially with old family recipes. "So," he chuckles, "rather than sharing a fish and chip recipe, why don't you try this delicate fish dish that relies on the fragrance of peppers. Oh, yes, do serve with basmati rice."

"Dinner is here!"
Anne Parsons

3/4 cup extra virgin olive oil
2 bay leaves
3 whole cloves
1 stick cinnamon
3 cardamom pods
1 teaspoon ground cumin
1/2 teaspoon chili powder
1 teaspoon finely chopped fresh ginger

1 medium-sized onion, chopped, optional
1 cup fish stock or bouillon
1 clove garlic, chopped
8 ounces plain yogurt
1/2 teaspoon saffron threads
1 sweet red pepper, cut into strips
1 sweet yellow pepper, cut into strips
1 1/2 pounds filleted white fish, such as halibut, hake, flounder, monkfish,
    or turbot
12 medium-sized shrimp, peeled
juice of 1 lemon

Put the oil and the bay leaves, cloves, cinnamon, and cardamom into a 12-inch skillet, and heat over medium-low heat. When the oil is hot, add the cumin, chili, ginger, onion if using, fish stock, and garlic. Stir and cook for 10 minutes. Remove the pan from the heat, and set aside to cool.

Return to the heat, and add the yogurt and saffron. Stir gently but constantly for 15 minutes, or until the oil and yogurt separate.

Add the red and yellow peppers, and cook until they soften but are still firm. Add the fish and shrimp, and cook for 7 to 10 minutes. Do not overcook. Add the lemon juice and serve immediately.

Serves 4.

 *English Sticky Toffee Pudding*

"When my niece and nephew (Anne and Simon Harrington) brought this dessert to my home for Christmas dinner one year, my family was delighted," says Alexandra Greeley. It has all the lush, rich, and fattening elements that holiday desserts must have to be decadent and sinful. Simon's mother, also named Anne Harrington, graciously shared the recipe (origins unknown), and it has since become a favorite holiday dessert in the Greeley family.

Pudding
6 ounces pitted dates
1 teaspoon baking soda
4 tablespoons (1/2 stick) unsalted
  butter
3/4 cup granulated sugar
2 large eggs
2 cups cake flour
1/2 teaspoon vanilla

"We want pud! We want pud!"
Nicci Greeley, MD

Sauce
1 cup brown sugar
6 tablespoons heavy cream
1 cup (2 sticks) butter
1 teaspoon vanilla extract

Preheat the oven to 350°F. Butter a 2-quart ovenproof baking dish.

Soak the dates in 1 cup water. Bring to a boil, and remove from the heat. Add the baking soda, and let stand.

Meanwhile, cream the butter and sugar until smooth; add the eggs, beating well. Fold in the flour, and stir in the dates with the water and the vanilla. Pour into the baking dish.

Bake for 30 to 40 minutes.

Meanwhile, make the sauce by heating the brown sugar, cream, butter, and vanilla extract in a small saucepan over low heat, and continue cooking and stirring until the sugar dissolves and the mixture become syrupy; stir often. When the pudding is firm in the center, pour 1/2 cup of sauce over the pudding, and continue baking 10 minutes more. Reserve the remaining sauce to serve with the pudding.

Serves 6.

France

- Buckwheat Galettes (Gallettes de Blé Noir)

- Soup with Milk (Soupe au Lait)

- Duck Breast with Port Sauce

- Potato Pastries (Galettes de Pommes de Terre)

France was my spiritual homeland. From [French chefs] I learned why good French food is an art, and why it makes such sublime eating . . . If one doesn't use the freshest ingredients or read the whole recipe before starting, and if one rushes through the cooking, the result will be an inferior taste and texture . . . But a careful approach will result in a magnificent burst of flavor, a thoroughly satisfying meal, perhaps even a life-changing experience.

—Julia Child, *My Life in France*

Eiffel Tower—a great place to meet friends.
Anne Parsons

*I*n this beautiful country of great food and celebrated wines, every meal is an epiphany of wonder. Although there are elegant restaurants serving superb haute cuisine, the best meals are the rustic, hearty dishes, or the unpretentious home-cooked fare that form the basis for many regional dishes. From high mountain plateaus to lush farmland, from ancient timbered villages to chic city streets, from soaring Gothic cathedrals to small village churches, it is easy to understand why the French people say they have it all.

French cuisine emanates from the strong kinship between the land and its people. With regional identities that are quite diverse—rocky terrain in the north, the broad fertile valleys in the central plateau, and the seductive beaches in the south—the French remain firmly connected to their rural roots.

Even with modernity bringing changes into their lives, meals still remain an important part of French daily routine; the French people cherish the time sitting around a table partaking in the pleasure of a leisurely meal and sharing good conversation with family and friends.

Buckwheat Gallettes
GALETTES DE BLÉ NOIR

Englishwoman Ruth Bown and her partner, Bob Bown, have lived in the small Breton village of Kerbras for thirteen years. She

Three villages barbecue in a farmer's barn in Bretagne.
Celine Crozier

cherishes the lifestyle of mellow sweetness in this bucolic environment. Recently she wrote to Anne Parsons, "I am sorry but we don't have any e-mail. We are a couple of techno-phobes, watching everyone else rushing to God knows where, like lemmings." Bown believes that life should be savored slowly, one day at a time. "For example, my neighbors, Yolande Crozier and her family," Bown says, "have lived here all their lives, rural and family oriented, coping with whatever the world can sling at them, yet they have a quiet knowledge of what is really worthwhile in life. These are Yolande's family recipes, simple but good."

The matriarch of the family, Grandma Puren (Salonge), explains Bown, "has lived in the village of Kerbras all her life. Born in the older part of the village, her mother had nine children and her family farmed the land. So there was plenty of milk, eggs, and flour, and her mother used to cook the gallettes and crêpes on the old forge in the cowshed. And that cowshed still has the forge and is Bob's workshop. Her mother also had the license to make l'eau de vie (a very potent apple liqueur). I once asked Salonge (Grandma Puren) how her big family fared during the Second World War. She tapped her nose with her finger and said, 'We never starved, and we never went without our wine.' After the War, her mother had a house built nearer the main road, and when Salonge married Pierre, they built their house attached to her mother's house, where they had six children. Her sister also built a house next door. Bob and I live in her mother's house now."

In Brittany, crêpes are usually cooked in a *pillig*, or pan, using a *rozell*, or spreader (looks like a large tongue depressor), to spread the mixture, and an *askelleden*, or spatula, to turn the crêpes at the half-way stage. A savory filling for these crêpes is goat cheese (*chèvre* cheese), but Crozier also suggests dotting the crêpe with butter, adding ham, eggs, or sausages, and folding it into quarters before serving.

Most Breton food is traditionally served with a *cul de fût* (bowl) of cider (a delicious farm cider).

14 ounces buckwheat or wheat flour
pinch salt
1/4 cup clarified butter, melted

Stir the flour and salt together; make a well in the center.

Gradually stir in 2/3 cups water, keeping the mixture smooth. Slowly, add another 2/3 cups of water, and beat well. Continue beating and add another 2/3 cups water until the batter is the consistency of thick cream. Beat in the butter, and let it sit for an hour. Add a little water, and beat again.

Grease a heavy skillet with buttered paper, and to test the readiness of the pan, put a drop of butter on its surface. When it sizzles, the heat is correct.

Pour 3 tablespoons of the batter into the skillet, and gently tip it back and forth, or use the *rozell*, until the batter evenly coats the bottom. Cook over high heat until set and lightly colored underneath. Turn and cook the other side. Serve with your choice of filling while still very hot.

Serves 6.

Soup with Milk
SOUPE AU LAIT

In the northwest corner of France, Brittany is formed by the sea and is culturally distinct from the rest of the country. The first Celts settled in this land that features the Megaliths at Carnac, and the incredibly beautiful Mont-Saint-Michel in the north. Between these two ancient towns, lies the small village of Kerbras. Here, Yolande Crozier's family has lived for generations; her friend, Ruth Bown, describes them as "the salt of the earth." Crozier writes that this is her father's recipe—a very simple peasant soup. She explains that butter is a prime ingredient in Breton recipes, and that together with milk, eggs, and flour, you have the base for many traditional dishes. Sup the soup with some local red wine like the ancient Bretons.

Yoland Crozier and her family at Sunday lunch in their garden. Celine Crozier

1 1/2 ounces salted butter
1 small onion, grated
1 quart whole milk
pinch freshly grated nutmeg
salt to taste
freshly ground black pepper
  to taste
1 baguette or 1 loaf French
  country bread

Brown the butter in a saucepan over medium heat, add the onion and milk, and bring to a boil. Add the nutmeg, salt and pepper, and cover; gently cook for 10 minutes.

Cut the bread into thin slices, and place them in a soup tureen. Pour the soup over the bread.

Serves 4.

Duck Breast with Port Sauce

After moving to Brittany from England, Ruth Bown stepped back from fast-paced living and changed gears to an enormously satisfying slow tempo. Bown explains to Anne Parsons that market gardening has been a way of life for many in this province for over two hundred years. In fact, she boasts, this area accounts for half of the artichokes in France. As an expat, she worried that the locals wouldn't accept her, but nothing could be further from the truth. "Not only," she writes, "are we accepted in the community, but also into their homes to share family meals. Many of my neighbors have been terribly generous in giving me their family recipes, many of which are now part of my family's repertoire of meals. This particular recipe was given to me a number of years ago by Madame Anne Duval from Bergerac." Bown describes her neighbors as warm and friendly, wedded to the land, and utterly modest.

2 duck breast fillets
2 teaspoons sea salt
1 teaspoon freshly ground black pepper
2 shallots, finely chopped
1 cup finely chopped onion
1 tablespoon granulated sugar
1 tablespoon wine vinegar
1/2 cup Ruby Port or Madeira
1 1/2 ounces butter

Ruth and Bob Bown take an evening stroll with friends.
Anne Parsons

Wipe the duck breasts, and score the skin side with a small sharp knife in a lattice pattern. Sprinkle with the salt, and season generously with pepper.

Heat a nonstick skillet over medium heat, and put the duck, skin-side down in it. Cook for 10 minutes, or until crisp and golden, then turn and cook for another 10 minutes. Remove the duck from the skillet, leaving about 1 tablespoon of fat in the pan. Keep the duck warm.

Add the shallots, onion, and sugar to the pan, and cook over a medium heat until softened and lightly caramelized. Add the vinegar, and boil until evaporated. Stir in the port and any juices that have come from the duck breasts, and boil for 2 to 3 minutes, until slightly reduced. Remove from the heat, and stir in the butter.

Cut the duck lengthwise into thin slices, and fan out on dinner plates. Spoon some sauce over each, and serve at once with a selection of vegetables.

Serves 4.

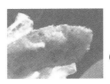

Potato Pastries

GALETTES DE POMMES DE TERRE

While the Loire Valley is known for its extraordinary chateaux—Chenonceau, Chambord, Blois, and Azay-le-Rideau—you will also swoon over the fresh cheeses and be seduced by the savory pastries. We rented a house in a tiny village, Beaumont-sur-Dême, with the intention of improving our French and getting to know the local villagers, especially the baker, greengrocer, cheese maker, and farmer. During those three summers, Anne Parsons, with friends Ruth Thompson and Beth Black and their daughters, made friends with many of the locals, were invited to their homes to sup with them, and swapped recipes with the family cooks.

Jen cycles to the lake.
Shaler Black

This recipe is a family favorite of Madame Ghislaine, whose family has lived in the Valley for as long as she can remember. She shared it with friends, Shaler Black, Jennifer Parsons, and Sarah Walsh, who took these pastries in their backpacks each day when they cycled to the local lake. And many evenings the girls would eat these pastries, sometimes filled with ham, or mushrooms picked in the caves in the local village (where Madame Ghislaine has worked all her adult life), with a large salad. They would also purchase the *chèvre* cheese (goat cheese) from Monsieur Corbeau, whose farm was across the field from our rented house, *L'Aitre Boutin*.

large salad. They would also purchase the *chèvre* cheese (goat cheese) from Monsieur Corbeau, whose farm was across the field from our rented house, *L'Aitre Boutin*.

1 1/2 pounds potatoes, peeled and diced
1 1/4 cups all-purpose flour
3 ounces fresh goat cheese
1 tablespoon minced chives
1 tablespoon minced garlic
1 tablespoon rosemary
4 tablespoons (1/2 stick) unsalted butter
1 egg yolk mixed with 1 tablespoon water, for glazing

Preheat the oven to 375°F.

Boil the potatoes until fork tender, and drain. Mash the potatoes until smooth, and set aside until cold.

Mix enough flour into the potatoes to form a soft dough. Blend the cheese, chives, garlic, and rosemary with the butter, and shape it into a flat block.

Flour a work surface, and roll the dough out into a 1/4-inch-thick rectangle. Place the cheese block into the center, and fold up the dough along the long sides to cover the cheese. Fold up the bottom third, and fold down the top third. Crimp the edges shut with a fork.

Cover the pastry, and chill for 15 minutes. Then repeat the rolling and folding twice more, and chill between each folding. Chill the last time for an hour. Roll out the dough, then cut into 12 to 15 rectangles about 3- to 4-inches long. Brush with the egg and water glaze.

Bake for 30 minutes, or until golden. Transfer to a wire rack to cool.
Makes 12 to 15 pastries.

Greece

- ♦ CHICKEN SOUP WITH EGG-LEMON FROTH (AVGOLEMENO)

- ♦ STUFFED CABBAGE ROLLS

- ♦ ROAST LAMB, GREEK-STYLE

- ♦ MOM'S CHICKEN AND ORZO

- ♦ SEMOLINA DESSERT (HALVA)

- ♦ SHAPED BUTTER COOKIES (KOULOURIA)

*A*nyone who has watched the movie *My Big Fat Greek Wedding* probably comes away believing that Greeks enjoy sumptuous repasts every day. And such a plan would appeal to everyone who loves good food. Greeks are proud of their cuisine, and, in fact, they proclaim that theirs may be the oldest cuisine, with a cookbook dating back to 300 BC; the Chinese would disagree.

Parashos's father herding sheep in the village of Ormenipo.
Parashos Parashidis

However, their earliest cooking became later influenced by the waves of invaders—Italians, Balkans, and Turks—who swept across Greece in intervening centuries, leaving behind the inspiration for such dishes as baklava, *dolmades*, pilaf, and moussaka. Yet what has inspired Greek cooks over the years has resulted in a cuisine that is the very model of the Mediterranean diet, a prescription for a long and healthy life based on eating whole grains, fresh vegetables, fresh fruits, seafood, olive oil, and very little meat. What particularly helps is that much of Greece, in general, has mild and wet winters countered by hot and dry summers, a climate that helps farmers raise their bountiful crops.

Greek cooking is replete with hearty, sturdy dishes that depend on olives and olive oil, sharp wines, and the regional, seasonal ingredients fresh from the land—assorted vegetables, rice, and whole grains—to plentiful seafood (Greece boasts about 2,000 islands and 15,000 miles of coastline). And that doesn't include the luscious sweets—the baklava, *halvas*, and *koulouria*—for which Greek cooks have become famous.

To help spread the appeal of Greek cooking, Nikki Rose, who is a Slow Food member of Greek heritage, now lives in Crete (the cradle of the Mediterranean diet), runs travel and cooking tours through Crete, and has her own website—www.cookingincrete.com—extolling the virtues of this simple country fare. Indeed, the main goal of her enterprise is to preserve the culinary heritage of that island. Perhaps Crete will be the microcosm of all that makes Greek cooking so memorable, lusty, and inviting.

Chicken Soup
with Egg-Lemon Froth
AVGOLEMENO

Nikki Rose—an American food writer and professional chef who now lives on Crete—writes about her Greek in-laws who live in northeastern Greece. "My in-laws, Christos and Vasiliki Moldovanidou, live in an isolated area on the rugged mountain border of Bulgaria and the Evros River that divides Greece and Turkey. The region is called Trigono (triangle). Their village, Dikea, is one of many small Greek farming communities where most residents are retired industrial farmers, and home farm-gardens are a basic necessity. Their house is built like a train car on a ridge overlooking the valley. A maze of cement walkways leads to rich, black soil gardens, barns and poultry coops. Chickens and turkeys occupy the rest of the property.

"Vasiliki recently retired at the age of 67, after running a sizable cereals farm, which she carried on with the help of her sons long after her first husband died. Her blue eyes are soft with a spark of whimsy, yet I've never met a woman as strong and strong-willed as she. Trim and vivacious, Christos only sits down to relax at mealtime. At 81 years of age, he's more fit than many men half his age. Judging from their storeroom shelves stocked with homemade wine and spirits, dried fruits, preserves, juices, pickled vegetables, sausages, herbs and garlic hanging from the rafters, I wonder if Christos and Vasiliki ever have time to sleep.

"Vasiliki is by no means a conventional Greek woman of her era. She drives a pickup truck (many women in her age group don't drive at all) and operates the farm tractor while juggling a host of domestic tasks. Around here, those tasks include raising and growing your own food, preserving enough for the winter, weaving textiles, knitting clothing; the list is daunting. I lovingly call her 'the general' because no one just sits around her house unless it's time to eat and she makes sure of that.

"With a stream of family and friends visiting, their house is rarely empty. We pack ourselves into the kitchen-living room with a wood-burning oven, the only heat source in the house. Vasiliki is much more than a great home cook; she is a master at combining flavors from recipe ideas shared with people from the north and the east. She makes a daunting range of savory and sweet pies and bread. We are all Vasiliki's assistant chefs and do whatever we can (or are instructed to do) in her kitchen.

"With the help of an electric beater, I have made *avgolemeno* soup (*avga* means "egg" and the rest is a good guess) since I was a teenager. It seemed so complicated—tempering eggs into hot soup. When I saw Vasiliki make it with great ease, while she whipped the egg whites with just two forks, I wanted to camp out in her kitchen until further notice. I was beginning to understand regional Greek cuisine—recipes begin with raising or grow-

Moldovanidou's poultry coop.
Parashos Parashides

ing your food first. After that, it's only natural to know how to treat those flavors with respect and master the heat of a wood-burning stove. Wasting food is not an option. The key to making this recipe successfully is using fresh and organic ingredients."

1 medium-sized chicken, about 3 to 4 pounds, preferably organic
1 1/2 quarts water
salt to taste
1/2 cup small-grain rice
3 large eggs, separated
1/2 cup fresh lemon juice
lemon wedges

To make the stock, in a large stockpot, cook the chicken in lightly salted water over medium-low heat until done, about 1 hour. Remove the chicken, divide it into serving pieces, and keep warm. Add the rice to the stock, and continue cooking over medium-low heat until tender, about 20 minutes. Remove from the heat, cover, and keep warm.

Meanwhile, to prepare the *avgolemeno*, separate the eggs. Place the yolks in a bowl, and whisk them until smooth. Place the whites in a large stainless steel bowl, and whip the egg whites to soft peaks. Very gradually whisk in the yolks, then the lemon juice just until incorporated.

Continue whisking the eggs while adding one ladle of hot stock in a very slow stream. This process of "tempering" the eggs will prevent them from curdling when they are added to the soup. Repeat the process with one more ladle of stock.

Using a spatula, gently fold the egg mixture into the soup to prevent the air bubbles in the egg sauce from breaking, and to form a nice blanket of froth on top of the soup. Do not bring the soup to a boil, as high heat might curdle the eggs and will deflate the frothy blanket. Serve immediately with pieces of chicken and lemon wedges.

Note: If the stock seems bland, add a cup or two of rich chicken stock. You can also add diced and sautéed aromatics, such as onions, leeks, and carrots. You may choose to put some of the chicken pieces into the soup or just serve it alongside.

Serves 6.

Stuffed Cabbage Rolls

Nina Alexiou, of Silver Spring, Maryland, was born and raised in northwestern Greece, where the meals consist of meat, potatoes, and vegetables of all kinds, often combined into sturdy, main-course pies like *spanakopita*, made from phyllo dough, meat, cheese, and spinach. "When I was growing up," she says, "we ate more vegetables than meat. A typical dinner consisted of a bean soup, plenty of rice and potatoes, and some meat to go with it. We used chicken, lamb, and pork, meats typical of the small towns and vegetables in that part of Greece. Breakfasts of milk, bread, cheese, and eggs resembled an American farm breakfast."

Nina Alexiou tasting treats at a Greek festival.
Alexandra Greeley

One of her mother's specialties was stuffed cabbage leaves, made from fermented cabbage leaves rolled around a filling of ground pork. Using sauerkraut in this recipe helps to replicate the flavors of her mother's version without having to use fermented cabbage leaves. You can serve these solo; they need no accompaniments besides bread and salad.

1 large head green cabbage, cored, or 16 large cabbage leaves
1 1/2 pounds ground pork or mix of ground pork and beef or ground
    pork and veal
1 large onion, peeled and chopped
1/2 cup medium-grain rice
1/2 cup plus 2 tablespoons ketchup
juice 1/2 lemon

1 tablespoon paprika, optional
salt to taste
freshly ground black pepper to taste
pinch allspice
3 tablespoons olive oil plus extra for brushing and drizzling
1 (29-ounce) can sauerkraut

Cut off the tough stem ends from the cabbage leaves. Parboil them in lightly salted boiling water for 5 minutes, or until soft enough to fold. Remove, and set aside to cool. Brush the bottom of a large stockpot lightly with olive oil.

Combine the meat, onion, rice, ketchup, lemon juice, paprika (if using), salt, pepper, and allspice, mixing well. Place one leaf, rounded edge towards you, on a flat surface. Depending on the size of the leaf, put 2 to 3 tablespoons of the mixture onto the leaf edge, and press it lengthwise to fit. Roll the leaf once away from you. Fold in both sides to contain the filling, and continue rolling it up. Place the roll, seam side down, in a large stockpot. Continue with the remaining leaves and filling.

After placing the first layer of rolled leaves in the stockpot, drizzle them with part of the olive oil and some sauerkraut juice, and spread about 1 cup sauerkraut over the rolls. Repeat with the second layer of rolls. Drizzle on the remaining olive oil, and pack the remaining sauerkraut over the rolls. Place a heatproof plate on top of the rolls, and cook the mixture over low heat for 2 hours; high heat causes the cabbage leaves to stick to the pot. Serve hot.

Serves 4 to 6.

Roast Lamb, Greek-Style

According to Aglaia (Lea) Nikides O'Quinn, who grew up in a Greek household in Dayton, Ohio, with her parents, maternal grandmother, two younger sisters, and one older brother, "My family was quite active in the church, and we kids were active in church activities as well as in Greek School, which we attended either after regular school, in the evening, or during summer vacation. As a result, we learned the Greek language, both by speaking Greek at home to my grandmother, but also by studying it in Greek School. We also participated in Greek plays and programs where we sometimes dressed in Greek costumes (as for Greek Independence Day), and we often were called on to perform Greek poems. All of this was a source of great pride for my mother, but we didn't always think it was so great, as you can imagine.

Succulent lamb ready to serve.
Anne Parsons

"My grandmother and my mother together would plan the meals for our family, and then my mother would bring home all the groceries, and my grandmother would cook. Occasionally my mother would help, but her specialty was the desserts.

"She also made an excellent *peta* (any dish that uses phyllo dough for a top and bottom crust encasing a filling) from a recipe she learned about from my father's relatives from northern Greece. My mother made the phyllo for this *peta* by herself, rather than buying ready-made phyllo. Although I watched her make this many times while I lived at home, I have not been able to duplicate the delicate phyllo, which she made. There is some secret which eludes me. I have tried to make this innumerable times, and my sisters have joined me, but so far we only approximated what my mother turned out with little effort.

"This *peta* was so special in our community that my mother was often asked to give demonstrations of how to make it. I can't tell you how many times women gathered at our house to watch the demonstrations, and then to enjoy eating the product. I wonder now if any of them were able to go home and repeat what they had seen done."

"Also when I was growing up, we mostly had roast lamb on special occasions, and especially at Easter. It was a very special meal for us. This recipe was the one used in my family, but it also is probably very similar to what most Greeks do with roast lamb—that is, it is not a unique recipe. Sometimes, my grandmother, who was the chief cook, would add peeled and quartered potatoes to the shallow pan in which the lamb is cooking, toward the end of the cooking time, and the potatoes would cook along with the lamb and would absorb the flavor from the mixture which had been used for the basting. Some water would have to be added occasionally to the bottom of the pan so that the potatoes did not burn."

1 (5-pound) leg of lamb
5 cloves garlic, gently crushed
1/2 cup olive oil
2 tablespoons crumbled fresh oregano
1/2 teaspoon fresh thyme
salt to taste
freshly ground black pepper to taste
juice of 1 lemon

Make 5 slits all over the leg of lamb, and push the garlic cloves into the slits. Combine the oil, oregano, thyme, salt, pepper, and lemon juice in a mixing bowl. Rub the lamb with the oil mixture, and put the leg onto a rack in the roasting pan. Set the meat aside for several hours.

Preheat the oven to 450°F. Line a second roasting pan with foil. Put the leg into the roasting pan.

Reduce the oven temperature to 350°F. Roast the lamb, basting it with the remaining oil mixture 3 to 4 times during the cooking period, for 1 1/2 hours for pink or medium-rare meat or for 2 hours for well-done meat.

Serves 6 to 8.

Mom's Chicken and Orzo

Nikki Rose—an American food writer who now lives on Crete—comes from a Greek family and is passionate about her native food. She writes from Crete, "When I asked my brothers and sister which of Mom's meals were their favorite, I got a list with wonderful descriptions and stories. Mom's love for us and for life was ever present in her cuisine.

Vasiliki Lapanoudi cooking at home. Parashos Parashides

"The atmosphere and scents from our childhood kitchen are so vivid. As hard-working Greek-Americans in the restaurant business (surprise, surprise but French restaurants, not Greek!), life revolved around cooking and eating together. Music and a little dancing is a given. Living in the suburbs of Washington, D.C., my family found that there was not much in the way of quality Greek retail products years ago. Greek food in the restaurants was usually mediocre then, too.

"But at home, Mom had the golden touch with food. She always managed to find gorgeous oregano and olive oil from Greece, and we often got our meats directly from restaurateurs, which was of a much higher quality than our local supermarkets sold back then. Mom cultivated other flavors of Greece in our tiny backyard—always tomatoes, figs, berries, cucumbers, and some years even corn! We really needed a bigger backyard for corn and it took up a lot of our kickball field. No one in our neighborhood grew anything but flowers, so this seemed very odd to them.

"Mom was a food purist before we knew what that was. She was a and flash (fancy presentations) was optional. When our friends were eating chips and pretzels, we were fighting over artichokes and yogurt. We didn't know then that we were the lucky ones—to develop good eating habits from day one.

"During the holidays, Mom invited everyone to our house —no formal RSVP was required. I still don't know how she gauged how much food we would need for 20 drop-ins, but she did. Over the years our friends never missed 'Greek' Easter at our house and the place was packed. It did not matter what, if any, religious beliefs our friends had, it was a celebration with family and friends . . . a taste of our family's homeland. We all just remember how fun it was and still carry on the Greek Easter tradition, which is easier today as far as finding products, but harder for friends to join us, since our lives are more hectic now.

"Many dishes were unfamiliar to our friends and there were certainly too many vegetables around for their taste. But today, my friends ask for those recipes they nervously but trustingly sampled and discovered they were delicious, like spinach pie or chicken with orzo. Chicken with Orzo is one of those heavenly, seemingly simple dishes. The exotic (for many!) pinch of cinnamon offers a familiar, comforting scent. Serve with lemon wedges, a nice hunk of feta cheese, and sautéed spinach or a big green salad."

Chicken
1 (3 1/2- to 4-pound) chicken, cut into serving pieces
3 tablespoons extra virgin olive oil
2 tablespoons dried Greek oregano, crushed
salt to taste
freshly ground black pepper to taste

Orzo
2 tablespoons extra virgin olive oil
1 medium-sized onion, chopped
4 cloves garlic, minced
2 medium-sized fresh tomatoes, chopped or 1 (14.5-ounce) can Roma tomatoes, crushed
1 1/2 cups orzo
1 tablespoon dried oregano, crushed
1/4 teaspoon ground cinnamon or one cinnamon stick
pinch salt
pinch freshly ground black pepper

pinch freshly ground black pepper
3 1/2 cups chicken stock
lemon wedges for garnish

Preheat the oven to 350°F.

To prepare the chicken, rinse the chicken pieces with cold water and dry well with paper towels. Rub the pieces with the olive oil and seasonings. Put the chicken into a large, heavy roasting pan. Roast for 30 minutes, basting once or twice with the pan juices.

Remove from the oven, and let the pan cool slightly. Transfer the chicken pieces to a plate, reserving most of the chicken juices and the fat in the pan.

Meanwhile, to prepare the orzo, heat the oil in a large skillet over medium-high heat, and sauté the onion until just golden. Add the garlic, and sauté 2 minutes more. Add the tomatoes, orzo, oregano, cinnamon, salt, pepper, and stock, and stir to combine. Bring the mixture to a boil, and reduce the heat to low. Cover the pan, and cook for 15 minutes, stirring occasionally.

Transfer the orzo mixture to the roasting pan, and stir it together with the pan juices. Gently shake the pan so the orzo becomes a bed for the chicken, but is not packed down. Place the chicken pieces on top of the orzo, and return to the oven.

Roast another 15 to 30 minutes, or until the chicken is cooked. Check the corners of the pan, and stir the orzo if it starts to stick. If it becomes too dry, add a little stock or water. Remove the chicken, and keep it warm. Stir the orzo to incorporate the juices, and gently transfer it (do not pack it down) to a large serving platter. Distribute the chicken pieces on top, and serve.

Serves 6.

Semolina Dessert
HALVA

Called *halva*, or *halvah*, this dessert is not really similar to the Middle Eastern *halvah* made with sesame seeds because this calls for coarse semolina, available at Greek or Middle Eastern markets. The dessert also remains spoonable or sliceable, rather like a very thick pudding; you cannot cut this into bars or cookie shapes. Nina Alexiou says her mother called this dish "1, 2, 3, 4" because of the ingredient measurements.

Nikki Rose's aunts grinding wheat. Nikki Rose

"We all loved these," she says, noting that it has a perfect consistency for molding into individual shapes or in one large mold. She says her grandmother used to scoop a portion into tablespoons as molds and serve the dessert in the spoons. This is a simple recipe, taking no more than 45 minutes to make from beginning to end. Before serving, sprinkle each portion with ground cinnamon. Although considered a family or informal dessert, halvah can be molded and dressed up with whole almonds.

3 cups sugar
1 cup vegetable oil
2 cups coarse semolina
cinnamon stick, optional
1/2 cup slivered almonds
ground cinnamon for sprinkling

Boil the sugar and 4 cups water over medium heat, stirring often, until the mixture becomes syrupy, 25 to 30 minutes. Set aside.

Meanwhile, in a second pot, heat the oil over medium heat, add the semolina and cinnamon stick (if using), and cook it, stirring constantly to prevent burning, until it begins to turn brown. Add the almonds, and let them brown slightly. When the color is uniformly brown-gold, re-move from the heat. Add the syrup all at once, taking care to avoid the splattering.

Put the pan back on the burner, and cook, stirring constantly, until all the sugar syrup is absorbed. Remove from the heat, cover with a clean towel, and set aside for several minutes until the mixture cools slightly. Pour it into one large or several smaller molds, and cool completely.

Shaped Butter Cookies
KOULOURIA

These round or twisted cookies, called *koulouria*, are a staple of the Greek household. Nina Alexiou notes that every Greek housewife has these on hand to offer guests who drop by for a cup of coffee. Alexiou says when her mother first came to the United States and asked for baking ammonia—a powdery, lemony product that works like baking powder—grocers handed her the ammonia for cleaning. She finally found the American equivalent—baking powder.

Delicious Greek pastries.
Anne Parsons

1/2 pound (2 sticks) butter
1/2 pound granulated sugar or 1
  cup granulated sugar
2 egg yolks
3 to 3 1/2 cups all-purpose flour
1 teaspoon baking powder
1/2 teaspoon baking soda
1/2 cup whole milk
1 teaspoon vanilla extract
1 egg beaten with 1 teaspoon water
  for glaze

Preheat the oven to 350°F. Lightly butter a baking sheet.

Using an electric mixer, cream the butter and sugar together until smooth. Add the yolks, one at a time, and beat well after each addition. Combine the flour, baking powder, and baking soda. Mix in the dry ingredients alternately with the milk and vanilla, starting with the flour mixture. The dough should be soft, but still hold a shape; add more flour, if needed.

To make the cookies, pinch off a piece of dough about 1 inch round, and roll it out to 6 inches long and the width of a little finger. Fold the length in half, and twist it to make a loop. Repeat with the remaining dough. Brush the cookies with the egg glaze.

India

- Steamed Shad or Hilsa (Ilish Machher Bhapa)

- Lamb Dumplings in a Special Sauce (Rishta Kofta)

- Tempered Red Pumpkin (Kaddu Ki Subzi)

- Fried Whole Wheat Puff Bread (Poori)

- Lamb or Chicken with Lentils (Dhansak)

*P*unjabi housewife and cookbook author Mrs. Balbir Singh in her 1961 edition of *Indian Cooking* sums up India's cuisine simply: "Indian food has an uncanny charm and those who once taste Indian food find that all other food is insipid and tasteless in comparison." For those people who have fallen in love with the cooking from the vast subcontinent, these words ring true.

But even its greatest fans may not know that the cuisine of India has evolved from numerous traditions, techniques, and ingredients imported from the many invaders who settled in the subcontinent, including Mongol and Hun, Portuguese and Jew, Hindu and Muslim, Greek and Turk, Saracen, Persian, and Tartar, to say nothing of the British. That means defining what is the heart and soul of Indian cooking is almost impossible, since the cuisine varies not only from region to region, but also from state to state, town to town, community to community, and possibly from household to household. Factor into that the number of existing cooking styles—the Handi, Kadhai, and Tawa, for example—that have a welter of interpretations. Added to that are other layers of complexity: for example, the ancient Ayurvedic medical philosophy links specific foods to health, providing the fundamental philosophy of Indian cooking and spicing. And differing religious practices consider some foods—such as pork for some groups and all types of meat for others—absolutely taboo. Plus climate and geography also determine who eats what where.

Yet despite the multiple complexities, Indian cooks do have something in common: they respect their ingredients and seasonings and devote time and energy to achieving the subtle and layered flavors that characterize fine Indian cooking. That is the single common culinary thread that binds India's diverse cooking styles together—the ingenious use of seasoning blends, or *masalas*.

The backbone of Indian cooking, the *masala* has as many versions and variations, it seems, as cooks. And *masalas* can transform humble portions of chicken, goat, or lamb into dishes fit for maharajahs. Cooks formulate *masalas* to suit their palate, their style, and a particular dish—for example, some spices are too potent for delicate poultry, fish, and vegetables. Northern *masalas* are a blend of dry spices, the most familiar being the *garam masala* ("hot spices"), whereas southern *masalas* are pastes of dried spices moistened possibly with lemon juice, yogurt, or coconut milk.

The majestic Taj Mahal.
Anne Parsons

And most Indians expect—and demand—freshly cooked meals. Dr. Sambhu Banik of Bethesda, Maryland, tells of relatives, who lived in America temporarily, finally moving back to India. The reason? The husband could not eat a meal that had been cooked earlier in the day or maybe a day before, and he could not tolerate processed foods. To modern Americans, that may seem unrealistic, but those who love good food probably understand the premise—fresh is best. And they might agree that thoughtfully and carefully prepared Indian meals may be among the most outstanding culinary treats in the world.

Steamed Shad or Hilsa

Ilish Machher Bhapa

According to Bengal native Dr. Sambhu Banik of Bethesda, Maryland, his parents always put a premium on serving good food and sharing it with others. He remembers that they were very religious and treated their guests with utmost dignity. Like all Bengalis, his parents believed that the body was a temple, and that food must elevate the soul. His mother was also a very good cook, he says, and like most Bengali women, had complete control over the kitchen, a sacred place. Every morning before striking a match to light the kitchen wood fires, his mother knelt to pray to the kitchen god Agni, and then began her daily meal preparations. This fish dish was one she prepared often.

He says that two elements characterize Bengali cooking: the use of mustard oil and access to some of the best freshwater fish in the world. As he says, among all the fish, *elish* (or *hilsa*, or shad) has a unique fascination for the Bengalis, an almost mythological element. To every Bengali, *hilsa* evokes some romanticism about fish preparation, and the fish represents either the Cadillac or Rolls-Royce of fish preparation. To a Bengali, nothing comes close to either Padmar (*hilsa* from the Padma River) or Gangar (*hilsa* from the Ganges), because it has an outstanding taste and flavor, which is not available in American shad. If you live near a well-stocked Indian market, you may be able to buy frozen *hilsa*; otherwise, wait until springtime and use shad.

You can easily prepare the special seasoning pastes at home. For the chili paste, use a good ground cayenne or Kashmiri red chili powder from an Indian market, and mix a teaspoonful with enough water to make a paste. For the cumin paste, he suggests toasting and then grinding cumin seeds, and mixing a teaspoonful of the ground seeds with enough water to make a paste. Likewise with the mustard paste, you simply pulverize yellow or red mustard seeds, and mix a teaspoonful of ground seeds with enough water to make a paste.

This dish requires that you partially cook basmati rice first, and use the hot rice as a bed and a covering for the banana-leaf-wrapped fish. Be sure to use a very deep pan to accommodate both the rice and the fish.

3 pounds fresh shad, skinned and boned and cut into 1/2-inch pieces
salt to taste
1 teaspoon ground turmeric
1 teaspoon red chili paste, or according to taste
1 teaspoon cumin paste
1 teaspoon mustard paste
1 cup mustard oil
banana leaves for wrapping

Put the fish pieces into a large, nonreactive glass baking dish to marinate. Mix the salt, turmeric, red chili paste, cumin paste, mustard paste, and mustard oil together, and coat the fish pieces with it thoroughly. Use two layers of banana leaves one on top of the other, cut to fit all the fish pieces in one packet. Place the fish on top of the leaves, fold the leaves over the fish tightly, and using toothpicks or bamboo skewers, secure the packet closed.

Dr. Sambhu Banik's family in Calcutta, 1957.
Banik family album

Make a well in the center of the partially cooked rice, removing enough so that the fish packet fits in the pan. Replace the rice in the pan, covering the packet with the rice. Cover the rice pot with a lid, and continue cooking the rice over medium-low heat until done, about 10 minutes more. This steams the fish.

Spoon out the top layer of rice, and carefully remove the packets, putting it on a serving platter. Put the cooked rice in a serving dish, and unwrap the banana leaves. Serve both fish and rice while hot.

Note: Although most cooks tell you to remove the strong taste of mustard oil by heating the oil to the smoking point and then cooling it before using it to cook, Dr. Banik says Bengalis don't do that because they love the strong flavor of mustard oil.

Serves 6.

Lamb Dumplings in a Special Sauce
RISHTA KOFTA

Ajit Kalra, raised in New Delhi, India, and the son of India's leading food guru J. Inder Singh, grew up appreciating fine foods. Yet, one of the dishes he remembers most clearly—and fondly—is one his grandmother cooked for the family, *rishta kofta* (lamb dumplings in a special sauce). "The memories I have of *rishta kofta* are that of my grandma making it in the kitchen, and my brother and I peering through the kitchen door totally intoxicated by the fragrance of mustard oil with fennel and ginger." He adds, "My grandmother was always famous for being an exceptional cook. Not exceptional as an excited expression, but exceptional in the real sense of the word. Friends and family were always findings excuses to come over for lunch, and most of them freely admitted that my grandma's food was the best that they had ever tasted. In fact, she was the inspiration behind dad's career in the culinary world.

"As is often the case in collective societies, my grandparents and my family lived in the same home. My grandmother was always planning the entire week's meals ahead of time. She was a little lady with a very pleasant face, and skilled in every walk of life. Creating foods was one of her many talents: She had a master's touch, and measuring instruments were never part of her cooking equation. Decades of knowledge and experience always translated into flavorful foods.

"Like all doting grandparents, she took great joy in cooking for my brother and me. Each morning, she would make her way from her bedroom to the kitchen where she would start the elaborate cooking process. The meal preparations started with the purchase of fresh foods everyday, peeling of vegetables, and the grinding of spices. Even though we had multiple refrigerators in the house, leftovers were never popular—yes, we were spoiled in that sense. My grandma had developed arthritis in her old age and could not stand for too long, so she used a stool for all her cooking. I distinctly remember her old-fashioned double-burner gas stove, which required more artistic skill than scientific knowledge to be used effectively. However, she worked magic with it every day of the year.

"The house was always filled with the fragrances of aromatic herbs from the kitchen, which helped keep everybody's appetite healthy throughout the day. If it wasn't the main entrees for the meals, it was the frying or baking of Indian snacks like *matthees* or *samosas*. Homemade pickles, chutneys, sherbets, and even ice cream (especially mango) were part of the food offering in every season. We would enjoy the fragrance of coriander, mint, cilantro, cloves, cardamom, and a million other aromas throughout the year. She was always inventing new combinations of foods, working with her little hands, taking such pride in all her creations. My brother and I were always hovering around her feeling a great comfort in her presence.

Samosas are also known as curry puffs. Hartini

"In my years growing up, grandma was always adamant about family time at the dinner table. Not only was the food scrumptious, she would also time meals perfectly so that there was never a painful anticipation. In return, she demanded that everybody was present and ready at the start of the meals. The whole family would be seated around several bowls of food, passing the food around, and savoring the flavors. It truly was a joyous experience every day."

Rattanjot is a medicinal herb—which is dried cockscomb flower—recommended as part of the Ayurvedic tradition for its various effects, and is apparently appreciated for its color-imparting properties. Look for it at Indian groceries or at online herbal or Indian food suppliers. You can also find such spices as black cardamom, ground fennel, and the red chili powder at Indian markets. Kalra notes that it imparts "a gorgeous orange color that makes this dish magical."

To make the *kofta*, or meatballs, the traditional way, you need to pound the meat on a flat surface with a meat mallet for about 1 1/2 hours. Kalra notes that cooks can replicate the process in a food processor, but that the texture really never is the same.

The Kofta
1 1/3 pounds minced or ground goat or lamb, preferably from the leg
4 ounces goat or lamb fat

2 pieces black cardamom
2 (1-inch) sticks cinnamon, toasted and broken into pieces
2 teaspoons ground fennel
1 teaspoon ground ginger
1 teaspoon Kashmiri red chili powder
salt to taste

The Gravy
1 ounce dried *rattanjot*
1 teaspoon ground fennel
1 teaspoon Kashmiri red chili powder
1/2 teaspoon ground ginger
salt to taste
2 tablespoons mustard oil
4 whole green cardamom, opened
2 teaspoons fried onion paste
1 tablespoon cornstarch mixed with 1/2 cup water

To make the *kofta*, mix all the ingredients together in a large bowl, put them in a food processor, and process until the texture is light and fluffy and mousselike. Refrigerate the mixture for about 30 minutes. Divide into 12 equal portions, and roll into meatballs.

To make the gravy, put the cockscomb extract in a large wok or saucepan, add 2 cups water, and bring to a boil over medium heat. Cook for 5 minutes, and strain through fine cheesecloth into a small bowl. Add the fennel, ginger, and red chili powder, mix well, and set aside.

Heat the mustard oil to a smoking point in a large wok, remove from the heat, and cool. Reheat the oil, add the green cardamom, and stir over medium heat until it begins to change color. Add the reserved cockscomb extract mixture, cook for 2 minutes, add about 2 cups water and the salt, and bring to a boil. Carefully add the meatballs, bring to a boil again. Reduce the heat to low, and cook 30 minutes more. Stir in the fried onion paste, and continue to cook for 15 minutes more. Remove the meatballs, and adjust the seasonings. To thicken the gravy, cook it down until it reduces by half, or use the cornstarch slurry. Serve hot.

Note: To make the onion paste, slice 1 large onion (about 1 pound) and saute the slices in 2 tablespoons peanut oil or vegetable oil. Cook until the onion turns golden brown. Drain on paper towels. When cool, put the onion and about 2 tablespoons plain yogurt into a food processor, and puree.

Tempered Red Pumpkin

KADDU KI SUBZI

A native of New Delhi, chef Sudhir Seth, owner of the restaurant Passage to India, in Bethesda, Maryland, remembers his childhood as very happy, with a houseful of delicious foods and aromas, and plenty of food-based celebrations.

He describes the red pumpkin as "a delightful mix of flavors and tastes, the musky pungent aroma of mustard oil, the slight bitterness of the fenugreek seeds, coupled with the natural sweetness of pumpkin enhanced with the earthy sugars of *jaggery* set off against the tart taste of powdered raw mango. The texture of soft pumpkin flesh contrasts really well with the cooked skin which remains al dente. We ate this mostly with *poories* [see the fol-

A batch of simmering, aromatic curries. Anne Parsons

lowing recipe], the deep-fried whole wheat puffed bread, on festive occasions when Hindus eat vegetarian foods without onion or garlic. The dish preserves pretty well, and in my childhood days with no refrigeration or iceboxes, the above combination was a great travel meal to pack and take on a train ride. In fact, the dish has such powerful memories that writing about it reminds me of two things: Diwali and train trips to Jaipur."

For this recipe, Seth suggests using a slightly under-ripe pumpkin or winter squash. These will take longer to cook, but unlike a fully ripe pumpkin or squash, the flesh cooks more slowly and stays firmer. Note that the Asian *kobacha* squash is not a substitute. *Jaggery* is India's version of brown sugar; look for it at an Asian or Indian market. Likewise, *amchoor* (or *amchur*, or raw mango powder) is another Indian favorite, and this seasoning adds a slightly sour taste to recipes.

3 tablespoons mustard oil

1/2 teaspoon fenugreek seeds

5 green chilies, slit lengthwise

2 pounds slightly under-ripe pumpkin or squash, peeled, seeded, and cubed

1/4 teaspoon ground turmeric

salt to taste

1/2 teaspoon ground *jaggery*, or more to taste

1/2 teaspoon *amchoor*, or more to taste

Heat the mustard oil over medium-high heat in a large skillet until the oil shows clear. Remove from the heat, and cool slightly. Add the fenugreek seeds, stirring until they turn golden.

Return the skillet to the heat, and add the chilies and pumpkin. Cook, stirring often, over medium heat until all the pieces are coated with oil. Cover, and cook for about 10 minutes.

Stir in the turmeric and salt, reduce the heat to low, and cook for 20 minutes more.

Stir in the *jaggery* and *amchoor*, mix well, and cook about 5 minutes more, or until the flavors are well combined. Serve hot.

Serves 4.

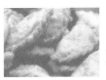

Fried Whole Wheat Puff Bread
POORI

A very healthful bread, *poori* calls for a dough that is part whole wheat and part white flours. You can also refrigerate this dough after kneading and cook it later in the day, or even the next day. Sudhir Seth explains that his mother taught him to add the oil after the gluten in the flour has started working. This prevents the dough from turning into a short crust paste, and allows the fried bread to come out crisp on the outside and soft on the inside without being crumbly.

3 cups whole wheat flour
1 cup all-purpose flour
1/2 teaspoon salt
1 tablespoon plus about 3 cups vegetable oil, or more as needed for deep-frying

Some pappadums *to accompany the curries.* Anne Parsons

Sift the flour and salt together into a bowl. Make a well in the center, add 7 ounces (almost 1 cup) water, and knead the dough until firm and elastic; knead in just enough more water to make the dough pliable. Cover the dough, and set aside for 15 minutes.

Brush the dough with the oil, and knead for 2 minutes more, or until the oil is incorporated. Divide the dough into 16 equal portions, and roll them into balls. Cover, and set aside to rest for 15 minutes.

Heat the remaining 3 cups oil to 250°F. Roll out the balls into 4-inch circles; the dough should be dry enough so that the work surface and rolling pin require no extra flour. When the oil is hot, fry the rolled-out dough pieces one at a time, turning once, until puffy and golden. Remove, and drain on paper towels. Repeat until all the dough is cooked.

Makes 16 pieces.

Lamb or Chicken with Lentils
DHANSAK

Tahmineh Parsons, a native Washingtonian, has Zoroastrian relatives in Mumbai (Bombay), India, who claim that this dish, *dhansak*, a Parsi dish that is served on Sundays in many homes, is the national dish of the Parsis. Although at first glance the recipe may appear formidable, it is really quite straightforward if you break down the process into six parts and then combine them. Companions for this hearty meal are browned basmati rice and onion *kachumbar*, a spicy tomato salad.

George and Tahmineh Parsons (couple on far right) on honeymoon, 1940.
Parsons family album

Legumes
1 cup dried yellow split peas, soaked overnight
1/2 cup dried yellow lentils, soaked overnight
1/2 cup dried red lentils, soaked overnight

Meat
4 pounds leg of lamb, boned and cubed, or 4 pounds skinless, boneless chicken
1 tablespoon salt, or to taste

Vegetables
1 medium-sized eggplant, peeled, seeded, and cubed
1 large potato, peeled and cubed
2 medium-sized onions, peeled and chopped
2 tomatoes, peeled, seeded and chopped
2 cups spinach leaves, well rinsed
2 cups peeled and cubed pumpkin

Wet Masala
6 dried red chilies, seeded and chopped
1/2 cup hot water
6 fresh green chilies, seeded and chopped
1 tablespoon chopped fresh ginger
10 cloves garlic, peeled and chopped
1/2 cup fresh mint leaves
1/2 cup cilantro leaves

Dry Masala
1 tablespoon ground coriander
1 tablespoon ground cumin
1 tablespoon ground turmeric
1/2 teaspoon ground cinnamon
1/2 teaspoon ground cardamom
1/2 teaspoon ground black pepper
1/2 teaspoon ground black mustard seeds
1/2 teaspoon ground cloves

Onion Paste
4 tablespoons ghee or vegetable oil
4 medium-sized onions, finely sliced

Drain the legumes, and set aside. Put the lamb into a large stockpot, and add the legumes with enough water to cover. Add the salt, and bring to a boil. Cover, reduce the heat to low, and cook for 15 minutes. Add the vegetables, and continue cooking for 30 minutes, or until the meat is almost tender.

Remove the meat, and set aside. Drain the legumes and vegetables, and puree them in a blender with enough liquid to help process them. Set aside.

Meanwhile, make the onion paste by heating the ghee in a large saucepan over medium-high heat until very hot; add the onions, and fry, stirring often, until they are browned, about 15 minutes. Remove from the pan, and set aside.

Combine the wet masala ingredients in a blender, and puree until smooth. Combine the dry masala ingredients in a bowl.

Combine the two masala groups in the empty stockpot, and stir-fry over medium heat until well cooked and fragrant. Add half the browned onions, the lamb, and the legume mixture. Bring to a slow boil over medium heat, and cook for 20 to 30 minutes, until all the flavors are blended. Garnish with the remaining onions, and serve.

Serves 10.

Iran

- ♦ Noodle Soup (Ash-e Reshteh)

- ♦ Chicken with Pomegranate and Walnuts (Khoreshe Fesenjan)

- ♦ Steamed Rice (Chelo)

- ♦ Subzi Polo with Fish

- ♦ Yogurt with Cucumbers (Mast va Khiar)

$\mathcal{F}$or many centuries, Greek historians, and then Europeans, referred to Iran (land of the Aryans) as Persia (so named from the southern province of Fars). It is a non-Arabic country (Farsi is the official language), and it was the center of the world's first empire. Born of invaders from distinct cultures, such as the Turks, Mongols, Greeks, and Arabs, Persian culture evolved with those cultural linkages to deeply imprint the social landscape of the country. Ultimately, Iran became the major scientific, philosophical, and artistic center in the world.

People who recognize Iran only as a major producer of oil, carpets, and caviar should taste its diverse cuisine. While the Iranian landscape is predominantly mountainous with high contrasting green oases, culinary traditions distinguish each region through particular dishes. Overall, Iranian food is exquisite but unpretentious. While the cuisine is rarely hot, it is rich in spices and herbs such as saffron, curcuma, cinnamon, mint, and dill. Iranian dishes also abound in fruits such as pomegranates, quince, apricots, and raisins. As the leading world producer of dates and pistachios, Iran offers plentiful domestic supplies; don't be surprised when you visit an Iranian home to find ubiquitous snacks in bowls, effortlessly emptied by visitors and families.

Persian painting on wooden box. Anne Parsons

Understanding the special link between cuisine and culture, it is no wonder that Iranians are passionate about food, a pleasure for all the senses, and that they cherish the intimacy of family meals. Almost as important as the preparation of food is the presentation—like a beautiful painting the table should impart a wonderful sense of elegant and delicate brush strokes.

Noodle Soup

ASH-E RESHTEH

When Tooran Shadman moved from Tehran to the United States almost forty years ago, she brought many family recipes and traditions with her. She admits that, in Iran, she never had to cook, but with help from her sisters and mother, she was soon preparing all the family favorites from the old country. Shadman explains that *ashe* is the Persian word for soup and that soups are an important part of this culture's cuisine. This recipe, combined with flatbread, is just as delicious on a cold, damp day as it is for family dinners.

Noodle Soup
2 tablespoons vegetable oil
2 small onions, thinly sliced
1 teaspoon salt to taste
1/2 teaspoon ground cinnamon
1/2 teaspoon freshly ground black pepper, or more to taste
10 cups water or chicken stock
1/2 cup chickpeas
1/2 cup kidney beans
1 pound boneless, skinless chicken thigh meat, cooked
2 cups dried noodles
1 cup chopped parsley
2 scallions, chopped finely

To make the soup, heat the oil in a large skillet over medium heat, and sauté the onions. Add the salt, cinnamon, and pepper, and mix.

Put the water into a large saucepan. Add the peas and beans, and cook over medium heat for 20 minutes. Add the chicken, noodles, parsley, and scallions, reduce the heat to medium-low, and cook for 40 minutes.

Garnish
1 tablespoon vegetable oil

1 onion, thinly sliced

3 cloves garlic, minced

2 tablespoons dried mint, rubbed between palms

1/2 teaspoon freshly ground black pepper

1/2 teaspoon ground cinnamon

Tom and Tooran Shadman relax after dinner. Sean Shadman

To make the garnish, heat the oil in a large skillet over medium heat, and sauté the onion and garlic for 5 minutes, or until golden. Add the mint, pepper, and cinnamon, and mix with the onion and garlic. To serve, stir half the mixture into the soup, and use the remainder for a garnish.

Serves 6.

Chicken
with Pomegranate and Walnuts
KHORESHE FESENJAN

Jennifer Parsons's great-grandfather, Dr. Ardeshire Irani, was from Yazd in Persia. For many years, Dr. Irani's family met at his house for Sunday dinner, and her great-grandmother, Louise, often prepared Persian dishes from old family recipes. Jennifer, an attorney, whose grandparents are Scottish, English, Irish, and German, and whose husband, Albert, is Chinese, thrives on her family's multicultural events and, as a wee lass, started collecting recipes from grandmothers and aunts. She suggests serving this dish with *chelo* (steamed rice).

Dr. Louise Schumann
Irani, 1906.
Parsons family album

5 tablespoons vegetable oil
3 pounds chicken thighs, boned
3 teaspoons salt
1 teaspoon freshly ground black pepper
1 tablespoon lemon-pepper seasoning
3 tablespoons butter
1 large onion, thinly sliced
3 tablespoons tomato sauce
2 cups finely chopped walnuts
1 teaspoon ground cinnamon
3 tablespoons lemon juice
1 cup pomegranate juice, or 3 tablespoons
    pomegranate syrup
2 tablespoons sugar, optional

Heat the oil over medium heat in a large saucepan, and sauté the chicken thighs with 2 teaspoons salt, pepper, and lemon-pepper seasoning until browned on all sides, about 15 minutes. Remove the thighs from the pan.

Heat the butter in the skillet over medium heat, and sauté the onions until transparent. Add the tomato sauce, and cook for 5 minutes more.

Add the walnuts, and cook 3 or 4 minutes, stirring constantly. Add 4 cups water, the remaining salt, cinnamon, lemon juice, and pomegranate juice. Cover the pot, reduce the heat to low, and cook for 40 minutes.

Adjust the seasonings. Add the chicken, and continue cooking for 30 minutes more. Serve hot.

Serves 6.

Steamed Rice
CHELO

Tahmineh Irani Parsons taught her granddaughter, Jennifer, to make this rice dish. Jennifer says it took many attempts before she made the fluffiest *chelo* with the crispiest *tadiq*. This is a basic Persian method of cooking rice, and it can be enhanced with fruits, nuts, and meats, depending on your fancy. Because Jennifer's family loves the added flavor of barberries, she adds them during the steaming process. What differentiates this Persian rice from other cooking methods is that a crust forms on the bottom, a golden-brown crispy *tadiq*. In fact, many Persian cooks are judged by the color and crispiness of their *tadiq*.

Mrs. Banee Sarouche, 1902.
Irani family album

3 cups uncooked basmati rice
1/4 cup salt
1 stick plus 1 tablespoon unsalted
  butter, melted

Wash the rice by hand in lukewarm water, drain, and repeat 2 more times. Soak it in 2 tablespoons of the salt and cold water to cover overnight, or at least 3 hours.

Bring 2 quarts of water to a boil, and add the remaining 2 tablespoons of salt. Drain the rice, and add it to the boiling water. Boil for 12 minutes, stirring occasionally to prevent sticking. Pour the rice into a strainer, and rinse with lukewarm water.

Put 1/4 cup of the melted butter into the bottom of a pot, and add 2 tablespoons of water. Taking large spoonfuls of rice, mold the rice in the pot to form a pyramid. Using a circular motion, pour the remaining butter over the rice, distributing evenly. Cover the rice with 2 paper towels, add the lid, and cover everything with dish towels.

Cook the rice over medium heat for 15 minutes. Reduce the heat to low, and cook for 40 minutes more.

Pour 1 inch or so of water into the sink, and put the pot into the water to help the crust on the bottom to separate from the pot. Spoon the white rice onto the platter, and put the *tadiq* on a separate plate.

Serves 8.

 *Subzi Polo with Fish*

Ezzat Parsa of Reston, Virginia, is a lifelong Baha'i who moved to the United States with her family many years ago from Iran.

With the various chopped herbs stirred into the delicate rice, plus the herb-stuffed whole fish, this dish is the ideal meal for dinner guests. Ezzat Parsa says that her family loves her way of preparing the fish: instead of frying fillets, she uses a whole, cleaned fish, fills the cavity with a flavorful mixture of herbs and other seasonings, and roasts it until the skin browns. To flavor the fish stuffing, Parsa uses a product called "pomegranate paste," which is really a slightly sweet syrup made from pomegranates; this is available at Indian and Middle Eastern markets.

In true Persian fashion, Parsa prepares the crusty *tadiq*, the cooked rice that browns in the saucepan while the remaining rice steams; towels absorb the water so that the rice grains remain firm instead of becoming sticky. Look for the already fried onions in a Middle Eastern or Asian market, where the product will be called "fried shallots."

Rice
3 cups long-grain rice, such as basmati
2 1/2 tablespoons salt
1/2 cup vegetable oil
1 large potato, peeled and thinly sliced
1 bunch dill, chopped
1 bunch parsley, chopped
1 bunch cilantro, chopped
1 cup chopped chives
1 cup fried onions

Rinse the rice well, and soak the grains with 2 tablespoons of the salt for 2 to 3 hours. Drain the rice.

Bring a large pot of water to boil, add the remaining 1/2 tablespoon of salt and stir in the rice. Cook over medium heat about 15 minutes, or just until the rice grains become tender. Drain and rinse the rice.

Combine the oil and about 1/2 cup of water, and pour into a large saucepan. Put a layer of sliced potatoes on the bottom of the pan. Toss together the chopped dill, chopped parsley, chopped cilantro, and chopped chives in a large bowl.

Layer the rice on the potatoes, sprinkle a layer of mixed herbs on the rice, and repeat this layering until the rice and herbs are used up. Rest a thick towel over the top of the saucepan, and then put a lid on it. Start cooking the rice over medium heat, and when the water begins to boil, reduce the heat to very low, and cook until the rice grains are fluffy and tender.

A superb repast of Persian-style fish. Anne Parsons

Spoon the rice mixture onto a large platter. Scrape out the crusty bottom layer of browned rice, the *tadiq*, and serve it on top of the steamed rice. Sprinkle the fried onions over all.

Stuffed Fish
3 tablespoons vegetable oil
2 large onions, thinly sliced
3 large heads garlic, peeled and separated
1 cup chopped dill
1 cup chopped parsley
1 cup chopped cilantro
2 tablespoons pomegranate paste
salt to taste
freshly ground black pepper to taste
1 large (3-pound) whole fish, preferably white fish, cleaned and scaled
1 large lemon, thinly sliced
grapes or other fruit, for decoration

Preheat the oven to 400°F. Line a large roasting pan with foil.

Heat the oil in a large skillet over medium heat, and sauté the onions, garlic, dill, parsley, and cilantro until the herbs wilt slightly, about 10 minutes. Spoon the mixture into a large serving bowl, and season it with the pomegranate paste, salt, and pepper. Stir well, and spoon the mixture into the fish cavity. Sew or skewer the cavity shut. Put the fish into the roasting pan, and cover it with foil.

Roast the fish for 10 minutes at 400°F, then reduce the temperature to 350°F. Continue cooking, covered with foil, for 20 minutes more, or until the fish flesh is flaky. Remove the foil, and brown the fish.

Carefully transfer the fish to a serving platter. Garnish the fish with the lemon slices, and decorate the platter with grapes or other fruit, as desired.

Serves 6.

Yogurt with Cucumbers

MAST VA KHIAR

When Tooran Shadman has guests to dinner, as she frequently does, they can expect to have this deliciously simple dish as an appetizer or as a light salad.

2 cups plain yogurt
1 large seedless cucumber, peeled
    and finely chopped
1 tablespoon fresh dill
salt to taste
white pepper to taste

Put the yogurt and cucumber in a bowl. Add the salt and pepper to taste and mix well. Put in refrigerator for an hour before serving.

Serves 4.

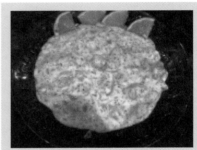

Mast va khiar is refreshing at any time. Anne Parsons

Ireland

- ◆ IRISH POTATO SOUP

- ◆ ST. BRIGID'S LAMB STEW

- ◆ IRISH SODA BREAD

- ◆ MARINATED GRILLED WILD DUCK BREASTS

There is no sincerer love than the love of food.

—George Bernard Shaw (1856–1950)

*T*here are few better places on the planet to visit than Ireland, a land of poets, artists, ancient cultures, and an evolving food culture. Politically divided into the Republic of Ireland (a country separate from the United Kingdom) and Northern Ireland (about one-sixth of the land mass that is part of the U.K.), all of Ireland has lush green pastures, breathtaking landscapes, idyllic country villages, meandering waterways, elegant manor houses, bustling towns, and ancient castles. Crafted into the rich tapestry of this land are compelling tales of heroes and saints who have dramatically shaped the boundless nature of the people in this small green island.

For centuries, impoverished conditions compelled most Irish home cooks to make the best of whatever was available. Nothing was wasted. Cooks used every part of the slaughtered animal and whatever they grew was the basis for their own meals. Like many other countries, great peasant dishes emanated from these conditions of scarcity. For example, the potato, a staple of the Emerald Isle is a food with infinite possibilities: colcannon, haggerty, collops, potato scones, and boxty, to name just a few. From its early Peruvian beginnings, the potato migrated around the world until it finally arrived in Ireland. Soon the Irish became so dependent on it, that when the fungus, *phytophthora infestans*, attacked it in the nineteenth century, famine ensued. The population was cut in half, either from starvation or emigration. High praise indeed goes to the farmers who stayed on and cultivated the land.

Now, a new marvel has taken over the land. Like many other northern European countries, Ireland has taken a huge gastronomic leap forward. Fiercely clinging to their roots, young, innovative chefs think they have made a remarkable discovery—by using local home-grown produce, meats, and fish,

Dunluce Castle, Ireland.
Alan Kiernan

they have created a "new" traditional cuisine. But, if you take a closer look, you might note that these sophisticated meals are classic comfort foods based on wholesome traditional peasant fare and unpretentious working men's meals.

Irish Potato Soup

Joyce Cleland MacLeod's family lived for generations in Magheralone, County Down. MacLeod says, "Shortly after Granny died, family and friends were sitting around her kitchen table at her home. For us,

Irish Potato Soup.
Joyce Cleland

Granny's kitchen was a cozy, warm place where folks congregated, food was cooked, and family shared their woes and joys. This kitchen was Granny's domain; it was the pulse of the family. Although we grieved her passing, we knew that she'd always be with us because we inherited her love of family traditions, good food, and many of her recipes. Her enthusiasm for bountiful family meals, especially during holidays and celebrations, is a legacy upon which my family has built, and, it is a living memory of my Granny.

"Granny always said that soups are as old as the hills, and that they should be substantial and filling. Most of our family soup stock was made from inexpensive soup bones—dad believed that the bone marrow was filled with essential nutrients. This soup is a quick and simple one to make, but it is equally at home on an old pine kitchen slab, or center stage on a fancy dining-room table."

5 ounces butter
3 pounds potatoes, peeled and diced
3 large onions, thinly sliced
3 cups chicken stock
2 tablespoons chopped parsley
salt to taste
freshly ground black pepper to taste

2 cups whole milk
6 slices bacon, chopped and fried until crisp

Heat the butter in a skillet over medium heat, and sauté the potatoes and onions for about 20 minutes, but do not brown; reduce the heat to medium-low, if needed.

Remove them, and place in a large pot; add 3 cups water, the chicken stock, parsley, salt, and pepper; reduce the heat to low, and cook for 45 minutes, or until the vegetables are tender. Remove the pot from the heat, and allow to cool.

Puree the mixture in a blender or food processor. Return the mixture to the pot, add the milk, and bring to a boil. Serve hot, and garnish with bacon.

Serves 8.

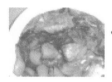

St. Brigid's Lamb Stew

In Ireland and Scotland, sheep were raised for their wool. Ordinary folk couldn't afford to eat lamb—the aristocracy devoured it—so they slow cooked mutton—the flesh of a mature sheep—instead. Alice Cleland, orphaned as a toddler, relied on her older sister, Rebecca, to raise her. Rebecca never used a recipe, so Cleland took notes and gathered recipes as a way of retaining some family history. Cleland says that many of the recipes didn't have a title other than stew, soup, or some such plain name. To distinguish her recipes, she named them after saints, and sometimes sinners. "This stew," says Cleland, "I called after the fertility goddess, St. Brigid, who is associated with livestock and other farming matters. Supposedly she was a 'fiery arrow' who gave absolute authority to the woman in the house. She was a wise woman!"

Alice Cleland, 1918.
Cleland family album

This dish tastes better the second day.

2 pounds lean lamb or mutton, cubed
3 tablespoons flour
1/4 cup unsalted butter
salt to taste
freshly ground black pepper to taste
6 medium-sized potatoes, peeled and thickly sliced
3 onions, peeled and thickly sliced
chopped parsley for garnish

Preheat the oven to 350°F.

Dredge the meat in the flour, heat the butter, and brown the meat on all sides. Season with salt and pepper.

Arrange a layer of potatoes in a 4-quart ovenproof casserole. Add a layer of onions and of lamb, and repeat layering until all the ingredients are used up. Season each layer with salt and pepper. Add 3 cups water, and cover the dish.

Bake for about 2 1/2 hours, or until the meat is very tender. To serve, garnish with the parsley.

Serves 6.

Irish Soda Bread

Donna Countryman, a native Bostonian who now lives on the Outer Banks of North Carolina, cherishes her Irish heritage. She recalls that when her Irish grandfather, Thain, married her grandmother, Millicent Maude, who was only half-Irish and from County Cork, his family was a trifle upset. Nevertheless, the marriage worked, and Countryman became the recipient of her grandmother's recipes that she, in turn, has passed on to her children and grandchildren. Countryman remembers her grandmother telling her, "Out of necessity the Irish used potatoes to make bread and cakes, because it made the flour go further." She notes that this traditional soda bread does not use yeast, and it is important to use buttermilk to get the proper flavor.

Donna Countryman's grandmother, Millicent Maude.
Anne Parsons

Caraway seeds add an unusual and distinctive taste to this country-style bread.

5 cups sifted all-purpose flour
3/4 cup granulated sugar
2 teaspoons baking powder
1 teaspoon baking soda
1 1/2 teaspoons salt
1/2 cup (1 stick) unsalted butter
2 1/2 cups raisins, soaked in warm water
3 tablespoons caraway seeds
2 1/2 cups buttermilk
1 large egg, beaten

Preheat the oven to 350°F. Spray two 9-inch loaf pans with nonstick spray.

Stir the flour, sugar, baking powder, baking soda, and salt together in a large mixing bowl. Cut in the butter until the flour mixture resembles cornmeal. Drain the raisins, and stir the raisins and caraway seeds into the dough. Stir in the buttermilk and egg just until all the flour is moistened. Divide the batter in half, and spoon it into the prepared loaf pans.

Bake the loaves for about 1 hour, or until a toothpick inserted in the center comes out clean. Remove from the oven, and cool the loaves on a rack before slicing.

Makes 2 loaves.

Marinated Grilled Wild Duck Breasts

Following recipes precisely is not Murphy's Law, not Richard Murphy's Law at any rate. Though devoted to his Irish family recipes, Richard Murphy keeps himself open to creative exploration. In the kitchen, he is adventurous and imaginative, it is where he takes risks—his cooking is powered by passion.

Richard Murphy testing an old family recipe. Susan Murphy

Murphy is a descendent of Irish immigrants; his maternal grandparents, Kelly and MacNair, emigrated to the U.S. through New Brunswick, Canada, circa 1900, and settled in Aroostook County, Maine. As a skilled hunter and fisherman, Murphy celebrates his Irish roots by bringing home his own take of venison, doves, geese, ducks, quail, rabbit, and whatever the sea and rivers have to offer. Herbal seasonings—sage, scallions, chives, basil, and rosemary—grow abundantly in his back garden. Needless to say, his enthusiasm for cooking reflects an artistic ability in which his masterpieces are created solely for delectable consumption by his family and friends—even if they aren't Irish.

The recipe for the marinade is a general guide; make this to suit your taste. Murphy suggests serving this dish with cranberry chutney or spiced salted apples and saffron rice.

3 wild ducks, skinned and cleaned
3 cups buttermilk, milk, or beer
1/4 cup soy sauce

3 tablespoons water
2 tablespoons sesame oil
1 tablespoon chopped fresh ginger
1 tablespoon garlic, minced
1 tablespoon hoisin sauce
salt to taste
freshly ground black pepper to taste
3 tablespoons rum

Pull the skin free from the breast, and cut the breast meat from the bone; there should be 2 good-sized pieces of meat per duck. Soak the breasts in buttermilk for 2 to 3 hours. Turn over once or twice while cooking.

Rinse the ducks, pat dry, and trim off any fat or skin. Put the duck meat into a glass or stainless-steel pan.

Combine the marinade ingredients, and pour them over the duck meat. Refrigerate for 4 to 8 hours, or overnight.

Fire up a charcoal or gas grill. If using a charcoal grill, when the coals are at the white-ash stage, grill the duck until medium rare, reserving the marinade and brushing the ducks during cooking. Serve the duck meat sliced on the diagonal.

Note: Murphy says that the following method is excellent and can also be used with doves. Split the breast meat in half—1 duck yields 2 pieces. Pound each piece lightly. Put a piece of serrano or jalapeño chili and a chunk of pineapple in center of each piece, wrap it up in bacon, and secure the meat with a toothpick.

Marinate as above, and grill 5 to 7 minutes. Serve with your favorite dipping sauce, such as honey-mustard.

Serves 6.

Italy

- STUFFED POTATO PASTA WITH LEEK AND SAUSAGE SAUCE (FAGOTTINI DE PATATE CON PORRI E SALSICCIA)

- STUFFED STEAK (BRACIOLE)

- LITTLE HAT SOUP (CAPPELLETTI)

- PASTA WITH SEAFOOD (PASTA CON FRUTTI DI MARE)

- SIDEBAR: PROSECCO WITH BASIL

*V*isitors have a difficult time leaving this country willingly because Italy has so much to offer—a remarkable history, a rich culture, and extraordinary food. For centuries, Italy has been a major center of literature, art, architecture, and music. Yet, for many of those centuries, Italy was also a land of political fragmentation in which sovereign states shared few traditions and had no common language. Even today, Italy remains a land with a plethora of distinct regional customs and traditions: Milanese, Roman, Venetian, Piedmontese, Bolognese, Tuscan, Neapolitan, and Sicilian. Furthermore, differences in the food vary not just from one area to another, but sometimes among towns in the same area. The contrasts in these regional cuisines are further defined by the landscape of the mountainous Alps and the exotic Mediterranean and Adriatic seas.

Close to France, Switzerland, and Austria and blessed with good soil and a good climate, it is not surprising that people in the north have a closer affinity to European cooking than their southern counterparts. In addition to the ubiquitous pasta dishes, you'll discover northerners eating prodigious amounts of polenta and risotto. Unfortunately, after the industrial north attracted labor from the south, factories usurped much of the pasta sales and began to mass produce it. Yet, if you travel to the south of the country, the discerning foodie will note how the strong influences of North Africa and the Middle East are embedded in regional cuisine through the range of sweet, sour, salty, and spicy dishes.

Whether you prefer the rich gastronomy of Emilio-Romagna or the simple fare of the Piedmont, Italy is a country for indulging in food forays. And, since 1989, Italy has been the home of Slow Food.

Founded by Carlo Petrini and located in Bra, Italy, Slow Food works locally and globally with policy-makers such as the United Nations Food and Agriculture Organization. The mission of Slow Food is "to defend biodiversity in our food supply, spread the education of taste, and link producers of excellent foods to consumers" through such events as fairs, farmers' markets, and the bi-annual international food festival, Salone del Gusto, in Turin, Italy. On a local level, members aim to celebrate and protect the traditional foods of their region by supporting local farmers, fishermen, growers, breeders, and artisan producers.

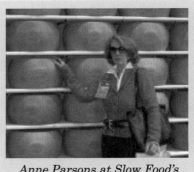

Anne Parsons at Slow Food's Salone del Gusto, Turin.
Alexandra Greeley

Many of you may ask about the appellation "Slow Food." Well, it is the converse of fast-food values. It denotes the slow rhythms and harmony of life and a convivial table where family and friends meet to "explore the pleasures of the palate."

Stuffed Potato Pasta
with Leek and Sausage Sauce
FAGOTTINI DE PATATE CON PORRI E SALSICCIA

Giovanna Biagi, owner and chef of the *Trattoria Pandemonio*, in Florence, offers her clients (read guests) a menu of delicious home cooking. The atmosphere in this well-organized family-run restaurant is definitely not pandemonium; rather, after Giovanna welcomes you to her establishment, you feel right at home in this tranquil setting. Rolando (the husband) is on hand to help you pair wines with dishes, and Giovanna will sit with you and discuss what she has cooked and prepared that day. The rest of the family participates as well—son Francesco is cooking, and his wife Francesca and brother Lorenzo are waiting tables.

While dining at the restaurant, Giovanna was too busy to write down this excellent recipe for the authors. Instead, she e-mailed it to them with a note, "Our English is not very good, but I'm sure you'll find the way to explain in a better way. Please tell your friends when they visit us, that in Florence is another street with a very similar name, and many books make mistake of our address which is Via del Leone, 50/r. Many thanks for the idea to use one of my family recipes in your book!!!"

Pasta
2 1/4 cups unbleached all-purpose flour plus more as needed
3 eggs, lightly beaten

Filling
1/4 pound pancetta, or bacon
1 1/2 pounds boiled potatoes
4 large eggs
2 ounces grated Parmigiano cheese
freshly ground nutmeg to taste
salt to taste

Sauce
2 tablespoons extra virgin olive oil
3 pork, or Italian, sausages

1 clove garlic, crushed
1 hot pepper, finely chopped
8 ounces white wine
3 leeks, washed and thinly sliced
2 tomatoes, seeded and chopped
salt to taste

Giovanna and Rolando Biagi at their restaurant, Pandemonio.
Anne Parsons

Place the flour in a mound on a work surface. Make a well in the center of the flour, and pour the eggs into the well. Using a fork, gradually incorporate some of the flour from the sides, taking care not to break the flour wall. When the eggs are no longer runny, work in the rest of the flour until the dough is no longer sticky.

Knead the dough by hand, dusting with additional flour, until the dough is smooth, about 2 to 3 minutes. Wrap tightly with plastic wrap, and let rest for at least 20 minutes before rolling out.

With a pasta machine, or by hand, roll dough out to desired thinness. Use machine or knife to cut into squares about 1/4-inch thin.

Cook the pancetta, or bacon, in olive oil, let cool, and chop finely. Put potatoes through a sieve. Put the pancetta, potatoes, eggs, Parmigiano, nutmeg, and salt into a bowl, and mix well.

Put a small amount of filling on each square, and close it, forming a triangle; seal the edges.

Remove the sausage meat from their casings, and sauté in olive oil. When halfway cooked, add the crushed garlic and the hot pepper. Add the white wine, and let it evaporate. Add the leeks. Cover and cook, stirring frequently. Add the tomatoes, and continue cooking over medium heat for about 30 minutes. Add some vegetable broth if mixture becomes dry.

Cook the *fagottini* (bundles) in salted boiling water, about 8 minutes. Drain and toss quickly with the sauce in a pan over medium heat.

Serves 6.

Stuffed Steak

BRACIOLE

W hen Fred Speno's Sicilian grandparents, Alfio Giovanni Spena, of Acireale, and Maria Concetta (née Belfiore), of Mascali, left Italy in April 1906, they first traveled to Marseilles, France, where Maria's father was a minor official in the Italian Consulate. There, they boarded a ship and sailed to their new life in America where an immigration officer changed the name to Speno.

Fred Speno's grandparents in 1906.
Speno family album

Speno writes, "Unfortunately, we have no recipes from my grandmother that survived in her writing—the fact is, she had only a sixth grade education and did not write well. Nevertheless, many of her recipes have survived through various generations, because the kitchen was the heart of the home and that's where family members learned their cooking skills from just watching and copying grandma." Speno goes on to say, "My favorite recipe from grandma was for *braciole*, but I must admit that I've tweaked it a bit by using canned tomatoes and paste." He explains that "*braciole* is any cut of pounded meat, stuffed with various herbs and eggs, then rolled and braised. Many immigrant Italians brought their own family recipe for *braciole* to the States, and if you attend any festive event, you'll be sure to taste this succulent dish."

As for mushrooms, you can use ordinary fresh white button mushrooms. (If you use dried mushrooms, hydrate them with Marsala wine for a special flavor). When you slice and serve the meat, or *braciole*, be sure the hard-cooked egg shows in the center. Serve over al dente rigatoni or penne pasta.

Special equipment: cotton kitchen twine

Meat

1 1/2 pounds top round steak cut about 1/2 inch thick
1/2 cup dry breadcrumbs
1 teaspoon chopped parsley
1 teaspoon chopped garlic
1/2 cup grated Parmigiano-Reggiano, or Pecorino-Romano cheese
1/2 cup thinly sliced cremini and morel mushrooms
3 hard-boiled eggs, shelled
2 tablespoons chopped fresh oregano
1 teaspoon finely chopped fresh rosemary leaves

Sauce

3 tablespoons extra virgin olive oil
1 medium onion, finely chopped
4 cloves garlic
1 pound chopped, fresh Roma tomatoes or canned pomodoro-type tomatoes
1 (4-ounce) can of tomato paste
1 cup of water, or more as needed
1/2 cup sweet Marsala wine
1/2 teaspoon fennel seed
1 tablespoon chopped fresh basil
1 tablespoon chopped oregano
salt to taste
freshly ground black pepper to taste
3 tablespoons chopped fresh parsley

Pound the steak with a butcher's mallet until it is nearly twice its original size.

Mix the breadcrumbs with parsley and garlic, and spread the mixture along the length of the meat. Top with the grated cheese, then cover with the mushrooms, oregano, and rosemary.

To make the sauce, heat the olive oil in a large skillet over medium heat, and sauté the onion and garlic until very soft. Add the chopped tomatoes, stir, and add tomato paste and water. Stir again, and add wine or sugar. Reduce the heat to low, and cook for about 30 minutes; if too thick, add more wine or water. Add the remaining ingredients, and stir.

Set hard-boiled eggs in a row across the steak. Starting with the long edge nearest you, roll the meat lengthwise over the filling and eggs to form a long, cylindrical log. Tie it shut with cotton kitchen twine. Set aside.

Place the wrapped meat in the sauce, and cook for about 40 minutes over medium heat. Remove and slice the meat into 1-inch-thick rounds with the egg displayed in the center.

Makes 2 large portions or 4 small.

Little Hat Soup
CAPPELLETTI

A few days prior to family celebrations, Italian-born Aida Cristofori had her children sit around the kitchen table in their New Jersey home making this pasta for her delectable soup. Her daughter, Renata (Rennie) Cristofori Hackmann, of North Carolina, says these memories are precious, and this soup can be made at any time of the year. So on winter days when the rain is pelting against the windows, she'll invite some friends over to share this special tradition. Note that a scoop probably equals about half a cup of flour and that, depending on the size of the eggs and the humidity, you should adjust the quantity of flour accordingly. The broth recipe is one Hackmann always uses for the pasta, but you may use any clear broth. You can make the broth in a pressure cooker in about 20 minutes after it begins to perk, or cook the bones in a large stockpot.

Broth
3/4 pound oxtails
2 carrots, peeled and cut into 1 1/2-inch pieces
2 celery ribs, cut into 1 1/2-inch pieces
1 onion, peeled and cut into 6 pieces
salt to taste

Cappelletti
3 to 4 large eggs
3 to 4 scoops (about 1 1/2 to 2 cups) all-purpose flour
4 tablespoons (1/2 stick) unsalted butter
1 boneless, skinless chicken breast, cubed
1/2 pound lean pork, cubed
1/3 cup grated Pecorino-Romano cheese

1. Stockpot Method
To make the broth, put the oxtails, carrots, celery, onion, and salt into a large stockpot, and add 9 cups water, or to cover. Bring to a boil over medium-high heat, and reduce the heat to medium. Cook until the meat

falls from the bones, about 1 1/2 hours. Strain the broth, discarding the bones and mashing the vegetables through a strainer into a large bowl.

2. Pressure Cooker Method

Place all the ingredients in a pressure cooker. After it begins to pulsate, cook for 20 minutes. Turn off the heat, and let cool until the valve drops.

The Mazzanti family in 1918.
Cristofori family album

Discard the oxtail. Strain the broth into a bowl, and mash the vegetables through a strainer into the bowl. Put the broth into a pot, and keep warm on low heat.

To make the *cappelletti*, mix the eggs and flour together, kneading to form a dough. Form into a ball, and set aside in a bowl for about 20 minutes.

Meanwhile, melt the butter in a large skillet over medium heat, and sauté the chicken and pork cubes until browned, about 10 minutes. Grind together with a meat grinder or in a food processor, adding the cheese. If the mixture seems too dry, stir in any remaining butter from the skillet to moisten. Set aside.

Using a pasta machine or a rolling pin, roll out the dough, working with small amounts of dough at a time. Using a biscuit cutter or glass, cut out a 3-inch circle of dough, and spoon 1 tablespoon of meat filling into the center of the circle. Fold the circle in half, and seal it by wetting the edges with water. Then, take the two corners and press them together to make a little hat. Repeat with the remaining dough and meat.

Bring a large saucepan of water to a boil over medium-high heat, and cook the pasta for about 10 minutes, or until they float to the surface. Drain, and pop them into the broth.

Serves 6.

Pasta with Seafood
PASTA CON FRUTTI DI MARE

Serena di Liberto is a native-born Italian from Palermo, who was raised in Bra, the home of Slow Food. She now lives in New York and has worked with the national office of Slow Food U.S.A. She remembers her family as she was growing up: "Basically, all the memories I have with my family are connected to the table. We were having lunch and dinner all together, every single day. Sunday was the day of the extended family, when my aunts, uncles, and cousins were also present at my parents' or grandparents' house. My mother's father was a hunter; I remember that every single Sunday, especially in the winter, my grandmother was cleaning and cooking all the poor animals he was bringing home. I was feeling bad because all the blood, but I was eating them because sooo good. The kitchen was hot, the oven was always on!

Shellfish at Slow Food's Salone del Gusto in Turin.
Anne Parsons

"My father's father was a fisherman (Sicily, summer, sea, sun, boats). When we were spending our summers in Sicily, the fish was fresh on the table every single day, cooked very simply, grilled with lemon and olive oil, or in a more complicated way, usually with tomatoes sauce and olives or as seafood soup or as pasta with fish. I remember one of my father's brother saying to everybody, 'Do not put cheese on pasta with fish!'. . . I do, because I like it. Everybody was laughing. So, I can say that my family has meat and fish tradition. My brother is a good cook, too, very sophisticated and fine. He follows recipes like my mother does; I follow my instinct like my father does."

Serena di Liberto says, "*Buon appetito!*"

If cherry tomatoes are unavailable, use a good brand of canned chopped tomatoes.

4 tablespoons tomato paste
3 tablespoons heavy cream
juice 1 lemon
1 1/2 pounds seafood, such as mussels, shrimp, and scallops
6 tablespoons extra virgin olive oil
1 teaspoon fennel
1 teaspoon oregano
1 teaspoon freshly ground coriander seeds
2 cloves garlic, chopped
20 cherry tomatoes, quartered
salt to taste
freshly ground black pepper to taste
1 pound dried spaghetti
3 tablespoons chopped fresh basil

Combine the tomato paste, cream, and lemon juice in a bowl. Add the shrimp and scallops, and marinate for 30 minutes.

Heat 4 tablespoons oil in a large skillet over medium heat. Add the mussels, fennel, oregano, and coriander seeds. When the mussels start to open, take the skillet off the heat. When they are cool enough to handle, remove the mussel meat from the shells; discard the shells.

Heat the remaining 2 tablespoons oil in the same skillet over medium heat, and sauté the garlic until golden, for about 5 minutes. Remove the garlic, add the tomatoes, and the shrimp mixture, and sauté for 3 minutes. Season with salt and pepper. Add the mussels, and set aside.

Cook the pasta in boiling water according to package directions just until al dente. Drain, stir in the seafood, garnish with the basil, and serve.

Serves 4.

♦ Prosecco with Basil ♦

Although Prosecco is often referred to as the poor man's champagne, a good Prosecco is delightfully uplifting. Ponder its Venetian heritage. Prosecco—the name of the grape, not the region—grows  in the hills near the lagoon city of Venice and is served in every bar and tratorria. Jill Sheffer of Martin's Point, North Carolina, says an Italian friend shared this recipe with her many years ago, and she in turn shared it with her own children and grandchildren. With her partner, Tim, she often slowly sips this aperitif as she watches the crimson sunset dropping over the Currituck Sound horizon and toasts their memories of the shimmering Venetian canals.

Put a few basil leaves in a pitcher with ice. Add about 4 tablespoons Cointreau, and stir well. Fill the pitcher with Prosecco, and stir again. Using a strainer, pour the beverage into champagne glasses, and enjoy.

Japan

- Egg Custard (Chawan-Mushi)

- Yoko's Scattered Sushi (Yoko's Chirashi Sushi)

- Braised Kabocha Squash and Chicken (Kabocha Soboro)

- Pork Shabu Shabu (Joya Nabe)

*P*erhaps most Westerners think of traditional Japanese cooking in terms of sushi and sashimi, sushi rice, miso, tofu, and seaweed. But the cuisine of Japan in its stunning simplicity is both elegant and quite sophisticated, and encompasses a whole range of dishes that go far beyond raw fish and rice. Based on the Buddhist (*kaiseki*) principles of simplicity and harmony with nature, much of the cooking keeps in step with the seasons, and home and restaurant cooks secure what's freshest from the fields.

Unlike the bolder flavors found in Indian, Thai, and Vietnamese dishes, this is one Asian cuisine that depends as much on artful presentations—consider the bento box arrangement or the variety of porcelain dinner dishes for an understanding of food as art—as it does for delicate and subdued seasonings. It's also a cuisine that offers lean fare, with few oils, sugars, and other refined foods. A typical meal might consist of a simple grilled fish, a clean-tasting miso soup, a salad, and tea; company might enjoy the communal hot pot cooking in the form of *shabu-shabu* or *sukiyaki*, when everyone cooks his or her own food in bubbling broth set in the center of the table. Noodles—*soba*, *udon*, and *ramen*—are comforting snack foods as are the sushi and sashimi offerings.

But in Japan as elsewhere, Western influences have crept into the Japanese kitchen, and Western products have found their way onto the pantry shelf. To be convinced of this, stroll through a Japanese grocery to view the numbers of soft drinks, canned goods, and packaged sweets and treats on sale. A Japanese father once exclaimed that his son's towering height resulted from eating a Western diet from birth; by age fifteen, the son dwarfed his father. And notes Chef Kaz Okochi, who cooks for his own upscale Japanese restaurant in Washington, D.C., the food available in Japan when he was growing up was very international and very Western.

Yet, traditional and classical Japanese fare is still revered, and if not always cooked at home, appreciated for its elegance, delicacy, and simplicity—and its beautiful presentations.

Ancient Japanese kimono.
Anne Parsons

Egg Custard
CHAWAN-MUSHI

This custardlike dish turns up often in Japanese restaurants and homes as a comforting appetizer. You'll know when it is thoroughly cooked as its surface becomes firm and slightly springy to the touch.

Kamaboko is a Japanese fish cake sold at Japanese or Korean groceries. When cutting the fish cake, undulate the knife to make each cake look wavy. Ginko nuts are sold dried or canned in Japanese markets. If you use canned nuts, rinse them well before using. They may be sold fresh at Asian markets during the cold months, but they must be soaked first to remove their skins. *Mitsuba* resembles parsley and is sold at Japanese markets. Tiger lily bulbs, or lily buds, are sold at Asian markets and impart a delicate flavor to dishes. Cook the gingko nuts and lily bulb separately.

Japanese garden.
Belinda Cummings

Now living in Washington, D.C., Yoko Zoll is a native of Okayama, Japan. She treasures her family traditions and shares this recipe, which is one of her mother's. As she reports, "My mother, Nobuko Hagihara, is a great cook and still lives in Okayama, which is located between Kobe and Hiroshima. I call her every Saturday morning; her time is Saturday night, fourteen hours difference. I always ask her how to make Japanese cuisine each call."

2 large shrimp, shelled and deveined
salt to taste
4 ounces cooked chicken breast meat, shredded
2 teaspoons light soy sauce
2 large eggs, beaten
1 1/2 cups chicken stock
4 ginko nuts, boiled

2 wavy slices *kamaboko*
1 tiger lily bulb, boiled
1 shiitake mushroom, stemmed and halved
6 sprigs *mitsuba*, cut into 1 1/2-inch pieces, for garnish

Sprinkle the shrimp with some salt. Dip the chicken in the soy sauce, and set aside. Combine the eggs and chicken stock, and season with salt and soy sauce.

Separate the shrimp, chicken, gingko nuts, lily bulb, and mushroom into two portions, and put the portions into two large soup bowls. Divide the egg mixture in half, and pour over the chicken mixture.

Fill the bottom of a large saucepan with water, and set a steamer rack inside. Heat the water over medium heat, and when it is boiling, place the soup bowls on the rack. Cover each bowl with a paper towel to prevent water from dripping into the custard, and cover the steamer. Reduce the heat to low, and steam for about 7 minutes. Set the lid slightly ajar to allow steam to escape, and continue steaming until the custard is set, about 5 minutes more.

To serve, remove the bowls from the steamer, and garnish with the *mitsuba*.

Serves 2.

Yoko's Scattered Sushi
YOKO'S CHIRASHI SUSHI

When Yoko Murase Ray grew up in Nara, Japan, she had three dolls given to her when she was eight or nine years old, and she re-

Doll in traditional Japanese kimono.
Anne Parsons

members dressing them up annually in very elaborate clothing, a practice she continued until she was a young adult. Her parents celebrated the day with a meal of *chirashi sushi*—vinegared sushi rice that her mother garnished with tidbits of vegetables, crabmeat, and eggs scrambled with sake and sugar—accompanied by sweet sake. But Yoko notes that her mother makes this dish several times during the year, whenever the family wants it. It's a simple dish, and one that is popular on Japanese restaurant menus.

Chirashi, or "scattered," sushi means that the cook has topped cooked sushi rice with a variety of ingredients, and in this case, the sushi itself need not include raw fish. Every family has its own recipe, for it is an easy one to prepare and can be adjusted to suit tastes and whatever is available in the pantry. It works well as an appetizer or main course. You can season this by serving the sushi with wasabi paste and soy sauce on the side. Serve this at room temperature. Use only the Japanese short-grain, or "sweet," rice for sushi, and rinse it well before cooking.

Rice
3 cups uncooked sushi rice, well rinsed and soaked for 20 minutes
3 tablespoons rice vinegar

3 tablespoons granulated sugar
1/4 teaspoon salt

Topping
2 tablespoons vegetable oil
3 large eggs
3 tablespoons sweet sake, or mirin
1 tablespoon granulated sugar
5 fresh shiitake mushrooms, or 5 dried and soaked in hot water until
  soft, diced
1 carrot, diced
1 cucumber, peeled and diced
1/4 pound snow peas, cut into thin strips
2 scallions, thinly sliced
1 small sheet *nori*, crumbled
1/2 pound fresh crabmeat, picked clean of cartilage
Japanese soy sauce and wasabi paste, to taste

Cook the rice in a rice steamer according to the manufacturer's directions. Meanwhile, combine the vinegar, sugar, and salt in a saucepan, and heat over low heat until the sugar is dissolved. Set aside to cool.

Put the cooked rice into a large flat bowl or onto a clean work surface, and spread it into a thin layer. Using a wooden spoon or paddle, toss it lightly with the vinegar mixture until the rice is dressed but not too moist. Put the prepared rice into a container, and allow to cool completely.

When the rice has cooled, heat the oil in a large skillet over medium heat. Stir together the eggs, sake, and sugar. Pour into the skillet, and stir until the omelet is firm throughout.

Arrange the cooled rice in a large serving bowl or individual bowls. Top with mushrooms, carrot, cucumber, snow peas, scallions, *nori*, crabmeat, and cooked eggs.

Serves 6.

Braised Kabocha Squash and Chicken
KABOCHA SOBORO

In Washington, D.C., Chef Kaz Okochi, of Kaz Sushi Bistro, remembers when he grew up in Japan—home and restaurant meals were very international. "Curry and rice and spaghetti, adapted to the Japanese way, were dishes children loved," he says. But braised dishes, such as the following recipe, were also very popular because they "kept mother's flavor."

Look for *kabocha* squash at Asian markets or well-stocked supermarkets. Serve this with steamed rice.

Stone statue of Buddha.
Jennifer Parsons

1 tablespoon vegetable oil
1/2 pound ground chicken
1 tablespoon minced ginger
1 piece (2 to 3 pounds) *kabocha* squash,
    peeled and cubed
2 1/2 cups plus 1 1/2 tablespoons water
3 tablespoons sugar
1 tablespoon mirin
2 1/2 tablespoons soy sauce
1 tablespoon potato starch

Heat the oil in a large saucepan, and sauté the chicken and ginger for about 5 minutes. Add the squash, and sauté 2 to 3 minutes more. Add the 2 1/2 cups water, reduce the heat to low, and cook 5 to 6 minutes.

Combine the sugar and mirin, and pour into the pan. Cook 5 to 6 minutes. Add the soy sauce, and cook until the liquid reduces in half. Meanwhile, combine the remaining 1 1/2 tablespoons water with the potato starch, and pour into the pan. Stir and continue cooking until the liquid thickens. Serve hot.

Serves 4.

Pork Shabu Shabu
Joya Nabe

Kaz Okochi enjoyed this dish growing up. Its simplicity exemplifies the austere beauty of Japanese food. You will need to use a fondue pot or other cook-on-the-table pot for this dish. Use chopsticks for cooking and eating this dish.

3 cups sake, or more as needed
1 to 3 cups water, or as needed
1 daikon, finely grated
1 cup soy sauce
1 cup lemon juice
2 pounds boneless pork, thinly sliced
1 pound fresh spinach, well-rinsed
    and trimmed

Chopsticks—"Shall we eat?"
Doug Arcos

Pour the sake and water into a large fondue or other cookpot to fill three-quarters up. Heat over a burner until boiling.

Meanwhile, combine the grated daikon, soy sauce, and lemon juice in a bowl for passing as a dipping sauce. When the sake-water mixture boils, put pork pieces and spinach, a few at a time, into the liquid. When they are cooked, dip the meat and vegetables into the daikon sauce, and eat.

Serves 4.

Mexico

- Mole Poblano-Style (Mole al Estilo Poblano)
- Flour Tortillas
- Egg Bread in Shell-Shape Design (Granddad's Pan de Huevo "Conchas")
- Pozole

*I*f you've grown up anywhere in the United States—except possibly along the Mexican border—you probably define most Mexican food as a composite of tacos, enchiladas, burritos, and fajitas (fajitas aren't even Mexican—they're a Texan invention), all enjoyed with glasses of icy margaritas. Such a curtailed view of the cuisine from our southern neighbor omits much of what makes Mexican cooking so exciting, special, and filled with seasoning surprises. Imagine pairing chilies with chocolate, as chefs do when making the regional specialty from Oaxaca, *mole poblano.*

Several ingredient basics, however, unite most of the country, including a vast array of chilies—ranging from the tiny *pequin* to the very large *poblano*—corn, and beans, plus tomatoes, avocados, squash, and tropical fruits. All these components plus seasonings and meat staples are combined for stews, soups, roasts, and side dishes, all accompanied by either corn or flour tortillas at virtually every meal. But what really defines the cuisine of Mexico are the contrasting regional differences, the climate, and the topography: what you sample in the coastal city of Veracruz, for example, with its emphasis on fresh seafood, tomatoes, and chilies differs from the beef-centric cuisine from the northern plains where cattle ranchers dominate the scene, and where hearty folk start the day with a heaping serving of refried beans and some burritos.

The food historian can also trace how the Spanish and then the French invaders influenced the foods of the vast country: Spaniards added sugar and flour to the Mexican larder. Frenchmen decoded the complexities of pastries and fine baking.

As tortilla maker Victor Vazquez of Virginia has noted in discussions about his native foods, eating is one of life's great pleasures, and food is the centerpiece of most Mexican family gatherings and the focus of daily activities. Consider that not so many years ago, the traditional Mexican businessman went home at midday for a multi-course meal, after which he took a siesta. Later in the afternoon, probably around 4 p.m., he returned to work, where he stayed until 7 p.m. or 8 p.m. Although pressures of modern life have altered that pattern slightly, people still revere the leisurely times spent around the table eating and drinking. As Vazquez concludes, "Food played a central role

Hot chili peppers.
Ali Taylor

in our family life, and it was a way of expressing the family unity. Food is also emblematic of who we are and where we came from," he says, noting the Indian, Spanish, and French influences that have shaped Mexican cooking.

Mole Poblano-Style
MOLE AL ESTILO POBLANO

A native of San Antonio, Texas, Victor Vazquez was born to parents who immigrated to the United States from Mexico during the early 1900s: his mother from San Luis Potosi and his father from Monclova, Coahuila. He remembers the family mealtime being a very structured event that followed traditional standards. The food was all placed in the center of the table, then everyone was called to dinner, but no one was seated until his father first took his place at the head of the table. As always, a large stack of corn or flour tortillas was in the center of the table. "Mealtimes were always abundant, but usually consisted of mostly vegetables. When meat was prepared, it was usually in some sort of one-pot dish, so that we all were able to share whatever meat was available," he says. Desserts were minimal and usually consisted of a piece of candy or a kind of pudding, usually a bread pudding called *capirotada,* a traditional bread pudding with ancient roots that one food historian suggests is in danger of extinction.

"One of my favorite dishes as a youngster," he says, "was chicken *mole*, and my own children also took a special liking for this dish. In our family, we established a tradition that for birthdays the child who was having a birthday would get to choose the meal he wanted. One of my sons always chose this dish for his birthday, and we still prepare it from my mother's recipe." The dish consists of chicken, which is first sautéed, then simmered in a rich sauce consisting of chilies, tomatoes, chocolate, peanuts, and spices.

"The traditional method for making this dish is to begin by steaming the chilies until the skins soften and the pulp absorbs moisture," says Vazquez. "They are then pressed through a colander or ricer, and the pulp is used as the base for the mole sauce. To the chili pulp is added the tomatoes and other flavorings and spices, and then it is either sweetened with Mexican chocolate, or as my mother preferred, using a combination of unsweetened baker's chocolate and peanuts and sugar. Today, I always use unsweetened chocolate and then chunky peanut butter, which makes it easier to reach the balance between the chilies, the chocolate, and the peanuts and sugar taste.

"In preparing traditional foods today, we must be aware that the ingredients available are no longer the same as they were years ago. Furthermore, recipes were varied by regions of the country as well as by family preferences. However, I always tell people interested in this food that using the freshest ingredients and following the prescribed preparation methods will surely yield you a dish of excellent qualities."

3 dried *ancho* chilies, stemmed and seeded
3 dried *guajillo* chilies
3 dried *arbol* chilies
3 cups chicken stock
1/4 cup olive oil
1 (5-pound) chicken, cut into serv-
    ing pieces and sprinkled with
    black pepper
1/2 medium onion, chopped
2 cloves garlic, chopped
1 pound ripe tomatoes, diced
1 cup homemade tomato sauce or 1
    (8-ounce) can tomato sauce
salt to taste
1 (1-ounce) square unsweetened
    baking chocolate
2 tablespoons peanut butter
3 tablespoons sesame seeds
3 tablespoons almond pieces
ground cinnamon to taste
ground cloves to taste

Chicken stuffed in chilies
poblanos with mole sauce.
Anne Parsons

Put the chilies and chicken stock in a large saucepan, and heat the chilies over medium heat until boiling. Reduce the heat to low, and cook for 10 minutes, or until soft. Put the peppers and some stock into a blender, and puree until smooth.

Put the olive oil into a large skillet, and heat over medium heat. Fry the chicken pieces until golden on all sides, and drain chicken on paper towels. Reduce the heat to low, add the onions, and cook, stirring, until the onion is lightly brown. Stir in the garlic.

Stir into the remaining chicken stock the ground chilies, tomatoes, tomato sauce, onions, garlic, salt, and the chocolate, and cook over medium-low, stirring until the chocolate is completely melted. Reduce the heat to low, and cook for 15 minutes. Taste, noticing the spicy flavor of the chilies and the bitter edge of chocolate.

Starting with 1 tablespoon peanut butter, stir in enough to add some sweetness and until the flavor of the peanut butter is present, but still keeping the flavors in balance for a good mole. Stir in the sesame seeds, almonds, cinnamon, and cloves.

Add the chicken pieces to the sauce, cover the pan, and cook over low heat for 30 minutes, or until the meat begins to fall from the bones. Remove from the heat, cool 15 to 20 minutes, and serve over Mexican rice or pilaf.

Tip: When handling chilies, wear rubber gloves and wash your hands immediately after working with the chilies.

Serves 4 to 6.

Flour Tortillas

As Victor Vazquez notes, "My mom did all the cooking, but where we helped her was making the tortillas. We had four griddles going all the time, each with a different temperature, and we just passed them from one to another until they were all cooked. In my thirty years of making tortillas, there have been some changes, but we have made every effort to insure that the traditional taste has remained."

Note: Mr. Vasquez owns Moctec Mexican Food Products, a tortilla factory in Landover, Maryland. These super flour tortillas are based on the Moctec formulation.

4 cups bread flour
2 teaspoons salt
2 teaspoons baking powder
1/2 cup shortening or lard
1 1/2 to 2 cups lukewarm water

Young woman making tortillas.
Victor Vazquez

Mix together the first three ingredients until well distributed. Add the shortening, and cut it into the flour mixture until it forms small beads.

Add the water, and mix and knead until it forms a soft smooth dough, adding enough water to make it soft enough to roll out. Rest the dough for 10 minutes before rolling out. Divide the dough into 16 balls by dividing it into half, then half again until divided into 16 pieces. Form each ball into a small, flat patty about 3 inches in diameter.

Roll each patty with a rolling pin on a lightly floured board, turning several times, until it is about 1/8-inch thick and 8 inches round.

Cook on a medium-hot griddle or skillet, turning 3 or 4 times, until the tortilla looks bright white with a few browning spots.

Makes 16 tortillas.

Egg Bread in Shell-Shape Design
GRANDDAD'S PAN DE HUEVO "CONCHAS"

Designed to resemble shells, or *conchas*, these just-sweet rolls are traditionally served with coffee very early in the morning—about 5 a.m., says Victor Vazquez—and then as a light dessert later in the evening. Although his grandfather made these regularly in large batches, Vazquez's mother often opted to purchase the rolls from a Mexican bakery.

Rolls
2 packages (2 tablespoons) dry yeast
1 tablespoon plus 1 cup granulated sugar
3/4 cup warm water
4 large eggs
1/4 cup shortening or lard
4 to 5 cups all-purpose flour
2 teaspoons salt
1 teaspoon vanilla extract

Topping
1/4 cup shortening or lard
3/4 cup granulated sugar
1 large egg
3/4 to 1 cup all-purpose flour

To make the rolls, combine the yeast, 1 tablespoon sugar, and water in a large bowl, and set aside to proof, about 5 minutes.

Beat the eggs until thick and pale yellow; set aside. Cream the sugar and shortening until fluffy. Add the egg mixture, and, using an electric beater, mix at medium speed until well blended.

Add 2 cups flour, the salt, vanilla extract, and the yeast mixture to the sugar mixture, and blend together at medium speed. Add the remaining flour, and using a dough hook or by hand, knead the dough, adding extra flour as needed, until the dough is silky, smooth, and no longer sticky. On a floured surface, shape the dough into a smooth ball.

Grease a large bowl lightly, and put in the dough, turning it once to coat all sides. Cover the dough with plastic wrap, and set is aside in a warm place, about 95°F.

Let the dough rise until doubled in bulk, about 2 hours. When doubled, punch it down, and let it rest for 10 minutes. Lightly grease a baking sheet. Divide the dough into half, then half again, repeating until the dough is divided in 32 balls. Round each ball, and put it on the baking sheet about 2 inches apart. Flatten each slightly.

To make the topping, cream together the shortening and sugar. Add the egg, and mix until well blended. Add enough flour to form a firm but kneadable ball that does not crack when rolled.

Divide the ball into half, then half again, repeating until the ball is divided into 32 pieces. Flatten each ball by patting it between your hands until it is large enough to cover the top of a roll. Place 1 on top of each roll, patting it down slightly. Score the tops with a knife to form a shell design, but do not cut into the roll itself. Set aside to rise for about 1 hour in a warm place.

Preheat the oven to 350°F.

Bake for about 20 to 25 minutes. Cool slightly before eating.

Note: Dough that contains shortening, sugar, and eggs must be placed in a warmer place to rise than ordinary bread dough.

Makes 32 rolls.

 *Pozole*

Growing up in Mexico and spending much of his childhood with his grandparents in Chapala, Mexico, Humberto Martinez at the Cultural Institute of Mexico in Washington, D.C., has very fond memories of their farm, where they raised vegetables, avocados, chickens, and pigs. His grandmother also used to cook, and one of her best-loved dishes—one that she served for special occasions and when family members gathered together—was *pozole*. A classic hearty Mexican soup/stew, *pozole* is based on pork (and often pig's feet and pork rind) plus chilies and hominy (a dried corn kernel product made from field corn). It is a very filling meal-in-one, and it is still so popular in Chapala that sidewalk vendors gather in town to sell their *pozole* three nights a week. But *pozole* is very popular elsewhere in Mexico, too, notes Martinez, and you can find green or white *pozoles* in different regions. He adds that the name "*pozole*" comes from the Náhuatl word "*pozzoli*," meaning "foam," which results when you cook the white big hominy in water, because when it is boiling, it forms a white foam.

He advises that you start this dish the day before you plan to serve it, and to remember that it makes enough to feed about a dozen people. He says his grandmother was concerned about reducing fat content in her recipes, so she used part pork and part chicken in her *pozole*, but you can stick to the traditional recipe of all pork; in the final cooking, you can also add bone-in pork chops for added flavor. His grandmother served this with tostadas and refried beans, plus bowls of garnishes, such as iceberg lettuce chiffonade, diced onions, diced radishes, dried oregano, ground chili *pequin* and chili *cascabel*, and lime sections for juice. Store leftovers in a covered container in the refrigerator.

1 (3-pound) frying chicken, cut into pieces
5-pound pork, fresh hock or shoulder, bone in but fat removed
5 to 6 pork chops, bone in
4 onions, peeled and chopped
5 to 6 cloves garlic
4 or 5 bay leaves

Woman making pozole.
Javier Raygoza

salt to taste

1 pound dry hominy (*cacahuazintle*), soaked overnight, or 2 (29-ounce) cans cooked hominy, drained and rinsed

4 dried chilies *guajillo*, soaked in hot water

4 dried chilies *ancho*, soaked in hot water

1 tablespoon dried oregano

Garnish

1 head iceberg lettuce, chiffonade

4 onions, peeled and diced

16 radishes, sliced

8 limes, halved

2 tablespoons dried oregano

ground chilies *pequin* and chilies *cascabel*

To make the *pozole*, put the chicken pieces, pork hock or shoulder, and pork chops into a large soup kettle, and add water to cover. Add the onions, garlic, bay leaves, and salt to taste, and bring to a boil over medium heat. Reduce the heat to medium-low, and cook for 3 to 4 hours. Remove from the heat to cool slightly. Strain, reserving the liquid, and remove the meat from the bones when cool enough to handle. Set aside.

Meanwhile, cook the hominy in unsalted water to cover. When the kernels are soft, drain and rinse the hominy.

Put the softened chilies and some stock in a blender, and puree until smooth. Pour the pureed chilies into the stock, add the hominy, and cook, uncovered, over medium-low heat for 2 more hours. Then add the meat, and boil, covered, over medium-low heat for 2 hours more. Let the *pozole* rest, and boil again before serving. Serve very hot in a soup bowl with high sides. Pass the garnishes in separate bowls.

Note: If you want a spicy *pozole*, leave the seeds in the chilies; otherwise, remove the seeds and veins before soaking. Do not cook the dried hominy with salt; otherwise, they will take much longer to soften. If you cannot find the dried hominy, look for canned hominy at Hispanic markets.

Serves 12.

Morocco

- ◆ SHREDDED CHICKEN PIE (B'STILLA)

- ◆ TAJINE OF LAMB WITH PRUNES AND APRICOTS

- ◆ QUINCE AND HONEY TAJINE WITH CHICKEN

- ◆ ALMOND COOKIES FOR AZIZ

- ◆ SIDEBAR: MINT TEA

- ◆ ORANGE SLICES WITH CINNAMON

*M*orocco is a feast for the senses and Marrakesh is la crème de la
crème. The Berber Almoravids founded Marrakesh in 1062, and
quickly expanded their empire to include southern Spain and the plains
of West Africa. The resulting exchange of cultures and architecture led
to European influences still felt in a city that sits at the foot of the snow-
clad Atlas Mountains. Although a patriarchal society, Morocco is one of
the Muslim world's most liberal and progressive countries. The current
king, Mohammed VI, promotes education for women and for
marginalized groups such as the Berbers. Most Moroccans are fluent in
French—a legacy of French colonial rule from 1912 to 1956.

Visit the *souks* (markets) in Morocco, and you will be overwhelmed
by the heady aromas of more than one hundred spices. Walk through
the narrow archways, and you will be enveloped into a melting pot of
the senses. Meander through the markets and you will be amazed by
the rugs, woodwork, metal, leather, spices, jewelry, perfumes, tapes-
tries, and textiles. Anything you can imagine, you can find in the maze
of *souks* where there is a powerful lingering scent of saffron, ginger,
cumin, orange blossoms, and where the sight of abundant sacks of almonds, dates, olives, and figs demand to be tasted.

Not only that, you will be enchanted with tales of splendor and glory.
With its striking mosques, magnificent palaces, beautiful gardens, and
tranquil fountains, this country is a magical oasis that sprang from the
Sahara desert of North Africa. Here, the fusion of cultures and history
has created a dazzling array of mouth-watering aromatic foods. The
abundance of grains, fruits, and nuts in Morocco are a main feature of

the cuisine. A typical meal includes: olives—red, black, green, hot, sour, and sweet (as Morocco's primary export, they are served with every meal)—pickled vegetables; salads of tender carrots, eggplant, peppers, and beets; *djez makalli* (chicken with olives and preserved lemons); lamb *tagine*; couscous; *b'stillas* (ancient in origin, it is a meat pie made with incredibly thin pastry); and fish (the coastline abounds in seafood). A traditional dessert is a deliciously airy concoction—*jouhara*—made of super-thin pastry and crème patisserie with orange water and cinnamon. Yes, indeed, tantalizing tastes await you in Morocco.

Berber woman churning butter.
Anne Parsons

Shredded Chicken Pie

B'STILLA

Malika Kaddouri, an English teacher fluent in four languages, cooks two huge meals daily, à la Moroccan tradition, for her husband and three sons. And, she still finds time to have elegant dinner parties where the *b'stilla* is so big it requires two to three people to carry it to the table! The individual *briouat*-style *b'stillas* are infinitely more manageable and no less delectable than the traditional version. This traditional pie has ancient origins and used to be made with pigeon—it is an essential part of every Moroccan feast.

1 (3-pound) chicken
1 large white onion, sliced
1 large bunch flat-leaved Italian parsley, chopped
1 bunch cilantro, chopped
1/2 teaspoon ground turmeric
1/2 teaspoon ground coriander
1/2 teaspoon ground cumin
2 teaspoons grated fresh ginger
2 teaspoons ground cinnamon
2 tablespoons vegetable oil

Sauce and Pastry
5 eggs, lightly beaten
1 1/2 cups confectioners' sugar
ground cinnamon to taste plus 1 teaspoon cinnamon
ground pepper to taste
1 1/2 cups ground almonds
1/2 cup (1 stick) unsalted butter, melted
1 pound phyllo dough

Preheat the oven to 350°F. Grease a 9-inch pie pan.
    To make the chicken, place the chicken, onion, parsley, cilantro, tur-

meric, coriander, cumin, ginger, cinnamon, and oil in a roasting dish with 1 1/2 cups water. Bake for 1 1/2 hours. Remove the chicken from the roasting pan, and cool. Shred the flesh, and discard the skin and bones.

To make the sauce, skim the fat from the liquid in the roasting pan, and transfer the liquid to a medium-sized saucepan. Heat the liquid over medium-low heat, and add the eggs, 1 cup sugar, cinnamon to taste, and pepper. Cook, stirring, until the sauce is thickened.

To make the pastry, mix the almonds, 1 teaspoon cinnamon, and remaining 1/2 cup sugar together. Place a sheet of phyllo dough in the prepared pie pan. Brush the phyllo lightly with melted butter. Place a second sheet on top, and brush with butter. Repeat layering and light

Local baker in Marrakesh souk.
Anne Parsons

buttering with 8 more sheets, sprinkling some of the almond mixture on the last sheet.

Spread the egg mixture and chicken filling on top, fold over the pastry edges, and brush again with butter. Butter and layer 4 more sheets, cut into a round, and cover the pie. Butter the top of the pie.

Bake for 40 minutes, or until golden brown. Sprinkle with the remaining almond mixture. Serve hot.

Serves 8.

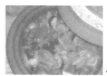

Tagine of Lamb with Prunes and Apricots

During a multi-cultural graduate class at George Mason University, Jane Buckley told her friend Anne Parsons that she met her Moroccan husband, Aziz Kaddouri, on a commuter train to Washington, D.C. When he tried to peer over Jane's shoulder to read her Balzac novel, she almost knocked him over—it was the beginning of a beautiful relationship, a marvelous marriage, and a beautiful daughter, Sufia. They love to cook and frequently serve *tagines*—traditional Moroccan stews featuring meat or poultry gently simmered with vegetables, olives, preserved lemons, garlic, and spices like cumin, ginger, pepper, saffron, and turmeric. Because Jane is not yet fluent in Arabic, she often gets recipes in French from her in-laws in Morocco, then Jane jots it down in English.

Buckley-Kaddouri says that sometimes she'll buy boneless lamb and "cut it into 4-inch pieces; that way, you can do as the Moroccans do, and use your bread to grab a piece of it, tearing a bit with the bread itself, or if you're serving non-Moroccans who tend more towards forks and knives, they have an actual chunk to go after." Buckley-Kaddouri also admits, "I don't cook the dates separately. Hate to dirty another pan! But I am chastised for not doing so by all the family's female Moroccans."

Chicken and lamb tagines cook slowly on grill.
Anne Parsons

2 tablespoons vegetable oil
3 large onions, diced
1/3 teaspoon ground saffron
1/3 teaspoon ground turmeric
3 pounds lamb, bone-in
3/4 teaspoon pepper
1/2 teaspoon salt
3/4 teaspoon ground ginger
1 stick cinnamon
1 tablespoon unsalted butter

3 tablespoons granulated sugar
1 cup pitted prunes
1 cup dried apricots
1/2 cup slivered almonds, toasted

Heat the oil in a heavy-bottomed pan over medium heat. Add the onions, saffron, and turmeric, and sweat the onions in the oil, adding a little water to prevent their burning and to speed the sweating, for about 10 minutes.

Add the lamb with enough water to cover. Add the pepper, salt, ginger, and cinnamon. Reduce the heat to low after the water starts to boil. Cover and cook for at least 1 hour, or until the meat is tender.

Meanwhile, melt the butter in a second pan; add 1 cup water, the sugar, prunes, and apricots. Cook over medium-low heat until they are almost falling apart.

Put the meat and its sauce on a platter, and pour the prunes and apricots over top so they don't break. Sprinkle the almonds over all, and serve.

Serves 6.

Quince and Honey Tagine with Chicken

Although many Americans don't like the tartness of the quince, which looks like a cross between an apple and a pear, Jane Buckley-Kaddouri insists that honey enhances its flavor. Quinces are available in supermarkets from October through December. Buckley-Kaddouri advises selecting those that are large, firm, and yellow with little or no sign of green. You can wrap quinces in plastic and refrigerate them for up to 2 months. Buckley-Kaddouri uses fryers because "they are just the right size, and they tend to be marvelously juicy, AND cheap!"

Spices for every dish are available at the souk.
Anne Parsons

5 tablespoons unsalted butter
2 large onions, grated
1 (3 1/2-pound) frying chicken, cut into serving pieces
salt to taste
freshly ground black pepper to taste
8 strands saffron, soaked in 1/2 cup boiling water
1 stick cinnamon
2 tablespoons superfine sugar
1 tablespoon ground cinnamon
1/3 cup honey
3 pounds quinces, seeded but un-peeled

Melt the butter in a saucepan over medium heat. Add the onions, reduce the heat to low, and cook until the onions are transparent. Add the chicken, salt, pepper, saffron, cinnamon stick, and 3 cups water.

Increase the heat to medium, and cook for 40 minutes, or until the meat is almost cooked. Remove the chicken to a platter.

Add the sugar, cinnamon, honey, and quinces, and cook until the quinces are cooked through. Remove each quince when it is cooked.

Continue cooking the sauce until it has reduced and become thick and rich. Return the chicken and quince to the sauce, each on its own side of the pan to avoid crushing the quince and reheat on medium-low. Arrange on a platter with the chicken on the bottom, then the quince, and the sauce poured over all.

Serves 6.

Almond Cookies for Aziz

For special feasts, and to indulge her guests' desire for something sweet, Jane Buckley-Kaddouri bakes these delicious cookies for her husband, Aziz. She cautions that the cookies "will be eaten like crazy by all and sundry, so do not put all the cookies out at once or you'll have none left."

Jane and Sufia bake cookies for Aziz.
Aziz Kaddouri

Dough
6 cups blanched almonds
1 1/4 cups granulated sugar
2 large eggs
2 tablespoons orange flower water
zest of 1 lemon

Syrup
1/2 cup sugar
1/2 cup water
2 tablespoons orange flower water

To make the dough, put the almonds and sugar into a food processor, and process until very fine. Add the eggs, and process again. Add 1 tablespoon of the orange flower water and half the lemon zest, and process again. Add the remaining orange flower water and lemon zest, and process well until everything is well combined. The dough will be very sticky.

Preheat the oven to 350°F. Butter 2 cookie sheets lightly.

Flour your hands, and break off one-quarter of the dough. Roll it into a fat cigar shape, and place it on the prepared cookie sheet. Pat it down to form a 1/2-inch-thick rectangle. Repeat with the remaining dough.

Bake for 20 minutes, or until the sides are golden.

Meanwhile, to make the syrup, bring the sugar and water to a boil; add the orange blossom water. Continue cooking until the mixture thickens and reduces slightly.

Remove the almond rectangles from the oven, and put them onto waxed paper. Cut the large rectangles into smaller ones, about 1x2 inches each. Using a pastry brush, brush all cookies with syrup. Coat 3 times.

Caution: Coating the cookies with syrup BEFORE removing from baking trays will make the dough too heavy. If you then try to lift it off to cut it, it will break apart. Trust me. This is experience talking. Put confectioners' sugar in a sieve or sifter, and shake gently over all cookies, coating lightly.

Makes about 3 dozen 4-inch cookies.

◆ Mint Tea ◆

In Morocco, no meal is complete without a cup of mint tea. Often, the host will pour the tea from one to two feet away into the traditional small glass cups.

4 tea bags green tea
1 cup packed fresh mint leaves
1/4 cup sugar
3 cups boiling water

Place the tea bags, mint leaves, and sugar in a teapot. Pour in the boiling water and stir to dissolve the sugar. Let steep 6 minutes and serve.

Orange Slices with Cinnamon

Dorothea Buckley has reaped the rewards of her daughter's marriage to Aziz Kaddouri. As she tells it, "Aziz's relatives have shared family recipes with Jane, who now cooks incredibly tasty *tagines* and other traditional Moroccan dishes. Yet, my favorite dessert is this one, perhaps because it is so simple, requires no cooking, and is so delicious." Jane says that Moroccans love to entertain. "Whether you are with wealth, or without, is not important. Moroccans will seize any opportunity to have guests dine with them. You can be sure the guest will be treated like royalty," says Buckley-Kaddouri, and adds, "My mother always gives it rave reviews."

Orange slices with cinnamon.
Anne Parsons

3 navel oranges
ground cinnamon to taste
sugar, if desired

Peel and slice the whole oranges thinly. Remove any pith and the seeds. Arrange the slices on a plate and sprinkle with cinnamon. Chill. Remove from the refrigerator about 10 minutes before serving.

Serves 4.

Poland

- Hunter's Stew (Bigos)
- Polish Cookies (Chrusciki)
- Dumplings Filled with Mushrooms (Uszka Pierogi)
- Christmas Eve Karp

*A*t the end of World War II, Poland, tormented by its history, disappeared behind the Iron Curtain to become part of the Soviet empire. From then until 1989, food was scarce for those in the populace who did not become communists. Food became a political tool. For farmers, it was not feasible to produce wholesale crops as the government set the market prices. So farmers, who could still own land, grew crops for their own consumption or traded on the black market for other goods. Today, however, now that Poland has a democratic government, markets are bursting with an abundance of excellent meats, pyramids of fresh fruits and vegetables, and stacks of newly baked breads.

Polish dancers in Warsaw.
Anne Parsons

Polish culture is a colorful quilt of Slavic, Turkish, German, Hungarian, and Jewish influences. Fortunately, these numerous cultures introduced such a diversity of new tastes and ingredients that only served to enhance the indigenous cuisine. Of course, with any culinary preparation, the success of the dish depends on the quality of its ingredients. In the home, Polish cooks believe early morning trips to the market are a crucial step in meal preparation. Here, the national dish is *bigos*, a hunter's stew of sauerkraut and wild game, or preserved meat. Other Polish specialties include *makowiec*, homemade poppy seed cake, borscht, *golonka* (pork knuckles cooked with vegetables), *kolduny* (meat dumplings), and *pierogi*.

To get a real taste of traditional cuisine, no visitor will willingly refuse a home-cooked meal. Lingering over dinner, you will believe that courtesy, good food, and conviviality began in a Polish kitchen.

Hunter's Stew

BIGOS

Before winter, Gosia Malicka, a student from Silesia, Poland, tells Anne Parsons that her family and friends pick mushrooms in the forest, dry them at home by hanging them from threads, and then store them in paper bags. If you use dried mushrooms, you will need to soak the mushrooms in hot water before cooking. This sauerkraut stew, the national dish of Poland, has variations that are almost infinite. It would be an ideal candidate for the slow cooker. Usually, people serve this stew with sour cream as a garnish, rye bread on the side, and plenty of dark, robust beer as the beverage. Boiled carrots and a green salad as accompaniments complement the dark stew. Note that this dish tastes better the next day.

Pots of bigos.
Michal Zacharzewski

1 1/2 to 2 cups beef stock plus more as needed
1 pound sauerkraut, drained and rinsed
1/2 head cabbage, finely shredded
6 large mushrooms, preferably porcini, chopped
1 pound smoked kielbasa sausage, sliced and fried
3 cups cubed pork
1/2 pound bacon, cut into small bits
1 onion, chopped
1 tart apple, peeled, cored, and cubed
1 tablespoon granulated sugar
12 peppercorns
12 allspice berries, or 1 teaspoon ground allspice
1 bay leaf

Heat the stock in a large saucepan over medium heat, and add the remaining ingredients. Reduce the heat to low, and cook for 3 to 4 hours, adding more stock as needed, or until all the flavors have blended. Serve hot.

Serves 6.

Polish Cookies

CHRUSCIKI

Regina Wojcik Wojtecki Bianchi O'Connor, born and raised in Poland, married a Pole, an Italian, and then an Irishman. She remembers her mother: "Although she never read a cookbook, she was a great cook, and everything was homemade. When asked the recipe for something, her answer was always, 'Whatever is on hand, a little of this, a little of that.'

"When preparing fish, she'd put them in a bowl, slice onions on top, put in a small bay leaf, salt, and pepper and let it sit like that so that the fish taste would disappear, then she fried them. She never broiled anything; everything was cooked on top of the stove. She even made her own cordials (blueberry and cherry, for example). The blueberries would ferment on the fire escape in a jar covered with sugar and a cloth on top. When ready, she'd add alcohol to the berries. If we had a cold, we'd be put to bed with hot tea and the blueberry mixture, put under a feather blanket, and wake up cured!

"In Poland, mushrooms were always picked wild and always very abundant. When she visited us in the U.S., she would go mushroom pick-

Regina and Henry Wojtecki on their wedding day in Poland, 1940. Wojtecki family album

ing in the woods near our home in Staunton. Her mushroom soup was outstanding; made of dried Polish mushrooms, it was meatless and finished off with homemade noodles and sour cream. Her stuffed cabbage was always made with ground pork. She made many types of *pierogis*—cheese, mushroom, meat, and sauerkraut.

Although she made her own headcheese, pickled eel, and *kielbasi*, her duck soup was particularly memorable. She always baked large *babki, pachki,* and *chrusciki.* At age eighty-one, I just remember that whatever her hands touched and made, it was out of this world."

Regina's daughter, Janet Colegrove, and her son, Tom Wojtecki, regret not having written recipes; however, they learned a lot from observing their *Babci* (grandmother), and they have re-created *Babci's* delicious *chrusciki* from notes their mother made in 1960 as she watched their grandmother make it. Colegrove suggests dividing the dough in half and working with one half at a time.

1 tablespoon granulated sugar
6 egg yolks
1/4 cup sour cream
1 tablespoon vinegar
2 cups all-purpose flour
3 cups vegetable oil, for deep-frying
confectioners' sugar, for dusting

Add the sugar to the egg yolks and beat until thick and lemon-colored. Add the sour cream and vinegar, and continue to beat. Fold into the flour, and knead until the dough blisters. The dough should not be stiff.

Lightly dust the work surface with flour to prevent the dough from sticking. Roll the dough out very thin (about the thickness of a penny), and cut into a 10x10-inch square. Slice the dough into 1.5x10-inch-long strips. Make a slit down the center of each strip to within 1 inch of each end. Knot into a bow shape.

Heat the oil to 350°F in a large, deep saucepan, and when it is shimmering, carefully put the dough bows into the pan and deep-fry until lightly browned (about 1 minute). Remove, drain on paper towels, and dust *heavily* with confectioners' sugar.

Makes about 20 cookies.

Dumplings Filled with Mushrooms
Uszka Pierogi

Asked to test some of her family's Polish recipes, Janet Colegrove readily accepted and later wrote this e-mail to her friends: "The REALLY big news is that—thanks to a good friend, Anne Parsons, who's writing a cookbook and her request of me to test some recipes—I've been discovering my 'Polish roots.' Yesterday I made *pierogis*. After a slight recipe adjustment, I achieved success! The delectable little mushroom-stuffed dough pockets awakened wonderful memories of my *Babci* and just about brought a tear to my eye. My mom is very proud of me! And a few days ago I rolled out and deep-fried some delicious *chruscik*. Yes, our meals are good and tasty around OBX (Outer Banks) town."

Dough
2 1/2 cups all-purpose flour, sifted
1 tablespoon sour cream
1 large egg
1/2 teaspoon salt
warm water
sour cream for garnish, optional

Filling
1 tablespoon unsalted butter
1 small onion, chopped
1/4 pound fresh mushrooms, diced

Janet Colegrove with mum and brother Tom, circa 1954.
Wojtecki family album

To make the dough, combine the flour, sour cream, eggs, and salt. Stir in enough warm water to make a soft dough that still holds its shape. Knead the dough in a bowl, wrap in a towel, and rest for 10 minutes.

Divide the dough into quarters, and roll out to 1/8-inch thick. Cut out circles 2 or 3 inches in diameter.

To make the filling, heat the butter in a large skillet over medium heat, and sauté the onion. Add the mushrooms, and continue cooking until the vegetables are soft.

Place 1 teaspoon filling on each circle, fold over, and stretch the edges, pinching them shut. Bring lightly salted water to a boil in a large saucepan over medium heat, and carefully drop the *uszka* pierogi in the water, a few at a time. When they float, use a slotted spoon to remove them from the water. Don't overcook.

Drain the *uszka* pierogi, and serve with hot soup.

Makes about 2 1/2 dozen.

Christmas Eve Karp

Gosia Malichka, a young woman from Silesia, Poland, spent some months working in the United States with Russian and Polish friends. When Anne Parsons asked what she really missed during her stay here, she quickly replied, "the food." After spending an afternoon drinking tea and discussing traditional family meals, Malichka agreed to e-mail her mother in Silesia for some family recipes. She said her mother is a great cook as was her grandmother, and remarked that Polish Christmas Eve and Christmas Day dinners are very traditional. "In fact," says Malichka, "Christmas Eve dinner was once a feast that consisted of twenty-one courses. Preparations often began months before the celebration."

Nowadays, this dinner consists of only four or five courses. Because hospitality is as important a tradition as food, Polish hosts always set an extra place at the dinner table for an unexpected guest. Malichka says that carp (spelled "karp" in Poland) is the main fish in the area of Poland where she lives, and it is therefore traditional for her Christmas Eve dinner. Serve this dish with cabbage and mushrooms.

A choice of karp for dinner.
Belinda Cumming

1 (3- to 4-pound) carp, cleaned and filleted
salt to taste
flour for dredging
1 to 2 eggs, lightly beaten
dry breadcrumbs
1/2 cup butter plus 1/2 cup vegetable oil for frying

Cut the carp into equal-size portions, and sprinkle lightly with salt. Let stand for 30 minutes.

Dredge the carp lightly with flour, shaking off the excess. Coat the pieces with the beaten eggs, using a pastry brush, or dip the pieces into the eggs. Coat the fish with the crumbs, shaking off the excess.

Heat the butter and oil together in a large skillet until very hot. Cook the fish on both sides until golden brown—about 5 minutes per side. Make sure the oil and butter mixture is half way up the sides of the fish. Drain the fish on paper towels, and serve immediately.

Serves 4 to 6.

Scandinavia/Iceland

- Swedish Meatballs

- Norwegian Caramel Pork Loin

- Icelandic Fish and Potatoes (Plokkfiskur)

- Danish Rice Pudding with Warm Cherry Sauce

- Sidebar: Wrapped Smoked Salmon

SCANDINAVIA

*A*re you geographically confused about Scandinavia? Not to worry, it's a familiar problem. The most commonly accepted definition is that Scandinavia, a region of northern Europe, includes Norway, Sweden, Denmark, Finland, and Iceland (the last one is culturally and historically included).

The traditional food of these countries might surprise you because it doesn't morph into something other than what it represents—the food tastes like itself. The ingredients for Scandinavian cuisine come fresh from the earth, the sea, and the lakes, and many Scandinavians eat the same foods as their Viking ancestors: mutton, chicken, geese, deer, fish, and bear. Because of its northern latitude, the winter months are long and yield only a few hours of daylight. Like their ancestors, modern Scandinavians smoke and salt their meats and fish to preserve them through the barren winters.

According to historians, the Vikings succeeded as invaders because the ship's pantry was filled with cured fish and meats allowing them to travel long distances. Today, the Vikings would surely approve of *gravlax*—a sugar and salt cured salmon (an alternative to smoked salmon) and one of Scandinavia's delicacies.

ICELAND

Iceland is one of the cleanest and safest places in the world. This small island, with Reykjavik as its capital, features a unique combination of art, architecture, and stunning natural beauty. In this unpolluted environment, the geysers, waterfalls (Dettifoss is the most powerful waterfall in Europe), volcanoes, bubbling mud pools, and abundance of wildlife are marvels of Mother Nature. The country's literacy rate ranks among the highest in the world, and the modern Icelandic language is still very close to the Old Norse spoken during the Viking era.

Reykjavik, capital of Iceland.
Alan Kiernan

Icelandic traditional food of the past is the meat of culinary legends—pickled ram's testicles, putrified shark, scorched sheep heads, blood pudding, and dried fish. Today, very few Icelanders partake in the consumption of this fare. A fine dining culture has taken hold that embraces a unique mix of ancient and modern traditional food, all of it sourced from local producers.

Swedish Meatballs

Dick Rodine, a former neighbor and friend of Anne Parsons, recalls: "My grandfather, Carl Johnson, came to America from Sweden when he was about twenty years old. When I grew up, my family lived a short distance from my grandparents' house in Des Moines, Iowa. Our holiday celebrations included several traditional Swedish dishes, with my favorite being Swedish meatballs. My wife Sharon's family has strong Swedish ties, so preparing Swedish meatballs became a tradition that we carried on with our children.

"Over the years, especially for Christmas, I adapted the basic recipe and included a 'secret ingredient'—eggnog. We'd drink a little eggnog, add a bit to the meatballs, and have a merry Christmas Eve. These meatballs can be made a day ahead and reheated."

An enticing Swedish smorgasbord. Anne Parsons

1 pound ground beef
1 pound ground pork sausage
2 cups soft breadcrumbs
2 (3-ounce) packages cream
  cheese, softened
1/4 cup dried onion soup mix
1/2 teaspoon salt
1/2 teaspoon ground nutmeg
fresh sage, chopped, to taste
1 cup eggnog
2 tablespoons vegetable oil
2 tablespoons all-purpose flour
1 1/2 cups whole milk

By hand, or using an electric mixer on medium speed, thoroughly combine the beef, pork sausage, breadcrumbs, cream cheese, soup mix, salt, nutmeg, sage, and 1/2 cup of eggnog in a mixing bowl. Shape the mixture into about 40 balls about 1 1/2 inches in diameter.

Heat the oil in a large skillet over medium heat, and brown the meatballs a few at a time, shaking the skillet and moving the balls with a wooden spoon to keep them round and to ensure they brown evenly on all sides. When browned, cover and cook for 25 minutes, or until done (check 1 or 2 meatballs to ensure they are cooked all the way through).

Transfer the meatballs to an ovenproof dish. Drain off the excess fat from the skillet, leaving 1/4 cup drippings in the skillet. Blend the flour into the drippings and whatever scraps remain from browning the meat; stir in the remaining 1/2 cup eggnog and 1 1/2 cups milk all at once. Cook and stir until bubbly. Pour the gravy over the meatballs, and heat in the oven or microwave until heated through.

Serves 10 to 12.

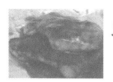

Norwegian Caramel Pork Loin

When Lindsay Neilson, a clothing designer who lives in New York City, was growing up, she loved to spend time with her mother, Jill, in the kitchen. Lindsay says her mother is an excellent cook with an artistic flair for entertaining. As a child, Lindsay remembers her mum making lots of foods to impress her Norwegian in-laws. Like many Norwegians who don't express their emotions, they never mentioned the food, but neither did they leave anything on their plates! Born and raised in Norway, Lindsay's great-grandma's (Norah Hanson) philosophy was that children "should eat lots of meat for good bones and strong bodies." Although Lindsay doesn't necessarily adhere to this viewpoint, she still loves to come home to her mum's home cooking, especially when she makes Norwegian foods.

Serve the pork with boiled potatoes, cabbage, and mashed, buttered turnips.

Lindsay preparing dinner.
Jill Neilson

3 pounds lightly salted and smoked pork loin, rolled and boned
kosher salt to taste
freshly ground black pepper to taste
9 tablespoons unsalted butter
1 tablespoon cardamom seeds, crushed
1 bay leaf
1 white onion, sliced
1 cup apple cider
3/4 cup granulated sugar
1/2 cup flour
3 tablespoons blackcurrant jelly

Wash the meat in cold water, and dry well. Rub with salt and pepper. Melt 4 tablespoons butter in a large, heavy pot over medium heat. Place the meat in the pot, and brown well on all sides, adding more butter as needed. Turn with two wooden spoons, or tongs, to avoid piercing the meat. When brown, cover the pork loin with boiling water. Add the cardamom seeds, bay leaf, onion, and apple cider. Insert a meat thermometer into the thickest part, and reduce the heat to medium-low. Cover, leaving the lid slightly ajar. Cook for about 1 hour, or until the internal temperature reaches 138°F.

Preheat the oven to 500°F.

Transfer the meat to a roasting pan. Coat the meat with the sugar, and roast until the sugar turns to caramel, about 8 minutes. Remove from the oven, wrap in aluminum foil, and let rest for 15 minutes.

Melt the remaining 5 tablespoons butter, and stir in the flour over medium-low heat. Gradually add 2 1/2 cups of the cooking liquid, salt, pepper, and jelly, and cook 10 minutes, stirring occasionally.

Serves 6.

Icelandic Fish and Potatoes
PLOKKFISKUR

Jon Gudbrandsson, of Reykjavik, admits to Anne Parsons that, as an Icelander, his culinary heritage was rather basic at best, and, for him, usually inedible. That is, until recently. He says that Icelandic cuisine is now bumping shoulders with European haute cuisine as it proudly presents some of the world's best lamb, cheeses, and fish. His mother, Asta Claessen, also a native of Reykjavik, loves family dinners when she and her son cook and show off the excellent fruits of the seas that surround this small island.

Gudbrandsson says that *plokkfiskur* is a traditional Icelandic dish, delicious and hearty. *Plokkfiskur* actually used to be an everyday meal made of leftover fish and potatoes. But recently, it has attained a new status in the finest restaurants where it appears on the menu, usually au gratin. Gudbrandsson suggests serving this dish with dark rye-malt bread (*rugbraud*), which is steamed, not baked! And, of course, butter.

It is traditionally not served with vegetables because, in Iceland, vegetables were a rare novelty.

1 1/2 pounds fish, traditionally haddock or cod
1 onion, diced
1/2 tablespoon vinegar
2 tablespoons salted or unsalted butter
2 tablespoons all-purpose flour
3 cups whole milk
1 pound cooked potatoes, cut into large chunks
salt to taste
freshly ground black pepper to taste

Put the fish, onion, and vinegar in a

Gudbrandsson and mother at his wedding in 2003.
Joe Menahem

large pot in lightly salted water to cover, and bring to a boil over medium heat. When the fish is cooked, drain, but do not discard the cooking water.

Melt the butter in a large saucepan over medium heat, and gradually add the flour, stirring constantly. Gradually add the cooking water from the fish, stirring constantly. Save the onions for garnish. Stir in the milk gradually, and continue stirring until the white sauce becomes smooth and a pourable consistency. Add the fish and potatoes, and heat through. Add salt and pepper, if needed. Garnish with the onions. Serve hot.

Serves 4.

Danish Rice Pudding
with Warm Cherry Sauce

In Scotland, a sixpence is hidden in the Clootie Dumpling; in Mexico, there's a bean in the Three King's Cake; and in Denmark, a whole almond is hidden in this pudding. Whoever receives the pudding with the almond expects not only good luck, but also a small gift. However, the lucky person cannot reveal his find until everyone finishes his pudding.

Birgitte Rasmussen making rice pudding. Anne Parsons

Birgitte Rasmussen, born in Stege the capital of Møen—where the high chalk cliff is one of the most famous natural areas in Denmark—now lives in Annisse, a medieval village about forty minutes from Copenhagen. When explaining the almond in the pudding, she mentions that this tradition was in effect when her grandfather, Hans Hansen, was born in 1870, so she believes it must be even older. As a child, there were three family generations living together in her grandparents' house, not at all uncommon at that time. "In fact," says Rasmussen in her delightfully accented English, "it was so much fun because there was always an adult willing to play with the children.

Nowadays, everyone is so busy, but my husband and I always make sure we're at home for all the family birthdays and holidays. Although it is traditional to eat this pudding on Christmas Eve and morning, it is so delicious all through the year."

Note: You cannot substitute any other rice. To prevent the rice from

Rice Pudding
1 3/4 pints whole milk
3 ounces short-grain rice
1/2 teaspoon salt
1 vanilla bean, slit open and cleaned
2 ounces blanched, coarsely chopped almonds
1 1/2 cups heavy cream, whipped

Cherry Sauce
1 (1-pound) can stoned cherries in their syrup
1 1/2 teaspoons cornstarch

To make the pudding, bring the milk to a boil in a heavy-bottomed sauce-pan over medium heat. Add the rice gradually, stirring constantly. Reduce the heat to medium-low, and cook the mixture for 50 minutes. Stir frequently to prevent the mixture from sticking. Remove the pan from the heat, and stir in the salt. Set aside to cool.

When the mixture is cold, stir in the extract from the vanilla bean and the chopped almonds. Fold in the whipped cream. Refrigerate until serving time.

Meanwhile, to make the cherry sauce, put the cherries and their syrup into a saucepan, and bring to a boil. Dissolve the cornstarch in about 1/4 cup water. Pour into the boiling liquid, stirring constantly. Serve immediately.

Serves 6.

◆ Wrapped Smoked Salmon ◆

Norwegian smoked salmon is a delicious and elegant appetizer at any time. Try it on dark bread with some mustard, fresh dill, and freshly squeezed lemon juice. Or, Rasmussen suggests wrapping 1 or 2 slices of smoked salmon around 2 pieces of freshly cooked asparagus and serving them with a mustard-dill sauce.

Scotland

- ◆ STEAK AND SAUSAGE PIE

- ◆ FINNAN HADDOCK SOUP (CULLEN SKINK)

- ◆ POTATO SCONES

- ◆ PHEASANT CASSEROLE

- ◆ CLOOTIE PUDDING (PLUM DUFF)

- ◆ SHORTBREAD

- ◆ SIDEBAR: GINGER WINE

If every French woman is born with a wooden spoon in her hand, then every Scotswoman is born with a rolling pin under her arm.
— *The Scots Kitchen* by F. Mariam McNeill

Scotland is a small but breathtakingly beautiful country with superior natural resources. Although the population is just over five million, there are five times that many Scots and many more would-be Scots living around the world who proudly claim this heritage.

Originally an isolated place, Scotland soon became home to the Picts, Celts, and Scots who inhabited the land and brought their language, culture, and a unique cooking style with them. The Celts introduced the girdle or griddle, one of the oldest cooking utensils in the world, on which they baked their daily bread. Hundreds of years later, in the thirteenth century, the French allied with Scotland against the English. This three hundred-year association left a mark in the language and in the kitchen.

Foreigners, many of whom have never been to Scotland, often confuse the excellence of Scottish food with the drab Sassenach (English) food south of the border. The natural resources, the rich, fertile farmland, and clean air are the foundations for Scotland's traditional cuisine. In a land of rushing rivers and lovely lochs, a land shaped by the sea, it is no surprise that fish is plentiful and delicious, whether cooked immediately or dried or smoked for later use. Also from the sea, the Scots harvest various seaweeds that are nutritious and economical. On the land, generations of canny Scottish farmers developed breeds of sheep and cattle that are much in demand because of the superior quality of their meat. Even the European Commission recognizes the unique regional characteristics of these breeds by awarding them Protected Geographical Indication (PGI) status. No wonder then that Scotland is proud of its rich larder of fish, meat, grain, and vegetables.

Local Highland games in Lanarkshire. Douglas Arcos

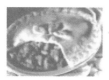 *Steak and Sausage Pie*

Transplanted from Auld Scotia (Scotland) to Virginia, Nancy Holmes has an old shortbread tin in which she keeps all her granny's recipes. "My granny," she says, "like most Scots, was very frugal and made good use of animal parts that are often discarded, such as the kidneys, liver, etc." Noting that her family refuses to eat animal organs, Holmes, rather than add kidneys to this pie, uses sausages instead: "My daddy always made this pie for our New Year's dinner and for special occasions because meat was expensive. Scotland has the best beef cattle in the world, the Aberdeen Angus. Because it matures so quickly and is of the finest quality, it is transported to the English markets where many butchers don't sell anything but the Angus. Beef today is plentiful, so I make this dish at least once a month."

Aside from her Sassenach bias, Holmes loves to tell friends that, in ancient times, pie crusts were actually edible cutlery for eating meat and scooping up the rich gravies or sauces. She says it helps friends understand that when husband, Rick, and daughter, Alexandra, "dook the crust in the gravy" it is part of their atavistic roots. Notwithstanding cultural dining etiquette, meat and game pies are still an integral part of Scottish cuisine.

Serve with mashed potatoes and green peas.

2 pounds stew beef or round steak, cubed, fat trimmed, and reserved
2 tablespoons unsalted butter or vegetable oil
1 large onion, minced
3 tablespoons all-purpose flour
2 cups beef stock, boiling, or 3 beef bouillon cubes, or 2 OXO cubes, dissolved in 2 cups hot water
2 tablespoons Worcestershire sauce
1 teaspoon salt
1/2 teaspoon freshly ground black pepper
1 pound beef link sausages
2 pounds flaky pastry for one-crust pie (recipe follows)
milk or beaten egg for brushing

Render the beef fat in a large skillet over medium heat; add the butter or oil, and sauté the onion over medium-high heat for 7 to 10 minutes until golden brown.

Dredge the meat in the flour, add to the skillet a few pieces at a time, and fry until the meat is well browned. Transfer the meat to a heavy saucepan.

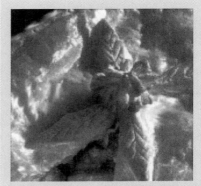

The hot pie is ready to serve.
Nancy Holmes

Add the boiling stock, Worcestershire sauce, salt, and pepper to the fat mixture in the skillet. Pour the mixture over the meat, and add the sausages. Cover the pan, and cook over low heat until the meat is tender, about 1 1/2 hours. Let cool. Meanwhile, make the Flaky Pastry (see recipe immediately following).

Preheat the oven to 425°F.

Place a pie bird or upside-down pie funnel in the center of a 10-inch *ashet* (pie pan) with 1/2-inch rim. Put the meat and half the gravy into the pan. Cover the pie with the pastry, leaving a hole in the center for steam to escape. Brush the pastry with the milk or egg, and crimp the edges of the pastry with a fork.

Bake for 25 to 30 minutes, or until the pastry is a rich, golden color. Reheat the remaining gravy, and serve in a separate dish.

Serves 6.

Flaky Pastry
Holmes says it's important to work fast in a cool place, without interruption, and to ensure your hands are cold when making pastry. This results in a very flaky crust.

2 cups sifted all-purpose flour
1 teaspoon salt
1/3 cup chilled unsalted butter
1/3 cup chilled lard
5 or 6 tablespoons ice water

Sift the flour into a bowl, add the salt, and cut in the butter and lard (both should be cold) with a pastry blender or two knives. Sprinkle the water over the dough. Mix well with a fork until the mixture is sticky, and press into a ball.

Roll the ball out on a lightly floured board and fit the pastry into the pie pan, trimming and crimping the edges with a fork.

Tips: My Aunt Aggie always told me that if you're right-handed, you should press more heavily with the left hand when rolling dough so the pin is more balanced and you form a more even dough.

She also cautioned me to never stretch the pastry to fit the pie dish because it will shrink when cooking, and not to glaze the edges as it prevents the pastry from rising.

From the leftover pastry, cut leaf-shaped pieces of dough to decorate the pie top.

Finnan Haddock Soup

CULLEN SKINK

Jimmy Smith, a coal miner from Nacherty, a student of ancient civilizations, a long-distance runner, and an avid gardener, loved to cook big pots of stews and soups—he needed to, since he had seven mouths to feed. He often served this dish for Sunday lunch. His grandson, Douglas Arcos of Machipongo, Virginia, remembers visiting his grandparents in Scotland, and says, "I always looked forward to the simple, no-nonsense meals at grandpa's home. The times I spent with him in his back garden, where he grew potatoes, turnips, carrots, lettuce, beetroot, peas, and rhubarb, are stamped in my memory. He taught me so much about gardening, and he'd take produce straight from the garden, put it into the pot, and then serve it at the supper table that same night. I try to grow as many vegetables as I can, and I'm teaching my son, Tucker, what grandpa taught me."

This soup is just one of many delicious soups that Arcos's granddad shared with him.

Tommy and Jimmy Smith at Nackerty Rows, 1913. Smith family album

4 pounds smoked finnan haddock fillets
2 medium-sized onions, sliced
5 cups whole milk
3 cups cooked mashed potato
4 tablespoons (1/2 stick) unsalted butter, cut into small pieces
salt to taste
freshly ground black pepper to taste

Put the haddock, skin side down, in a shallow saucepan, and cover with water. Bring it to a boil over medium heat, and cook for 5 minutes. Remove from the pan.

Turn the fish over, and slice off the skin. Put it back into the pan, add the sliced onion, cover, and reduce the heat to medium-low. Cook for 10 minutes. Take out the fish, remove the bones, and cut the fish into large chunks. Put the bones back in the pot, and cook for about 20 minutes; strain, reserving the liquid.

Combine the liquid and milk in a large saucepan, add the fish, bring to a boil, and add enough potato to make the mixture creamy. Add the butter, some of which should remain firm, and season to taste. Eat hot.

Note: Smoking is a traditional way of preserving fish. Sometimes smoked, or finnan, haddock is dyed to produce a golden color, but they are actually pale in color. When using this type of fish, it is best to poach them with a wee bit of milk.

Serves 8.

Potato Scones

Isabel Kirkwood McPhee says her granny, aunties, and mum were all grand cooks and beautiful bakers. "So what happened to me?" she moans. "My mum told me I'd need to either marry a rich fellow with a personal chef, or an ordinary lad who liked to cook." She remembers the delicious tarts, pies, and shortbread her mother baked. "Och aye," recalls Isabel, "mony a time she'd try to teach me, but I jist wisnae interested; anyway, she said my *hauns* (hands) were too heavy for baking." So Isabel took her mum's advice and married a fine chap who is also handy in the

A Scottish girdle *with scones.*
George McPhee

kitchen. On weekends, her husband George often makes breakfast for Isabel. Like most Scots, he doesn't waste food and always puts leftovers to good use. When asked for a recipe, McPhee replies, "Most Scottish food is simple yet nutritious, and the recipes are passed from one generation to the next through word of mouth. Sometimes I'll scribble down a note or two from the '*auld yins*' but mostly you learn from watching them cook and bake." He says that these scones should be eaten while still hot; you may use butter or jam, but they are especially good with fried or scrambled eggs, sausages, black pudding, and fried tomatoes.

2 baked potatoes, scooped out, or 1 cup leftover mashed potatoes
3 tablespoons unsalted butter, melted
3 tablespoons whole milk, or more as needed
salt to taste
1/2 cup all-purpose flour

Combine the potato flesh with butter, milk, and salt. Stir in the flour gradually, making a stiff dough.

Flour a surface lightly, and roll dough out until thin, about 1/4 inch thick. Cut the dough into a round, cut into quarters to make 3-inch triangles, and prick with a fork.

Bake on a hot girdle (griddle) until golden brown, flip over, and brown on the other side, about 5 minutes. Serve hot.

Serves 4.

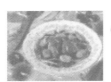 *Pheasant Casserole*

Thomas Cleland Smith, from Viewpark, Scotland, says that autumn is game-hunting season, and his family has cooked wild game since before they can remember. "One generation taught the next, so we never had recipes tae speak of—so this might be a guid time tae dae it," he says. With his wife May nodding her head in agreement, Smith explains that hunters catch their game during the autumn months when the birds such as pheasant, partridge, duck, snipe, woodcock, guinea fowl, geese, and grouse are at their fattest. Also, since ancient times, the ritual of flushing game is still alive today. On the Scottish moors, the peasants or servants stood in line with sticks beating the bushes to flush out the birds. As they flew out, the hunters shot at them. Because shot often remains in the birds, the Smiths advise checking them carefully. Also, when cooking game, they suggest covering the breast with fatty bacon and basting the meat frequently to prevent the flesh from drying out.

Thomas Cleland (Gordon Highlanders) Glasgow, 1940.
Ronald Cleland

1 pheasant, plucked and cleaned
flour seasoned with thyme and oregano
4 ounces lard for frying
6 ounces mushrooms, brushed, cleaned, and sliced
2 slices bacon, chopped

3 tablespoons port wine
1 cup chicken stock
salt to taste
freshly ground black pepper to taste
chopped parsley for garnish

Cut the pheasant apart at the joints, and dredge the pieces in the seasoned flour. Set aside.

Preheat the oven to 350°F.

Heat the lard in a cast-iron skillet over medium heat, and fry the pieces until golden brown. Put them in a casserole, and add the mushrooms, bacon, port wine, chicken stock, salt, and pepper, to cover half of the bird.

Cook for 1 hour, or until tender. Just before serving, sprinkle with chopped parsley.

Serves 4.

Plum Duff

CLOOTIE PUDDING

In the early 1920s, Annie Dingwall emigrated from Scotland to Detroit, Michigan, where her husband found a position with the burgeoning auto industry. At the age of ninety-six when Mrs. Dingwall died, her Scottish accent still was as broad as if she'd "just stepped off the boat." When her daughter, Helen Bigelow of Seattle, Washington, tried to sort out her mum's recipes, she said they were amazing—a list of ingredients, no "how to," and no oven temperature. But, after consulting with her daughter Alison, they shared memories of a handful of this, a pinch of that, and perhaps a wee bit of the other! In any event, they tested and tasted until the foods tasted like Alison's granny had made them.

Helen remembers that this pudding, a traditional Scottish dessert, had to have surprises in it. She and her brothers had to shine a few dimes, and sometimes even a quarter, by rubbing them on the rug. Helen said it took a long time before the coins were shiny. "But, oh," Helen says, "the excitement when you found a coin in your piece of pudding. I'm sure the Health Department would not approve, but just think of the sterilizing properties of steam." It's also important to use suet (the solid white fat surrounding the cow's kidneys)—a butcher once tried to give Annie Dingwall some ordinary beef fat; she was indignant! Dingwall also insisted that "raisins must be sultana (golden raisins); if it didn't say 'sultanas' on the box, they are simply bleached raisins." To add additional flavor to the pudding, Dingwall soaked the pudding cloths in brandy.

The pudding can be cooked 6 to 8 weeks ahead of any event and reheated. It's excellent served with a custard, brandy, or rum-butter sauce.

1 cup all-purpose flour
1 cup brown sugar
1 cup chopped suet
2 cups sultana raisins

A clootie pudding undressed and ready to be devoured.
Anne Parsons

1 cup currants
1 cup grated carrot
1 cup breadcrumbs
1 teaspoon ground cinnamon
1/2 teaspoon ground ginger
1/2 teaspoon ground nutmeg
2 ounces citron
juice of 1 orange
juice of 1 lemon
1 tablespoon molasses
1 tablespoon orange marmalade
1/2 teaspoon baking soda
1/2 cup stout
1 cup brandy
2 large eggs, lightly beaten

Butter a 3-quart ceramic bowl with a lip; butter the parchment paper for wrapping. Set aside.

Mix the flour, sugar, suet, raisins, currants, carrot, breadcrumbs, cinnamon, ginger, nutmeg, citron, orange juice, lemon juice, molasses, marmalade, and baking soda. Stir well. Add the stout, brandy, and eggs; mix well. Put in a greased ceramic bowl, cover with the buttered parchment paper, and tie with a string under the lip to make a handle.

Alternately, it can be cooked in an old piece of linen that has been soaked and wrung out in really hot water, and rubbed well in flour. When the mixture is spooned into it, ensure it's tied loosely to allow room for expansion.

Place the bowl or linen-wrapped mixture on a rack or trivet in a pot of boiling water to keep the mixture off the bottom, and steam for 5 to 8 hours. Add boiling water to the pot as the water evaporates. Remove, place on a wire rack, and keep wrapped until ready to serve.

Serves 12.

 *Shortbread*

Helen Bigelow, of Seattle, Washington, inherited a wee book of her mother's recipes. Actually, it was a book of notes with ingredients (no amounts) and few instructions. Among the notes for empire biscuits, currant scones, and Inverness gingerbread, Annie Dingwall was quite specific about her excellent shortbread recipe. Although delicious at any time, it's traditional to have shortbread, a Scottish creation, on the Hogmanay (New Year's Eve) table. Bigelow's mother, Annie, insisted that you must use only the finest ingredients—butter is essential, it is pointless to use margarine. Bigelow also says, "Mother always worked the ingredients with her hands. If young women find that too icky or are worried about contamination, if the latter, then they should learn to wash their hands."

The edges of shortbread are traditionally indented with the thumb, to symbolize the sun's rays, presumably from the early days of sun worship.

Petticoat tails and shortbread fingers. Heather Arcos

1 pound (4 sticks) unsalted butter, at room temperature
1/2 pound extra-fine granulated sugar
5 cups unsifted all-purpose flour
1/2 cup rice flour

Preheat the oven to 300°F.

Using an electric beater, cream the butter and sugar together in a large mixing bowl, and gradually stir in the flour. Work the ingredients together very lightly with the hands. Do not knead the dough as it will toughen.

Divide the dough in half, and roll it out, 8x10x1/2 inches, on sheets of waxed paper to make it easier to transfer to cookie sheets. Prick all over with a fork, and indent the edges with a thumb.

Bake for 45 minutes. Slice, and remove edge pieces. Separate remaining slices, bake for another 10 to 15 minutes, and WATCH IT (Helen's mother's words).

Remove from the oven, and let cool before turning out on to a rack.

Makes 16 pieces.

♦ Ginger Wine ♦

Bunty Fernon, of Hamilton, Scotland, always has a few bottles of this nonalcoholic wine on her Hogmanay table. Of course, guests are always welcome to add a wee nip o' whiskey to make a toddy. Fernon also recommends it for winter colds, as she says it "clears the tubes." She mixes together 10 cups of water with 3 pounds of sugar, and boils the mixture until the sugar dissolves. When the mixture cools, she stirs in a concentrated ginger flavoring called Yu-Lade, a fermented ginger extract available at health food stores. She sets them aside in a cool, dark place for 2 to 3 weeks before serving.

Spain

- White Garlic Soup with White Grapes (Ajo Blanco)

- Sea Bream (Hurta a la Gaditana)

- Sizzling Prawns (Gambas al Pil-Pil)

- Andalucían Crullers (Pestinos Andaluces)

*F*lamenco, bullfights, idyllic fishing villages, unspoiled beaches, and miles of undulating hills covered with endless olive groves are only some of the enticements of Spain, one of Europe's most important cultural centers for millennia. In the eighth century, Muslims crossed the Strait of Gibraltar, conquered the indigenous peoples, and introduced new sciences, architecture, and art. In the eleventh century, Cordoba, the mythic capital of Andalucía, was one of the most important capitals in Europe. At that time, it was the model of unity in diversity with people of various cultures and religions—Jews, Christians, and Muslims—living peacefully together. It was also a city that spawned eminent scientists, philosophers, and artists. Queen Isabel and Ferdinand came to the throne in the fifteenth century, and in 1492, after the discovery of America by Christopher Columbus, Spain became a rich and powerful country.

In Spain, you can meander down narrow, twisting old city streets, then turn a corner and be confronted by some of the most daring architecture in Europe. But whether you follow the trade winds from the lush green meadows to the rugged coastline to the snow-capped mountains, you will find the people friendly, the climate benign, and the food irresistible. This is not a country where you need to watch your diet, rather you want to join the moveable feast and taste the history of Spain through its cuisine.

Intriguing flavors and spices beckon you to taste the tapas and Serrano ham, an integral part of Spanish food culture. Serrano hams have been salted and cured since ancient times and are a fundamental part of every family's life. Almost an art form, tapas are complex and flavorful bite-sized morsels of food, like appetizers, although some could pass for miniature entrées of meat, chicken, spicy sausages, Serrano ham, manchengo cheese, or fish in a sauce. Before the free market arrived, tapas were served gratis with a glass of wine; there are still a few establishments that offer this service. Also, today, it is customary to move from bar to bar and savor tasty tapas spread out like a *smörgasbord*. Tapas also translate easily to home entertaining where conviviality is the order of the day.

The Alhambra in Granada.
Anne Parsons

As you watch boats enter the hospitable harbors along the Spanish coastline, as they have for millennia, you hope that the culture of tradition won't be usurped by the culture of convenience.

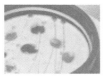

White Garlic Soup with White Grapes

AJO BLANCO

When Elmira Arcos Friedman's father left Andalucía, Spain, at the beginning of the twentieth century, he planned to live in New York but ended up living in Houston, Texas. Like his father before him, he raised milk cows and farmed the land in an area where Houston airport now stands. Friedman's mother grew all her own vegetables and peppers and took great delight in entertaining masses of relatives who came for dinner on most Sundays. Like a number of our recipe-givers, Friedman kept a scrapbook with her mother's recipes. And, like many others, the recipes lacked specific amounts and sometimes those ingredients were in a shorthand code!

From the many recipes she shared, we chose some that reflected the Andalucían area—a white gazpacho soup, a fish plate, a shrimp dish, and some crullers. In Andalucía the Parsons tasted an *ajo blanco* in a parador at Arcos de la Frontera. In this town, they discovered that *ajo blanco* is not white gazpacho, but a white garlic soup that, according to food historians, probably originated when Spain was part of the Islamic world in the Middle Ages. Gazpacho was introduced much later with its tomato and pepper ingredients. *Ajo blanco*, made with garlic, almonds, bread, olive oil, vinegar, salt, and fresh grapes, is divine and addictive. Parsons almost swooned when she tasted the *ajo blanco*, garnished with a scoop of tart green apple ice cream and four translucent cubes of raisin confit.

Based on Friedman's fragmentary recipes, Parsons asked family friend and Slow Food member, Bryan Ellis, to help reconstruct Friedman's family recipes that reflect the fresh produce and home cooking particular to Andalucía. Ellis, co-owner of the Meridian 42 restaurant on the Outer Banks, had chefs Chuck Arnold, Grant Sharp, and Evan Hayes help restore these recipes that are now part of the updated Arcos' family recipe album.

1 1/2 cups blanched almonds, coarsely chopped
2 garlic cloves, chopped

4 slices stale country bread, crusts removed

1/2 cup olive oil, preferably fruity flavored

4 tablespoons wine vinegar

2 cups white grape juice

2 cups iced water

3 teaspoons sea salt

24 seedless white grapes, halved

Bryan Ellis, Chuck Arnold, Grant Sharp, and Evan Hayes.
Anne Parsons

Combine the almonds and garlic in blender and blend until finely ground. Do not remove from the blender.

Soak the bread in cold water 15 minutes. Squeeze out excess water, add to the almonds, and process until smooth. With the motor running, add the oil in a stream. Add the vinegar, scraping down the sides. Pour in the grape juice and iced water slowly, and season with salt to taste.

Process in the blender for 2 minutes. Chill for 8 hours. Blend for 30 seconds before serving in chilled soup bowls with the grapes, or green apple ice cream, for garnish.

Serves 6.

Sea Bream

HURTA A LA GADITANA

Doug Arcos remembers his recently deceased grandmother, Elmira Friedman, proudly recount stories of her father's Spanish heritage—she was his window into the rich and complex culture of Andalucía. Arcos said his grandmother "placed great value on family time and always encouraged him to remember his forbears." Arcos says that preserving family recipes teaches children about their heritage through food.

Although *hurta* is the red-banded sea bream common to the Cadiz coastline, any large bream or saltwater fish may be used in this recipe.

A street in Arcos de la Frontera.
Anne Parsons

1 (3- to 4-pound) whole fish such as perch, bream, or bass, cleaned
2 cups all-purpose flour
6 tablespoons olive oil
3 tablespoons brandy
1 white onion, chopped
4 green bell peppers, cut into strips
2 tomatoes, peeled, seeded, and pureed
3 tablespoons dry sherry
1/2 teaspoon dried thyme
1 bay leaf
salt to taste
freshly ground black pepper to taste

Fillet the fish, and cut into 4-inch pieces. Dredge the fish in flour. Heat 3 tablespoons oil in a *cazuela* (earthenware pot), and brown the fish on both sides.

Pour in the brandy, set it alight, and gently swirl the casserole until the flames subside. Remove from the heat.

Meanwhile, in another pan, heat the remaining oil over medium heat, and sauté the onion and peppers.

Add the pureed tomato, sherry, thyme, bay leaf, salt, and pepper. Cook the sauce until reduced, about 15 minutes. Pour it over the fish, and cook until the fish is tender, about 10 minutes more.

Serves 6.

Sizzling Prawns
GAMBAS AL PIL-PIL

Doug Arcos's father-in-law, Stephen McCready, has access to lots of fresh seafood because he lives on the Eastern Shore of Virginia, between the Chesapeake Bay and the Atlantic Ocean, and many of his friends are commercial fishermen—one reason that Arcos and his wife Heather like to use his grandma's seafood recipes. Family friend Bryan Ellis remarks that, although the combination of spices and prawns are typical of many cuisines, this particular recipe is a classic, traditional Andalucían dish. Because Andalucía produces over 20 percent of the world's olive oil, most of the regional cooking employs many varieties of the oil in lots of dishes. Arcos uses Ellis's advice by using a good quality olive oil to bring out the flavor of the sauce. Sometimes, when Arcos makes this dish for his mother, he uses truffle oil.

Perfect as a tapa, this dish can be transformed to an entrée by doubling the recipe and serving it with Spanish rice.

Around the Arcos's dinner table in Machipongo.
Lulu Parks

16 raw jumbo shrimp
salt to taste
1 cup olive oil
4 cloves garlic, chopped
3 bay leaves
3 dried red chilies
1/4 teaspoon paprika
1/2 chicken bouillon cube
1 cup white wine
1 tablespoon chopped parsley

Season the shrimp with salt. Using a medium-sized *cazuela* (earthenware pot), heat the olive oil over medium heat.

Add the garlic, bay leaves, and chilies, stirring gently. When the garlic begins to turn brown, add the shrimp. Increase the heat to medium-high, and add the paprika and bouillon cube. Stir continuously until the prawns are cooked, for 2 to 3 minutes.

Add the wine, and remove from the heat when it starts to simmer. Sprinkle with parsley, and serve with bread.

Serves 4.

Andalucian Crullers

PESTINOS ANDALUCES

Douglas Arcos, grandson of Elmira Arcos Friedman, delighted in researching his roots back to the village of Arcos de la Frontera, in Andalucía. "Now," he says, "I have a better understanding of my roots. It's awesome that we traced some of our family legacy through old recipes."

The coupling of the orange sorbet with the cruller results in a scrumptious dessert. Family friend and Slow Food member Bryan Ellis suggests topping off this dessert by accompanying it with Emilio Lustau "Los Arcos" Solera Reserva Amontillado Sherry.

Shopping for fresh produce at the local market in Andalucía.
Anne Parsons

zest 1 lemon
juice 1 lemon
1 1/3 tablespoons heavy cream
2 tablespoons olive oil
1/2 teaspoon ground cinnamon
1/2 teaspoon salt
4 tablespoons dry liqueur, such as anisette
4 cups all-purpose flour
1/4 cup canola oil
sugar for sprinkling
mint leaves for garnish

Syrup
3/4 cup granulated sugar
1/4 cup dry liqueur, such as anisette
1 teaspoon five-spice powder (readily available in most grocery stores)

Put the grated rind, lemon juice, cream, olive oil, cinnamon, salt, and liqueur in a bowl. Mix well. Stir in the flour until the dough is stiff. Let the dough rest for 1 hour in a cool place.

Divide the dough into 4 parts. Lightly flour a surface, and roll each part out thin. Cut into rectangles about 3x2 inches. Heat the oil in a large skillet over medium heat until almost smoking. Roll up the rectangles, and fry a few at a time. Drain on a rack.

To make the syrup, dissolve the sugar in 1/2 cup water over medium heat. When it boils and begins to thicken, add the liqueur. Dip the fried crullers in the hot liquid, and drain on a rack. Sprinkle with sugar, and let cool before serving with a scoop of orange sorbet that has been softened and mixed with 1 teaspoon of five-spice powder.

Garnish each with a mint leaf.

Makes 36 crullers.

Thailand

- Pork Burger, Thai-Style (Mu Sap Tod Kratiam)

- Braised Cumin Beef

- Grilled Marinated Pork and Sticky Rice with Dipping Sauce (Kao Neow Mu Yang)

- Sidebar: Steamed Sticky Rice

- Noodles with Fish Curry Sauce (Khanom Jeen Nam Ya)

- Sidebar: Thai Chilies

*T*hailand is the Promised Land for food lovers, filled with every sort of edible creature and plant and so many layered tastes that the palate is dazzled and the senses reel. It's all there: fragrant jasmine rice, fresh noodles, hot condiments, exotic produce—from the familiar long beans and marble-sized eggplants to unfamiliar leaves and roots and stalks—sweet palm sugar, salty fish sauce, and chilies, chilies, chilies.

But what sets Thai cooking apart from all others are the flavors—levels of hot, sour, sweet, and salty that fuse to form a tantalizing whole. To achieve these ends, Thai cooks rely on such basic seasonings as Thai fish sauce, garlic, lemongrass, *galangal*, coconut milk, lime leaves, palm sugar, cilantro, shallots—and, of course, chilies. Thais make a fuss about their chilies and incorporate numerous varieties in their cooking, each one seemingly hotter than the next. Of course, most Westerners regard Thai food as overwhelmingly hot, and restaurant menus usually indicate heat levels by coding their hot dishes with chilies, one or several depending on the fire level.

And no dish is ever as simple as it seems. In fact, much of Thai food is breathtaking in its sophistication and cleverness. And the dressy Thai table, when set with intricate ice and vegetable carvings, or the simpler meals, when serving platters are garnished with one or many eye-catching vegetable or fruit carvings, demonstrate how much Thais care about the beauty of their cuisine. In short, Thai food can be an overtly sensual experience.

Sociable Thais prefer communal eating, gathering together to enjoy the main meal, which usually consists of several courses, often including a soup; a curry; a grilled, stir-fried, or steamed meat or seafood; rice and/ or noodles; and fruit or a sweet for dessert. Breakfasts and lunches are lighter and may center on fried rice or noodles; the overwhelmingly Western favorite, *pad Thai*, is among the lunchtime staples. And when not at the table, Thais snack on portable goodies offered at every turn. Common sights on Bangkok sidewalks are the vendors with their baskets, stands, and grills full of everything edible.

Section of ancient Thai door.
Anne Parsons

Bangkok is the perfect place to start out on a Thai eating spree and the obvious place to get your culinary bearings. The curious food traveler should make at least one market tour to the Floating Market up the Chao Prya river from Bangkok, and then go to Bangkok's famed weekend market out near the airport. Everyone in Bangkok goes there, on Sundays in particular, to buy everything under the sun, and shoppers will find all the raw ingredients for Thai cooking displayed in splendor. Bangkok is also home to assorted cooking schools—the most famous of which is probably the Oriental Thai Cooking School offered by the Oriental Hotel—that offer cooking classes for the food-serious tourist. And after Bangkok? All of Thailand is your bowl of noodles.

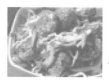

Pork Burger, Thai-Style
Mu Sap Tod Kratiam

A passionate chef and the successful restaurant owner of Thai Basil, in Virginia, Nongkran Thongkham Daks remembers this dish fondly from her childhood. As she writes, "As a child in the South of Thailand, during and just after World War II, we were quite poor. On those few days when my mother could scrape together a little more money, she made this special treat for our family." Even today, she still serves it to her family—she loves using the meat patty as a sandwich filling, but her husband Larry enjoys it with rice. You can prepare this easy dish in advance.

Nongkran Daks choosing a mortar and pestle in Bangkok market. Ampha Thongkham

4 to 6 cloves garlic, peeled
1 teaspoon whole black peppercorns
3 cilantro roots, coarsely chopped
1 tablespoon fish sauce
1 tablespoon soy sauce
1/4 teaspoon salt
1 pound lean ground pork
1 tablespoon vegetable oil
1 cucumber, sliced into thin circles
1 tomato, sliced into thin circles
1 sprig cilantro, coarsely chopped, as garnish

Pound the garlic, peppercorns, and cilantro roots with a mortar and pestle until the peppercorns are crushed. Add the fish sauce, soy sauce, and salt. Put the meat into a mixing bowl, and spoon the seasoning mixture in, stirring well to combine completely with the meat. Refrigerate for at least 1 hour.

To cook, shape the meat into four 1/2-inch-thick patties. Heat a large wok or skillet over medium heat until hot. Add the oil, and pan-fry the meat until brown on one side, about 5 minutes; turn, and cook the other side until brown, 4 or 5 minutes.

Arrange the cucumber and tomato slices on a platter, and put the meat patties on top. Garnish with the cilantro.

Note: You may substitute ground beef or ground chicken for the pork. The peppercorn-cilantro roots-garlic mixture—which Ms. Daks calls "Thai pesto"—freezes well for several months. You may have to search to find bunches of fresh cilantro with roots intact as not every supermarket sells them that way. There are no substitutes.

Serves 4.

Braised Cumin Beef

Presently a resident in the Washington, D.C., metro area, Nittaya Maphungphong grew up in a large family in Bangkok, and her parents kept all the children very busy. She remembers, "We didn't have too much free time. Even on Sundays we went to our sewing teacher's house for lessons. We all studied Thai classical music and took piano lessons. My father kept the routine going even after my mother died, and he was raising eight of us on his own. One important tradition in our house was that at 6 p.m., we would all get cleaned up, and after the gong chimed, we ate dinner. Typically, we were served three courses, a curry, a vegetable, and a companion third dish, and always rice. My father thought about what would go well together, and set the daily menu for the cook." Maphungphong remembers that this dish was a family favorite, and it goes well with steamed rice and a nice Pinot Noir. Look for palm sugar at any Asian market; if it is unavailable, use light brown sugar instead, although the taste will not be exactly the same. If you use canned coconut milk, use the thickest part.

Nittaya Maphungphong is ready to eat dinner.
Alexandra Greeley

1 1/2 tablespoons cumin seeds, soaked for 20 to 30 minutes
6 cloves garlic
4 Thai "bird" chilies
1/2 teaspoon black peppercorn
2 tablespoons vegetable oil
1 pound ground beef
palm sugar to taste
fish sauce to taste
1 cup coconut milk
fresh Thai basil leaves, rinsed and stemmed
6 to 8 Thai "finger" chilies, cut into strips lengthwise on the diagonal

Using a mortar and pestle, mash the cumin seeds, garlic, "bird" chilies, and black peppercorn into a paste, and set aside.

Heat the vegetable oil in a large wok or saucepan over medium-high heat. When the oil is hot, add the paste, and stir-fry until it is golden and fragrant. Add the ground beef, stirring to combine with the paste. Reduce the heat to medium.

Cook for about 5 minutes, stirring often, and when the meat is fully cooked, pour off the excess fat. Add the sugar and fish sauce to taste. Stir in the coconut milk, and continue stirring until the mixture comes to a boil. Add the basil leaves and Thai finger chilies, stir, and remove from the heat. Serve hot.

Note: The cooked meat should have a balanced taste between sugar and fish sauce plus heat from the bird peppers. Keep in mind that coconut milk will add a little more sweetness to the dish. You can increase the amount of sauce by adding more coconut milk, but be sure to balance the flavors by adding more sugar and fish sauce to taste.

Serves 4.

Grilled Marinated Pork and Sticky Rice with Dipping Sauce

KAO NEOW MU YANG

Native Thai Nick Sriwsawat from Hua Hin, a small oceanside town about 300 km south of Bangkok, has become a mega restaurant celebrity in Washington, D.C. Starting off with just one Tara Thai res-

Grilled marinated pork satay.
Anne Parsons

taurant, Srisawat has parlayed his vision of Thai food popularity into a major restaurant group that blankets the Washington metro area. Clearly, his passion for Thai food sets him apart from competitors. As he writes about his childhood, "My mom used to prepare this dish for me as one of an after-school snack. I always looked forward to it every time I saw the meat being mari-

nated in the 'fridge, because it is not a quick dish to make so I don't get to have it as often as I like. Now that I know how to make it, I still don't have time to do it for myself. But it's a perfect dish for a barbecue party so it is one of a must-have dishes at my parties and my guests always enjoy it every time. Because of its popularity among my friends, I decided to put it on the menu of my new restaurant as an appetizer."

This dish calls for roasted and ground rice. To make the rice powder, roast the rice (Srisawat prefers a half-and-half combination of jasmine rice and sticky rice together), and adds some chopped up *galangal* and several slivered *kaffir* lime leaves. He heats this mixture in a wok or skillet over medium-high heat until the rice becomes fragrant and begins to darken. Then this mixture is cooled down before it is pulverized in a blender; a food processor will not produce a fine enough powder. Srisawat also recommends using pork that still has some fat, explaining that lean pork gets too dried out after cooking. He also notes that the amount of sugar is approximate; adjust the sweetness to suit your taste. This dish is served with cooked sticky rice; see the sidebar on "Steamed Sticky Rice."

Marinade

1 whole head garlic, peeled and separated
1 bunch cilantro, roots on, chopped
1/2 can condensed milk
4 tablespoons oyster sauce
2 tablespoons sweet Thai soy sauce
2 tablespoons palm sugar
2 tablespoons freshly ground black pepper

Dipping Sauce

4 tablespoons palm sugar
4 tablespoons fish sauce
2 tablespoons tamarind juice, preferably fresh
chopped grape tomatoes for garnish
chopped cilantro for garnish
ground chilies, optional

◆ Steamed Sticky Rice ◆
Soak Thai glutinous, or sweet, rice (1 cup) in room temperature water about 1 hour or up to 6 hours. Scoop the rice into a bamboo steamer cone—or other steaming container that can hold rice grains—and steam the rice, covered, over simmering water for about 30 minutes, or until the grains are tender and sticky. Transfer the rice to a covered container to keep it warm and moist until use.

Pork

1 pound pork with a little fat, sliced about 1/2 inch thick

To make the marinade, process all the marinade ingredients in a blender, and transfer the mixture to a large bowl. Marinate the meat in it for 2 days, and cover and refrigerate.

To make the dipping sauce, put the sugar, fish sauce, and tamarind juice in a blender, and process on low until smooth. Pour the mixture into a saucepan, and bring it to a boil. Put it into a serving bowl, and garnish the sauce with the tomatoes, cilantro, rice powder, and ground chilies, if using.

To cook the meat, ready a gas or charcoal grill. Thread the meat on bamboo or metal skewers, and grill, turning often, until the meat is cooked, about 5 to 7 minutes. Heat the remaining marinade, brush it on the cooking meat, and pour it over the cooked meat before serving.

Serves 4 to 6.

Noodles with Fish Curry Sauce
KHANOM JEEN NAM YA

According to Petch Vailikit, a native of the village of Petchburi in central Thailand, this noodle dish is popular throughout Thailand and is often sold at street vendor stands or by mobile food vendors who drive through residential neighborhoods to sell this curry; this version was one his sister-in-law routinely made for his family. He remembers coming home from school or from swimming in the nearby river in the afternoon and finding this dish ready for the family to eat. Now a native of Potomac, Maryland, Vailikit cooks his favorite Thai foods at home for his wife and extended family.

Petch Vailikit and family enjoy the khanom jeen nam ya.
Alexandra Greeley

1 (13.5-ounce) can coconut milk
1 (4-ounce) can red curry paste
3 (4-ounce) cans Thai noodle sauce
4 (6-ounce) cans water-packed tuna, undrained
2 to 3 ounces *rhizome**, shredded
2 tablespoons fish sauce
2 to 3 cups fish balls, cooked, optional
4 bundles (3 ounces) somen noodles

Spoon the thick portion (the top, or solid, layer) of coconut milk into a large stockpot, and heat over medium heat, stirring, for about 5 minutes. Stir in the red curry paste, and cook for about 5 minutes. Add the noodle sauce, and continue stirring and cooking 5 minutes more. Add the tuna or other fish, the *rhizome*, and the remaining coconut milk, and stir well. Pour in 5 to 6 cups water and the fish sauce, and continue cooking and stirring until an orange slick forms on the surface. Add the fish balls, and reduce the heat to low.

Meanwhile, bring a large pot of water to a boil, and add the noodles. Cook for 5 minutes after the water returns to a boil, or until all the noodles float to the surface. Drain, rinse, and pour the noodles into a

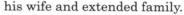

basin of cold water. When the noodles are cool enough to handle, take a small clump and wrap it around a finger to form a small bundle. Repeat until the remaining noodles have been bundled. Arrange the garnishes on one serving platter and the noodles on a second platter, pour the curry into a serving dish, and eat.

Note: This curry is traditionally served with several vegetable garnishes, including Chinese pickled cabbage, bean sprouts, sliced chilies in fish sauce, fresh mint, and shredded fresh cabbage. Petch Vailikit says that for a more traditional—but lengthier—version, use 1 1/2 pounds

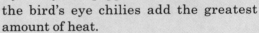

◆ Thai Chilies ◆

Many Asians love the fiery kick of fresh or dried chilies, but Thai food is notoriously hot, fired up primarily by two of Thailand's famous—or infamous—chilies, the long slender Thai "finger" chili, or *prik khee noo*, and the small, potent Thai bird's eye chili (also known as "rat dropping"), or *prik khee noo suan*. A third variety, the *prik chee far*, is the same variety as cayenne peppers. On the heat scale,

the bird's eye chilies add the greatest amount of heat.

Many Asian cooks, accustomed to working with chilies, don't bother to wear rubber gloves when handling chilies, but Westerners, unaccustomed to chilies' burn, should protect their hands by wearing rubber gloves, particularly if they have sensitive skin. Even with gloves, you should never touch your face or eyes after handling chilies unless you wash your hands first. Also rinse both the knife and any counter surface well after slicing chilies. If you prefer milder foods, be on the safe side and start with fewer chilies than the listed amount. You can always add more, but you cannot subtract.

Asian chili varieties are increasingly available in well-stocked supermarkets and specialty food stores. If you cannot find any Thai chilies, substitute jalapeños. If you want to stock up on chilies, or if you have several left over, you can refrigerate them in a plastic bag for about a week. Fresh chilies also freeze well in plastic bags, but they do not usually retain their shape or texture when thawed.

of fresh fish such as salmon or tuna, poach the fish until the flesh flakes apart, and use the reserved cooking fish stock as part of the liquid in the curry. You can also make the red curry paste and the Thai noodle sauce, or *nam ya*, from scratch. Otherwise, find the commercial products at an Asian market.

Rhizome, also known as "lesser *galangal*," is a member of the ginger family and is a seasoning Thais often use in fish- or seafood-based dishes. Look for it frozen at Southeast Asian markets. Thais eat this curry with chopsticks and a soupspoon.

Serves 6 to 8.

U.S.A.

All-American

- ◆ Dad's Pancakes
- ◆ Smoked Barbecued Chicken
- ◆ Sidebar: Texas-Style Barbecue
- ◆ Bread and Butter Pickles
- ◆ Pumpkin Bread
- ◆ Fresh Fruit Cake
- ◆ El's Chocolate Pie
- ◆ Grandma Bertha Wack's Christmas Opera Fudge

Southern American

- ◆ Daddy's Greens
- ◆ Traditional Red Beans with Ham and Sausage

African-American

- ◆ Meat Loaf
- ◆ Mashed Sweet Potatoes, Plantains, and Apples
- ◆ Granny's Rum Pound Cake

Jewish

- ◆ Tzimmes
- ◆ Potato Pancakes with Sour Cream and Applesauce (Latkes)
- ◆ Passover Brisket
- ◆ Grandma Greenbaum's Nut Torte

*A*merican cooking is many things, from Mom's apple pie to the ubiquitous snack foods and chips, cheese-covered pizzas, hot dogs, and juicy hamburgers. Often described as a "melting pot," America and American cooking are so much more than the term implies, since America's cuisine encompasses all the regional, ethnic, traditional, avant-garde, fast food, and family favorites that make up the complex whole of America's kitchens.

Regardless of one's allegiance, dietary preferences, or location, however, the typical American has at his fingertips a whole range of fresh, frozen, canned, and vacuum-packed foods that are probably the envy of other countries and other nationalities. It's often reported that newcomers to the United States become overwhelmed on their first trips to our supermarkets. Several years ago, a newspaper recounted the experience of one newly arrived Russian immigrant, who burst into tears and ran out of her supermarket. Apparently, she had never seen so much food and so many choices in her life.

With all this food at hand, Americans seemingly are disposed to overeat with a corresponding rise in the rates of obesity and diabetes. Americans are also inclined to depend on fast foods or commercially packaged meals to simplify mealtimes, a trend that serious food people are countering with an upsurge of food magazines, discourses on healthful eating, gourmet groups, wine tastings, farmers' markets, and consumer organizations dedicated to honoring America's culinary heritage.

Among these is a small, but increasingly vocal, visible, and public-spirited group with international roots and Italian origins: Slow Food.

As described on the international website, www.slowfood.com, the organization was founded to "counteract fast food and fast life, the disappearance of local food traditions and people's dwindling interest in the food they eat, where it comes from, how it tastes and how our food choices affect the rest of the world."

This message must be resonating with the American consumer, who has increasingly sought out farm-fresh fare, preferably organic, in restaurants, on supermarket shelves, and in fast-food outlets. And the amazing rekindling of the small American farm, which, thanks to community support of local farmers' markets, may actually reverse past trends and bring people back to small farming as a career option. And judging by the

Old Glory at Sunset.
Nathaniel Dodson, Uniment1
Design & Photography

output of cookbooks dedicated to preserving and honoring heirloom recipes, our culinary history may not be an endangered species after all.

According to an interview with Dr. Dean Ornish, founder of the Preventive Medicine Research Institute in Sausalito, California, published by *Parade* magazine in November 2006, Americans are increasingly realizing that a change in diet for long-term health benefits is more "powerful than medicine or surgery." As organizations such as Slow Food and others dedicated to informing consumers about good food and good health continue to deliver their messages, more people will wish not only to eat healthily but also may start honoring America's food traditions. It's possible that the next generation may actually slow down and enjoy the food they are eating.

ALL-AMERICAN
Dad's Pancakes

Christopher Greeley, MD, a pediatrician in Houston, Texas, has fond memories of family weekend breakfasts, when his dad regularly made very special pancakes. As he writes, "Almost every Saturday morning when I was growing up, my father made us three children pancakes accented with lemon juice, yet they were perfectly sweet. Now that I am an adult, and have a wife and family of my own—my wife Nicci and I are both pediatricians, and we have triplets—I will treat my children to these pancakes on Saturday mornings, and make them just the way my dad made them." (The recipe is adapted from one in *The Pancake Cookbook* by Myra Waldo, published by Bantam Books in 1963.)

2 large eggs
1 3/4 cups skim or whole milk
3 tablespoons fresh lemon juice
1/4 cup melted unsalted butter
1 teaspoon lemon extract
1 teaspoon lemon zest
2 1/2 cups all-purpose flour
1/2 teaspoon salt
1 teaspoon baking soda
3 tablespoons granulated sugar
warm maple syrup

Chris Greeley makes his dad's pancakes.
Nicci Greeley, MD

Using an electric beater with a whisk attachment, beat the eggs in a large mixing bowl until thick, about 5 minutes. Stir in the milk, lemon juice, butter, lemon extract, and lemon zest.

Sift the flour, salt, baking soda, and sugar together into a second bowl. Slowly fold the egg mixture into the flour mixture, stirring until smooth.

Butter a large griddle or skillet, and over medium heat, cook the batter about 1/4 cup at a time. Cook each until it is browned on the bottom and bubbles form on the surface, then carefully flip over to cook the second side until browned. Serve while hot.

Serves 4.

 *Smoked Barbecued Chicken*

On Maryland's Eastern Shore, Keith and Wendy Underwood operate an organic farm that offers consumers all-natural grass-fed beef, pastured eggs, wild honey, homemade beer, and artesan wine. All of their activities are family-oriented—bicycling, sailing, hiking, gardening, and cooking. Although son Nathaniel and twins, Seth and Lindsey, are good cooks, Seth is passionate about cooking. Not only does he have a repertoire of old family recipes (especially from the English, Persian, and German sides of his family), he is constantly adapting them to use the meat, dairy, and produce raised and grown at home. This barbecue chicken recipe is a family favorite and is always on hand during family reunions.

Underwood prefers using lump, rather than briquette-style charcoal, and adding apple or oak wood chips in equal parts to prevent the wood from producing unsavory soot. He notes that putting butter under the skin over the breast meat keeps the meat moist.

Seth Underwood cooking barbecue chicken for friends.
Lindsey Underwood

2 (3 1/2- to 4-pound) broilers/fryers at room temperature
1/2 cup (1 stick) salted butter, cut into eighths
olive oil for rubbing
1 tablespoon kosher salt
1 1/2 tablespoons onion salt
1 tablespoon celery salt
1 tablespoon freshly ground black pepper
barbecue sauce for rubbing

Using a chimney starter and a sheet of newspaper coated with 1 tablespoon vegetable oil, fire up a charcoal grill. Arrange the lit charcoal on one side of a kettle grill, and on the other side, place an aluminum drip pan underneath where the chicken will be. Place a handful of equal parts apple and oak chips along the edges of the charcoal pile. Cover the grill, and allow the smoke to start rolling before adding the chickens.

Prepare the chickens by working the butter underneath the skin covering the breast meat. Continue by rubbing a thin layer of oil over the entire chicken to crisp the skin and for the spices to adhere. Combine the three salts with the pepper. Sprinkle over the birds.

Place the birds side by side on the grill rack, legs facing the center of the grill. This lets the darker meat face more of the heat and cooks the meat more evenly. The grill should be around 400 to 500°F when you first place the chickens on the grill. Use a probe thermometer to monitor the internal temperature of the birds, and another thermometer to read the grill temperature.

Allow the coals to burn down as the chickens cook but don't let the temperature go below 200°F. The chickens need to reach an internal temperature of 170°F.

Brush some barbecue sauce on the birds during the expected last 15 minutes of cooking. Remove the chickens from the grill, and let rest for 20 minutes before slicing and serving.

Serves 6 to 8.

◆ **Texas-Style Barbecue** ◆

Outdoor grilling has become an American passion, and probably never more so than in Texas, where barbecue must seem almost synonymous with entertaining. Native Texan Niccole White Greeley tells of her father, John White, and his favorite barbecue this way, a way that has probably fed generations of her family: "Get a bunch of baby back ribs, try to remember the combination of dry rub, and or sauces you used last time; start the fire at approximately sunrise; seer the ribs on both sides, then move them to the smoking cylinder of the pit (as you create a drip pan of sauce, rub and some beer); try to keep the fire low and smoking; remember to check the ribs hourly; then pull the ribs off after 5 to 6 hours."

Bread and Butter Pickles

Deborah Burns, of Kennebunk, Maine, makes this family favorite annually—a summertime staple to use up her garden crops. And if you're lucky enough to enjoy a New England Thanksgiving dinner at the Matthew Burns's, you'll find a bowl of these served alongside the turkey. Kathy Burns, wife of Michael Greeley, grew up enjoying these pickles, and makes sure she has plenty on hand herself from her mother's pantry when summer ends. It's a very simple recipe, and keeps well in vacuum-sealed canning jars.

6 onions, sliced
6 cups sliced cucumbers
1 cup coarse salt
1 1/2 quarts cider vinegar
6 cups granulated sugar
1/3 cup mustard seeds
1 1/2 tablespoons celery seeds
1/2 teaspoon ground cayenne

Put the onions and cucumbers into a large enameled bowl. Combine with the salt, and set aside for 5 hours. Shake the salted cucumbers and onions, and strain off excess water. Rinse well.

Put the vinegar, sugar, mustard seeds, celery seeds, and ground cayenne into a large stainless steel or enameled stockpot. Bring to a boil over high heat. Add the onions and cucumbers, and boil for 5 minutes. Remove from the heat, cool, and store the vegetables in sterile vacuum jars, adding some of the cooking liquid to cover.

Yield: about 6 pints.

Pumpkin Bread

Peg Williams, of Long Valley, New Jersey, is an explorer of cooking traditions. She mostly concentrates on ones that might disappear, especially if they aren't handed down from one generation to the next. When she is testing new recipes, her husband, John, and daughters, Kim, Gretchen, and Allie, are always on hand to taste and comment on her baking and cooking. Many years ago, she retrieved this recipe from her mother-in-law, Anna Williams. Her family gave it a big thumbs-up and it has been part of her repertoire for Thanksgiving dinner ever since.

1 2/3 cups all-purpose flour
1 1/2 teaspoons baking powder
1 teaspoon baking soda
1 teaspoon ground cinnamon
1/2 teaspoon salt
2 large eggs
1 1/2 cups granulated sugar
1 1/2 cups canned pumpkin purée
1/2 to 1/3 cup vegetable oil
1/2 cup chopped walnuts
1/2 cup shredded coconut

The Williams's daughters with friends, 1988.
John Williams

Preheat the oven to 350°F. Butter generously a 9x5-inch loaf pan.

Combine the flour, baking powder, baking soda, cinnamon, and salt in a large bowl. In a second bowl, whisk the eggs until foamy, and stir in the sugar, pumpkin, and oil. Whisk in the dry ingredients. Stir in the nuts and coconut.

Bake for 70 minutes, or until a toothpick inserted in the center comes out clean. Cool slightly, then remove the bread from the pan, and cool on a rack.

Makes one 9-inch loaf.

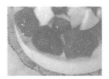

Fresh Fruit Cake

Brother and sister Michael and Susan Greeley have a favorite dessert. As they write, "Our mom has been making this very simple fruit cake for us and our families for many, many years." Because you assemble and mix the cake in a food processor, it comes together in no time. Best of all, it's very versatile, and you can adjust seasonings and fruit toppings to suit your taste and the occasion. It doubles easily and travels well. This is delicious as a breakfast cake, but it also works equally well for dessert, served plain or with whipped cream, ice cream, yogurt, or lemon curd, or even topped with streusel. This cake is the basis for some wonderful kitchen memories for generations to come.

1/4 pound (1 stick) unsalted butter, softened
1 teaspoon lemon extract
1 teaspoon vanilla extract
1 cup granulated sugar
2 large eggs
1 cup all-purpose flour
pinch salt
about 2 cups fresh or frozen fruit, such as blueberries, raspberries, straw-
　berries, mangoes, peaches, apricots, apples, or pears
1/2 cup slivered almonds or other nuts, optional

Preheat the oven to 350°F. Butter and flour a 9-inch cake pan

　Put the butter, lemon extract, vanilla extract, and sugar into a food processor, and pulse to cream the mixture. Add the eggs, flour, and salt, and process until smooth. Scrape the batter into the prepared cake pan. Top the batter with the fruit and nuts, if using.

　Bake for about 1 hour, or until the center is firm to the touch, and the sides are browned. Cool in the pan.

　Serves 4 to 6.

El's Chocolate Pie

Mary Hager, of Falls Church, Virginia, is the keeper of many family recipes in old trunks, recipe boxes, and notebooks filled with scraps of handwritten recipes. She writes, "Clearly this is an old recipe. It has at least two strikes against it these days—the two cubes of butter and the four raw eggs. Nonetheless, we enjoyed it many times, as did many others, and we've all survived to remember El's pie with fond memories. I have four copies in the recipe box, one in mother's handwriting, one in El's, one in mine. The fourth is a mystery. El used to make it with Ritz crackers for the 'crust.' Nothing fancy, just lining the pie tin. As I recall, it worked the best with its slight bit of salt. We've done it with the chocolate wafer crust, the vanilla wafer crust, graham cracker crumb crust, and a flaky piecrust. Never heard any complaints, though, as I remember, the chocolate wafer crust was overkill—though lots of chocolate is 'in' these days." Long beating is the secret to success with this. Don't underbeat. The more you beat, the creamier the texture. It should be like chocolate velvet.

1/2 pound (2 sticks) unsalted butter (no margarine!)
1 1/3 cups granulated sugar
4 eggs
4 squares unsweetened baking chocolate
1/8 to 1/2 teaspoon flavoring (mint is pretty intense, so 1/8 vanilla, but almond, rum, lemon, and orange have also been used)

Cream butter and sugar until light. Add eggs, one at a time, beat five minutes. Melt chocolate, add (when slightly cooled), and beat another five minutes. Pour into the shell and chill.
Serves 6.

Grandma Bertha Wack's Christmas Opera Fudge

Despite its name, opera fudge is not fudge at all but a rich mixture of heavy and light creams cooked into a fondant and coated with chocolate. Associated with Lebanon, Pennsylvania, where it possibly originated, opera fudge was a seasonal treat for cold weather months and popular elsewhere in the United States. Traditionally, candy makers used a sturdy marble slab for making the confection, and according to one member of Bertha Wack's family, using anything else, even the new in-vogue granite countertops, does not seem imaginable. "If I remember our stories correctly, the 'original' marble slab of grandpa's was actually from a candy store. That may not be true, but I can assure you that this recipe has nothing to do with 'new stone-type counter tops,'" writes her granddaughter, Tammy Lewis.

For the Lewis family, Grandma Wack's opera fudge, a family recipe handed down through the Pennsylvania Dutch Wack family, always made its appearance during the holidays. Her granddaughter, Jenny, reports that her grandmother would bake her way through Thanksgiving and Christmas with tons of different cookies and candies, but this opera fudge was always the favorite. Her recipe calls for using a very large stainless or enamel kettle and wooden spoon, plus a candy thermometer and a marble slab. As Tammy Lewis also writes, "Perhaps at some point I will try another technique, but then it wouldn't be Grandma's opera fudge, would it? For me, making the opera fudge, especially with my relatives (Mommy and I laughed so much last year!!!), is as much a sentimental and reminiscent journey as it is a means to an end, *i.e.* candy to die for!"

3 1/2 pounds granulated sugar
1 pint heavy cream
1 pint half-and-half
1/2 teaspoon cream of tartar
about 2 pounds couverture chocolate for coating, melted according to
   package directions

Bring the sugar and the two creams to a full rolling boil in a large saucepan over medium heat, and add the cream of tartar. Boil until the mixture reaches 238°F on a candy thermometer, or to the soft-ball stage, stirring constantly.

Turn the mixture out onto a dampened marble slab, using iron bars (or other sturdy objects) to contain the syrup. When it is cool to the touch, work with spatulas until the mixture becomes white and turns to sugar. This takes a little while. Scrape together on the slab, cover with a dampened tea towel, and place a heavy bath towel on top. Allow to "steam" for 1 hour. Line a cookie sheet with foil.

Carol Ann (Wack) Lewis making opera fudge.
Tammy Lewis

Work with your hands to knead the mixture until all the sugary lumps are gone and the mixture is creamy. Roll the candy into rolls or shape into logs, as desired. If making logs, roll them to about 6 inches long and 2 inches round, and, using a spatula, spread them with chocolate. Place the logs on the cookie sheet, and refrigerate until the chocolate hardens. When it is firm, turn the logs upside down, and, using a spatula, coat the undersides with chocolate. Refrigerate the logs again until hardened. Then wrap the logs in plastic wrap, and refrigerate until ready to slice and serve.

Note: If you do not have a marble slab or iron bars to contain the hot sugar mixture, you can pour it into a large baking dish, perhaps 9x13 inches, or larger as needed. You can also use your hands to mix the cooled fudge before you wrap it in towels to firm. Grandma Wack's recipe does not call for salt or vanilla extract, but a pinch of salt and two teaspoons vanilla extract add a flavor profile.

Makes about 4 1/2 pounds.

SOUTHERN AMERICAN COOKING
Daddy's Greens

Elizabeth Williams, president of the Southern Food and Beverage Museum, New Orleans, and a writer of legal and policy issues related to food, remembers her childhood family meals, especially this recipe. "My father loved greens. He cooked them when they were in season, changing the greens to reflect what greens were available. When I was old enough to help, I was the one who was assigned the task of washing the fresh greens to make sure that they were not gritty. This was a very important job."

Willliams's family loved tart, salad-like greens, but for those who desire a milder flavor, she suggests using 2 tablespoons vinegar added to dress the greens just before serving.

A plate of Daddy's greens.
Brian Chou

2 pounds greens, including mustard greens, collards, turnips or any other peppery and tough green leafy vegetable
1/4 cup bacon fat
1/4 pound fat back, chopped into 1/4-inch cubes
1/4 cup cider vinegar
salt to taste
freshly ground black pepper to taste

Rip greens from the tough stems. Wash thoroughly to remove grit. Shake dry. Roughly chop the greens. Set aside. In a heavy pot, like a cast-iron Dutch oven, heat the bacon fat over medium heat. When it is melted, add the chopped fat back. Cook until crispy. Remove the crispy bits and set aside. Add the slightly wet chopped greens to the hot bacon fat. Toss briefly, and cover. Reduce the heat to low. Cook, stirring occasionally, for about 30 minutes. (Depending on the type of greens, you may have to cook a bit longer. Taste after

30 minutes. If the greens are still tough, cook 15 more minutes.) Just before serving add the vinegar and salt and pepper (remember that the fat back and the bacon fat are salty). Toss to distribute the vinegar, and serve hot.

Serves 6 to 8.

Traditional Red Beans with Ham and Sausage

Elizabeth Williams, president of the Southern Food and Beverage Museum, in New Orleans, writes, "Everyone in New Orleans has a personal recipe for red beans. No two recipes are alike, nor are they expected to be alike. This dish is the ultimate New Orleans' comfort food. The way that my mother cooked her beans, always the same way, always made me feel safe and cozy. We had red beans and rice once a week, but not always on the traditional Monday. I knew that we would have red beans the next day, because my mother would set them to soak the night before. As a child, that was the first thing I was allowed to do—soak the beans. That meant getting out the big ceramic bowl, filling it with water, setting it on the counter, pouring in the beans, and covering the bowl with a cloth. In our family comfort food wasn't macaroni and cheese, it was red beans and rice. It was predictable and welcome. And, of course, my mother's were the best in the city."

1 pound dried red kidney beans
ham bone with about 1/2 pound meat
1 pound hot smoked sausages, sliced
1 cup coarsely chopped onions
1/2 cup coarsely chopped celery
1/2 cup coarsely chopped green bell pepper
1 carrot, grated
1 cup sliced scallions
3 cloves garlic, minced
2 bay leaves
2 tablespoons minced fresh thyme
minced parsley for garnish

Soak the beans overnight in 6 to 8 cups cold water. Just before cooking, drain the beans, and place them in a large pot with about 8 cups of cold water and the ham bone. Slowly heat the water over medium heat, and add all of the other ingredients, reserving half of the scallions for garnish.

Reduce the heat to medium-low, and cook, covered, for about 2 hours, or until the beans can be mashed easily against the side of the pot with a spoon. Mash about one-quarter of the beans, and stir them in to make a creamy sauce for the rest of the beans.

Remove the bone. Pick off any meat clinging to it, and add the meat back to the beans. Taste the beans, and add salt if needed. Place in a tureen, and garnish with minced parsley and sliced scallions.

Serves 6.

At Slow Food's Salone del Gusto hams and sausages are plentiful.
Anne Parsons

AFRICAN AMERICAN
Meat Loaf

Carla Hall Lyons, a caterer in the Washington, D.C., area, grew up in the South and has many fond food memories. As she writes, "When I talk about my food memories, it's usually involving my Granny and not my mother. To this very day, my mom will say that she isn't the cook of the family, but she does make an incredible meatloaf. If we were lucky there was enough left over for a classic meatloaf sandwich with white bread, mayo, and ketchup the next day."

Meatloaf
1/2 onion, coarsely chopped
1 medium-sized carrot, coarsely chopped
1 celery stalk, coarsely chopped
3 cloves garlic
1/2 red bell pepper
1 1/2 pounds ground chuck
1 1/2 pounds ground sirloin
1 cup fresh bread crumbs
1/2 teaspoon freshly ground black pepper
1/2 teaspoon dried thyme
1/2 teaspoon cayenne pepper
2 tablespoons Worcestershire sauce
1 1/2 teaspoons kosher salt
1 large egg, lightly beaten

The Glaze
1/2 cup ketchup
2 teaspoons ground cumin
dash Worcestershire sauce
1 tablespoon honey

Preheat the oven to 325°F. Line a baking sheet with parchment paper.
   Put the onion, carrot, celery, garlic, and red bell pepper into a food

processor, and process until the mixture is finely chopped but not puréed.

Combine the vegetable mixture, ground chuck, ground sirloin, breadcrumbs, pepper, thyme, cayenne, and Worcestershire sauce. Season the mixture with the kosher salt. Add the egg, and combine thoroughly, but avoid squeezing the meat.

Pack this mixture into a 10-inch loaf pan to mold the shape of the meatloaf. Turn the meatloaf out of the pan onto the center of the baking sheet. Place the sheet in the center rack in the oven.

Meanwhile, to make the glaze, combine the ketchup, cumin, and honey. Brush the glaze onto the meatloaf after it has been in the oven for 10 minutes.

Granny serving dinner to Walter Moxley and Marvin Head, taken about 1953.
Photographer unknown

Cook the meatloaf for about 1 1/4 hours, or until the center registers 155°F. Let the meatloaf rest for at least 15 minutes before slicing.

Serves 8.

Mashed Sweet Potatoes, Plantains, and Apples

Carla Hall Lyons, a Washington, D.C., caterer, remembers family meals, and this dish in particular. She says, "Mashed sweet potatoes were everybody's favorite at our Sunday family dinners—with or without the almost-burnt marshmallows. It was a way for the kids to get away with a sweet before dessert was served. The addition of the plantains—an African and Caribbean staple—and the apples update this dish and add both sweet and tart flavor notes. The black-ripe plantains are sweeter and softer than both the green and the yellow plantains."

Alexandra Greeley shops at local Reston market.
Anne Parsons

3 small sweet potatoes
2 black-ripe plantains
2 Granny Smith apples, peeled and quartered plus extra slices for garnish
3 tablespoons unsalted butter
1/2 cup packed brown sugar
1/2 teaspoon ground cinnamon
1/2 teaspoon ground ginger
1/2 teaspoon salt
cinnamon sticks for garnish

Preheat the oven to 350°F.

Place the whole sweet potatoes on a baking sheet, and bake until fork tender, about 40 minutes.

Line a baking tray with parchment paper or aluminum foil. Spray with cooking spray. Cut each end of the plantains off, and cut them in half lengthwise. Remove the peel. Place the plantain pieces and apple quarters on the pan, and set aside. Halfway through the cooking time of the potatoes, put the plantains and apples in the oven.

Bake the plantains and apples until fork-tender. When the potatoes are cool enough to handle, peel them, and put the potatoes, plantains, and apples in a large bowl with the butter, brown sugar, cinnamon, ginger, and salt. Mix all ingredients with a potato masher, beating until smooth and well mixed. Spoon mixture into a baking dish, and heat through before serving. Sprinkle with cinnamon, and garnish with cinnamon sticks and apple slices.

Serves 8.

Granny's Rum Pound Cake

"Everybody loves a really great rum cake, which is quite popular in the Caribbean," writes Washington, D.C., caterer Carla Hall-Lyons. "The typical rum cake is very moist and almost melts in your mouth because it's full of rum. In my family, Granny's plain pound cake was the most popular, but on those occasions when she would spike her treasure with rum that was certainly welcomed as well. This was the cake that all her grandchildren would beg her to send us after we moved away."

3 cups all-purpose flour
1 teaspoon baking soda
1 teaspoon salt
1/2 pound (2 sticks) unsalted butter
2 1/2 cups granulated sugar
6 large eggs
8 ounces cream cheese, softened
1 teaspoon vanilla extract
2 teaspoons rum extract
1 teaspoon coconut extract
1 teaspoon lemon extract
1 teaspoon almond extract

Preheat the oven to 350°F.

Sift more than enough flour, then measure flour, salt, and baking soda into medium bowl. Sift again, and set aside.

Cream the butter and sugar using the paddle attachment of an electric mixer. Add the eggs one at a time, allowing each egg to be incorporated.

Add the flour alternately with the cream cheese, beginning and ending with the flour. Mix for at least 2 minutes on medium speed.

Add the extracts one at a time, allowing each to be incorporated in the mixture. Continue mixing the batter until it is shiny, about 3 to 5 minutes.

Pour batter into a decorative tubular pan or a regular tube pan sprayed with nonstick spray. Place the pan in the center of the oven, and bake for 1 hour or until the cake is golden and a toothpick is inserted and comes out clean.

Let the cake cool on a wire rack for 10 minutes before turning it out onto the serving plate. While the cake is cooling, prepare the rum syrup. Brush the rum syrup on the top and sides of the cake. Let cool completely before cutting.

Preparing to bake.
Anne Parsons

Rum Syrup
1 cup granulated sugar
1/4 pound (1 stick) unsalted butter
3/4 cup dark rum
2 teaspoons vanilla extract

Combine the sugar, butter, and 1/4 cup water in a medium-sized saucepan. Bring to a boil over medium-high heat, and cook, stirring constantly, until the sugar has dissolved.

Add the rum. Reduce the heat to medium, and cook for 5 minutes. Remove from the heat, and stir in the vanilla extract. Use immediately, or a film will form on the top of the syrup.

Serves 10 to 12.

JEWISH
Tzimmes

Norma Auer, of the Outer Banks, in North Carolina, is known among her friends as the "Perle Mesta of the OBX" —because she is such an excellent hostess, chef, and baker. As an older teenager, Auer decided to cook a French dinner for her beau. When her mother asked her, "What do you think you're doing? You don't know how to cook." Auer remembers saying, "If I can read, I can cook!" Using Julia Childs's *Mastering the Art of French Cooking*, Auer cooked a complete meal. Obviously her beau was suitably impressed, since they were later betrothed and had a beautiful daughter, Dr. Jennifer Perlman. Auer's grandson, Max, is just a toddler but Auer already has plans to introduce him to many generations of her family's recipes.

Auer explains to Anne Parsons that centuries ago matzoh was only eaten dry, because it was not allowed to ferment. Eventually that concept changed when a Rabbi ruled that it was perfectly fine to soak the matzoh in water, since no fermentation could take place once it had been baked. Not surprisingly, the matzoh ball (*knaidle)* was invented. As Auer comments, "It isn't Passover without matzoh balls." *Tzimmes*, a hearty casserole with meat and sweet vegetables, makes the perfect backdrop for a *knaidle*.

Knaidle
3 large eggs, well beaten
1 cup matzoh meal
1 tablespoon granulated sugar
1 teaspoon salt
1/2 cup hot water

Tzimmes
2 bunches carrots, scrubbed, trimmed, and sliced
2 pounds sweet potatoes, peeled and sliced
1 large *knaidle*
1 pound flanken steak

1/2 cup granulated sugar
1/2 cup honey
1 large onion, diced
1/2 cut hot water

Preheat the oven to 325°F.

To make the *knaidle*, combine the eggs and matzoh meal in a large bowl. Stir in the sugar, salt, and hot water. Gather up the batter in your hands, and roll into a ball to form the *knaidle*. Set aside.

Four generations of the Cohen family (Norma is the young girl in photo). Schwartz family album

Put a layer of sliced carrots on the bottom of a large ovenproof casserole. Put a layer of sweet potatoes on top of the carrots. Repeat, alternating layers, until all the ingredients are used up. Nestle the *knaidle* in the center of the vegetables.

Cut the flanken steak into chunks, and add them to the casserole. Cover the meat and vegetables with the sugar, honey, onion, and hot water. Cover the casserole.

Bake for 2 hours, or until the meat and vegetables are fork-tender. Serve hot.

Serves 8.

Potato Pancakes with Sour Cream and Applesauce

LATKES

Estelle Cohen Schwartz, Norma Auer's mother, (who now lives in Florida), used to tell Norma stories about her great cousins, the famed Marx brothers. Often, when one of them popped into Schwartz's New York apartment for a quick nosh, especially for her mum's *latkes*, he'd toss Norma in the air (she was just a toddler) and have her giggling and rolling on the floor.

Auer now makes these *latkes* for her family and has passed the recipe to her daughter, Jennifer. Auer's mother told her that the potato and onion must be hand-grated, and even if some skin gets in the mix, don't worry because it is what makes the *latkes* authentic! However, be sure to use a metal grater to ensure the correct, uniform texture of the *latkes*. These recipes make 6 servings as a side dish, but since you can never eat enough *latkes*, just multiply the quantity proportionally.

Schwartz family portrait 1935.
Schwartz family album

1 cup grated raw potato
1 cup yellow onion, peeled and grated
2 large eggs, beaten
pinch baking powder
1 1/2 teaspoons salt
1 tablespoon all-purpose flour
2 tablespoons vegetable oil, or more as needed
applesauce for topping
sour cream for topping

Wrap potato shreds in a kitchen towel or several layers of cheesecloth, and wring them until they are as dry as possible. Put the shreds into a large mixing bowl. Add the onion, eggs, baking powder, salt, and flour, and mix well.

Heat the oil in a large skillet over medium heat. When hot, scoop the potato mixture by tablespoonfuls into the oil, and fry until brown on the bottom. Using a spatula, turn the potato pancakes over to brown on the second side. When golden, remove from the skillet, and drain on paper towels.

Repeat until all the mixture is used up, adding more oil as needed. Keep cooked *latkes* warm in a 200°F oven.

Serve warm with applesauce and sour cream.

Serves 6.

Passover Brisket

Norma Auer, an ex-Manhattanite and now a co-leader of Slow Food on the Outer Banks of North Carolina, is an advocate of buying locally and buying in season. She insists that her cooking is so popular with guests because she always uses the freshest ingredients. Auer suggests making this dish a day ahead because, like stew, it always tastes better the second day. She also suggests serving the brisket with potato pancakes.

Auer preparing brisket for her dinner guests.
Anne Parsons

2 teaspoons all-purpose flour
1 1/2 teaspoons kosher salt
freshly ground black pepper to taste
1 teaspoon paprika
5 pounds first-cut brisket
2 large garlic cloves, quartered
2 large carrots, sliced into 1-inch-thick pieces
4 stalks celery
2 large onions, sliced
1 (3-ounce) can tomato paste

Preheat the oven to 325°F.

Combine the flour, salt, pepper, and paprika, and dredge the meat in this mixture until it is well covered. Place the meat in a large ovenproof casserole.

Layer the meat with the garlic, carrots, celery, and onions. Mix together the tomato paste and 1/2 cup water, and pour into the casserole. Cover the casserole.

Bake for at least 3 hours, basting the meat occasionally and turning it over several times. When the meat is very tender, check for the amount of gravy; if there is too much, remove the cover and cook, uncovered, until the gravy reduces and thickens.

Remove the vegetables and meat, trim off the fat, and slice the meat. Put the meat and vegetables back into the casserole, pour the gravy over top, cover, and refrigerate overnight.

To serve, skim off the fat, and reheat the meat and vegetables in the oven until heated through.

Serves 8 to 10.

Grandma Greenbaum's Nut Torte

Bunny Polmer of Washington, D.C., says that her grandmother, Anna Grossman Greenbaum, "was the designated cook among her siblings. She was amazing. She was from Austria-Hungary; I think her hometown might have become part of the Czech Republic. I'm not sure. At any rate, when she was sixteen, a friend had a steamship passage to America and chickened out. My grandmother took the ticket instead and came. She landed in New York City, but didn't find her 'people' there. Most of the Jews in New York were Russian-Polish, spoke a different language, and ate different foods. She learned that Hungarians (Jews and Gentiles) were in Cleveland. So there she went and there she met my grandfather. Together they settled in Barberton, outside Akron. He opened a men's wear store, and they became pillars of the community. They both died in the 1970s, so they were a big part of my childhood and young adulthood.

"Her Hungarian cooking was legendary in our family. This recipe, a family tradition, appears every year at our Passover Seder. During Passover, we do not eat anything leavened, so this cake is dependent on heavily beaten eggs to help it rise. The mocha frosting was added by my mother, Stella Greenbaum Rosen, and is now an integral part of the dessert. By the way, Grandma's cooking was strictly Hungarian. Strudels, goulashes, *paprikashes*, stuffed peppers, brined banana peppers. A few years ago, my sister and I, with our husbands, went to the Czech Republic, Austria, and finally Budapest together, and it wasn't until we got to Hungary that we recognized—and ate—Grandma's cooking. It was a poignant food moment!"

The Torte
10 large eggs, separated
10 tablespoons granulated sugar
1 tablespoon Passover wine
1 pound walnuts, chopped fine
5 tablespoons matzoh meal

Mocha Frosting
1 cup unsalted butter
3 cups confectioners' sugar, sifted
2 ounces unsweetened chocolate, melted and cooled
2 tablespoons instant coffee, dissolved in hot water
1/2 teaspoon vanilla extract
few drops milk, optional

Lots of dough at Slow Food's Salone del Gusto. Anne Parsons

Preheat the oven to 350°F. Butter two 8-inch cake pans.

To make the torte, beat the egg yolks until lemon-colored. Add the sugar and wine. Add alternately the nuts and matzoh meal. Combine. Beat the egg whites until stiff. Stir a large spoonful of the whites into the yolk mixture to lighten it. Fold in the remaining whites, making sure the batter is well combined. Divide the batter between the two pans, smoothing the top of each.

Bake 25 to 30 minutes. Allow the torte to cool on a rack before unmolding and frosting it.

Meanwhile, make the mocha frosting. Cream the butter, and gradually beat in the sugar. Add the chocolate, coffee, and vanilla. Smooth out by adding a few drops of milk, if needed. Spread mocha frosting on top and sides.

Serves 8.

Vietnam

- VIETNAMESE SUMMER OR GARDEN ROLLS

- DAVID QUANG'S CARAMEL PORK

*N*eed some comfort food to ward off a chill, dispose of a headache, or soothe an aching heart? If you were Vietnamese, you might very well head to the nearest *pho* restaurant for a bowl of bracing, steamy beef soup topped with your choice of meat cuts and vegetable garnishes. Or if you just want a good breakfast, a midafternoon pick-up, or a midnight snack. you'd still order a bowl of *pho*. This Northern specialty, which is now enjoyed equally as much in Central and South Vietnam, is perhaps the one dish most Westerners associate with Vietnam.

Or perhaps that honor of best-known dish belongs to the ubiquitous Vietnamese spring rolls, filled with meat, noodles, and veggies and wrapped in a crunchy skin made of rice paper, then pan-fried. As popular and familiar as these two dishes are, neither truly represents the depth and breadth of Vietnamese cooking, influenced as it has been by the Chinese to the North (hence the use of chopsticks, soy sauce, and tofu), the French colonials (the love of baguettes and sausages), and the neighboring Thais (the use of fish sauce, herbs, and sugar as a seasoning).

As a result, Vietnamese cooking is an artful composite of various culinary influences, and for many dishes, quite elegant. While rice, noodles, fresh produce, pork, and seafood form the foundation of the national cuisine, Southern cooks have really perfected the art of using fresh vegetables in myriad ways, from garnishes to using vegetables as integral parts of the finished dish. Think chilies, lime juice, lemongrass, fresh cilantro, shallots, mint, garlic, and ginger and you have the vegetable and seasoning basis for many Southern dishes. Southern cooks have also garnered praise for producing a truly light, delicate array of dishes that, nonetheless, rely on layers of subtle flavors for their overall success.

Should you receive an invitation to eat at a Vietnamese home, you will find basically simple fare, with several courses shared communally. Chances are your meal will include a soup or stewlike dish, a piece of grilled fish or meat, vegetables, rice or noodles, and hot tea. You can't go wrong ordering this type of menu at a restaurant either, though you may want to add spring or summer rolls to the meal. But whether you eat at home or in a Vietnamese restaurant, you won't soon forget the taste of *nuoc mam*, the seasoning staple in every Vietnamese kitchen.

Local fishing boat.
Anne Parsons

A Vietnamese friend, David Quang, talks about living on the island of Phu Quoc, famous for its fish-sauce-making factories. He tells how the most valued sauce comes from the first pressing of the fermented fish—much like the Italians, Greeks, and Spanish prize the first pressing of the olive—and this sauce is reserved for the very best customers. Second and third "pressings" end up as the commercial seasoning—*nuoc mam*—that every Vietnamese treasures. This salty-fishy seasoning is a requisite component in most indigenous dishes and is the basis for making a more complex seasoning sauce used as a table condiment.

Fish sauce or no, Vietnamese cooking regardless of its region of origin, is one of Asia's most unforgettable.

Vietnamese Summer or Garden Rolls

Many folks on Colington Island, North Carolina, know that spring is officially here when they spot Lan Kaufman marching into her garden in full battle gear. Armed with her only gardening tool, a spade, and wearing a woven triangular shaped hat and cotton pantaloons, Lan plunges her weapon into the heart of the enemy, the winter weeds. Lan is a petite, energetic woman who came to the United States from a small village in the central part of Vietnam, just north of Cameron Bay.

Lan Kaufman serving her summer rolls.
Anne Parsons

"In Vietnam," Lan tells Anne Parsons, "fresh herbs and greens play a critical role at mealtimes because a typical meal includes an enormous platter filled with *rau thom,* or aromatic herbs." Lan explains that the herbs served will depend on the meal; for example, with *pho* (rice noodles with beef soup), there will be Asian basil and saw-leaf. With grilled meats, there will be lots of green and red *perilla* and other varieties of mint. Knives and forks are unnecessary," continues Lan, "because we either tear the greens into small pieces and add them to our bowls, or use them to wrap little pieces of meat or seafood and dip them in sauce. The idea is similar to the wrapped sandwich concept."

Lan prepares the pork butt for the following recipe by boiling it, then plunging it immediately into cold water, so it doesn't continue to cook. To test for doneness, she inserts a chopstick into the thickest part of the meat. She also notes that grilled chicken with bean sprouts and ginger could be substituted for those who do not eat pork. In fact, Lan suggests that one may fill the roll with whatever takes one's fancy.

She explains that Vietnamese cooking relies on fresh vegetables and subtle seasonings, that's why the cuisine has a delicate and light taste. Vietnamese cuisine is also perfect in this health-conscious society because it is based on fresh herbs and vegetables.

"A successful eating experience," Lan believes, "needs three ingredients: good food, good presentation, and good company."

Spring roll wrappers—also known as rice paper wrappers when used for Vietnamese recipes—are available in many grocery stores. Kaufman uses the 9-inch-round Thai wrapper with either the letters OK or a picture of a *sampan* (sailboat) on the label.

1 pound boiled pork butt with 2 cups cooking liquid reserved
24 spring roll wrappers
1 large bunch of Vietnamese or regular mint
1 head romaine lettuce, leaves separated, rinsed, and trimmed
1 (8-ounce) package Asian vermicelli, cooked and drained
48 medium-sized prawns, shelled, deveined, and cooked
24 stalks garlic grass

Boil 1 pound pork butt in lightly salted water to cover. While cooking, skim off any surface scum or fat. To test for doneness, insert a chopstick into the thickest part of the meat; it should slide in and out easily. Reserve 2 cups of stock for the dipping sauce. Plunge the pork into ice-cold water so it won't continue to cook. When cool enough to handle, slice the pork thinly.

Fill a large, flat plate with hot water, slide wrapper through the water, and place it on a large dinner plate with the shiny side down.

Fold the wrapper into the center on each side, and place mint, lettuce, vermicelli, and pork on the near end of the wrapper; the amounts will depend on how thick you want the rolls.

Roll the wrapper up tightly three or four times away from you, add 2 shrimp end to end and 1 stalk of garlic grass, and finish rolling the wrapper up tightly. Set aside, and repeat the procedure until all wrappers are used up.

To serve, offer 2 rolls per person with the Dipping Sauce.
Makes 24 rolls.

Dipping Sauce
2 cups pork stock
5 tablespoons hoisin sauce
2 tablespoons creamy peanut butter
1 tablespoon Vietnamese rock sugar
2 teaspoons crushed roasted peanuts

Put the stock in a pot, and cook over medium heat, bringing it to a boil. Make a paste with the hoisin sauce and peanut butter. Add the paste to the stock, and keep stirring until thoroughly mixed. Remove the sauce from the stove, and put it in bowls. Top with crushed peanuts.

David Quang's Caramel Pork

Born to Chinese parents in Saigon, David Quang grew up in Saigon's Chinatown, and remembers that the line between Chinese and Viet-namese cooking often blurs. His grandmother lived with them, providing them her maid who also cooked. Nevertheless, Quang's mother, even though she did not have to cook daily meals, was famous for her *nuoc mam*, the traditional Vietnamese fish sauce and also a fish-sauce-based seasoning.

Rice paddies.
Kwang-Yen Hsu Fine

Even today Quang makes this dish often for his family, just the way he remembers it from his childhood, when families made pots of this dish to use for more than one day's meals. Then cooks used fresh young coconut juice, but you may use canned coconut milk; this will give the finished dish a totally different taste and texture. Serve this with steamed rice and sliced cucumbers and Vietnamese pickles and bean sprouts pickled in a mixture of vinegar, salt, pepper, and sugar. Look for coconut juice in the frozen foods section of your Asian market; some stores also stock it canned.

1 pound meaty pork belly or bacon, cut into 1x2-inch pieces
dark soy sauce for marinade
2 tablespoons vegetable oil
2 tablespoons crushed garlic
1 cup coconut water
2 tablespoons *nuoc mam*

Marinate the pork strips in dark soy sauce to cover for about 1 hour. Drain.

Heat the oil in a large wok over medium heat, and stir-fry the garlic for about 30 seconds; remove from the oil. Add the pork, a few pieces at a time, and stir-fry for about 10 minutes, or until the pork is browned; repeat until all pieces are browned and crunchy. Pour off excess fat. Add the coconut water, *nuoc mam*, garlic, and cooked meat, and continue cooking until the mixture boils. Reduce the heat to medium-low, and cook for 30 to 40 minutes, or until tender.

Serves 4.

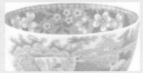

Wales

- CREAM OF LEEK SOUP (CAWL CENNIN A HUFEN)

- CHEPSTOW ONION PIE

- WELSH SALTED DUCK (MWYADEN HALLT GYMREIG)

- WELSH CURRANT TEABREAD (BARA BRITH)

*W*ales is a land of music, literature, and myths—tales of King Arthur, Merlin, Lancelot, haunted castles, and battles between dragons are captivating legends of honor and glory. In this small western peninsula of almost three million people, Wales boasts the second highest mountain and waterfall (second only to Scotland). When you cross the border from England there is a sign—*Croesco I Gymru* (Welcome to Wales)—you are now in *Gwlad hud a lledrith* (the land of magic and enchantment). While many Gaelic languages are dying, the Welsh language is not only alive but also growing. Visitors are often surprised to see and hear Gaelic everywhere, from roadway signs to the speech heard in many pubs, shops, and villages, especially in the north and west of Wales.

Another distinguishing feature of Wales is the cuisine. Like many other countries, the locals are rediscovering their native dishes. In Wales, many of the dishes evolved from the diet of coal miners, farmers, and fishermen who needed hearty dishes to sustain them in their hard and difficult work. Now that many restaurants are promoting this peasant fare on their menus, the result is a boost in production

A Welsh cottage near Chepstow.
Anne Parsons

of local foods. The rapid growth in food festivals and farmers' markets across the country has closed the gap between food producers and consumers resulting in a demand for local seasonal produce. A particular delicacy in Wales is the saltmarsh lamb; although it has been around forever, the demand for this rare treat has recently become very high. The Welsh Black breed is one of the most primitive in Europe; rearing of this cattle helps maintain the ecological balance of the Welsh countryside while providing consumers with outstanding flavorful beef. Most of all, we must not forget the Welsh tradition of ending dinner with a cheese board piled up with local artisanal cheeses. In particular, is the famous-for-hundreds-of-years Caerphilly cheese from the town of the same name.

Cream of Leek Soup
CAWL CENNIN A HUFEN

The Flenleys of Chepstow say their ancestors probably lived in Wales when St. David (the patron saint of Wales) was born in Pembrokeshire in the middle of the sixth century. One of their three children, Helen, has worked in Bosnia, the Falkland Islands, Washington, D.C., and Germany, but she is always anxious to get home to Wales and to her mum's comfort food. As a vegetarian, Mrs. Flenley draws heavily on spices and herbs to achieve a balance in the simple family fare she prepares for her family. She hopes that her children and grandchildren will continue to use these family recipes.

Hint: Because the leek is the national emblem of Wales, it is not surprising that leeks appear in many Welsh dishes. But many people resist using leeks because they seem difficult to rinse clean. The best way to rinse a leek thoroughly is this: trim all but one inch of the green part of the leek, insert the point of a knife at the root end of the white part of the stalk, and cut along its length to the top of the leftover green. Turn the leek a quarter of the way around, and repeat to make a cross. Hold the leek by the root end, and plunge it into a bowl of cold water, swishing it around. This removes the sand.

3 tablespoons unsalted butter
3 large leeks, washed and sliced
1 celery root or celeriac, trimmed and sliced
8 cups chicken stock
3 tablespoons minced parsley
3 ounces cooked chicken, diced
salt to taste
freshly ground black pepper to taste
1 cup heavy cream
sippets (bread cubes) for garnish

Heat the butter in a large, heavy saucepan over medium heat, and sauté the leeks and celery until the leeks are tender, about 10 minutes.

Add the stock, increase the heat, and bring it to a boil. Reduce the heat to low, and cook for about 1 hour.

Put the leeks and celery into a blender, and puree them until smooth. Return the mixture to the saucepan, and add the parsley and chicken. Season with the salt and pepper. Stir in the cream, and reheat the soup over medium heat; do not let it boil.

Chepstow High Street.
Patricia Fernon

Serve with *sippets* in the soup as garnish or on the side.
Serves 6.

Chepstow Onion Pie

Caerphilly, the cheese used in this pie, is an almost white, hard, crumbly cheese made from cow's milk, and originates near the town of the same name in Wales. When Patricia Fernon, of Chepstow, was serving in foreign countries, she'd often serve this family recipe to remind her of home.

Cheese, cheese, and more cheese at Slow Food's Salone del Gusto in Turin, Italy.
Anne Parsons

2 to 3 ounces fresh breadcrumbs, lightly crisped
3 large potatoes, peeled and thinly sliced
2 large onions, diced
8 tablespoons unsalted butter, plus extra for glazing the top
2 cloves garlic, mashed
3 ounces Caerphilly cheese, grated
salt to taste
freshly ground black pepper to taste
fresh herbs, such as oregano, thyme, and marjoram for garnish

Preheat the oven to 375°F. Butter a 1-quart baking dish, and sprinkle with the breadcrumbs, pressing them into the base and sides with a spoon.

Place a layer of potatoes on the bottom of the pan. Top them with a layer of onions, dot with butter, and sprinkle with some garlic, cheese, salt, and pepper. Repeat the layers, finishing with the potatoes on top. Melt the extra butter and brush the top of the pie.

Bake for 75 minutes, or until the potatoes are tender. Before serving, garnish with herbs.

Serves 6.

Welsh Salted Duck
Mwyaden Hallt Gymreig

In Wales, this dish is a traditional specialty, and, although it is extremely simple to make, many cooks fine-tune it by varying the herbs. According to Patricia Fernon, many of her Welsh compatriots boil the duck and let it simmer for two hours. When friends and family visit, Fernon prefers to roast the duck, after salting it for two days, and serve it with fresh vegetables and potatoes, or turnips, roasted in the duck fat.

Fernon says the process of salting the duck for a few days infuses it with a particular flavor that is really mouthwatering.

Salted Duck
1 (5-pound) organic duck
2 tablespoons rock or sea salt
1 shallot, finely chopped
2 teaspoons finely chopped thyme
2 teaspoons finely chopped sage
1 tablespoon finely chopped fennel
  bulb
watercress stems for garnish

White Onion Sauce
1 1/2 cups skim milk
1/2 cup organic cream
1 small onion, peeled
pinch nutmeg
1/4 cup (1/2 stick) unsalted butter
1/4 cup all-purpose flour
salt to taste
white pepper to taste

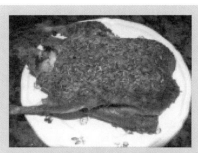

Duck straight from the oven.
Anne Parsons

To prepare the salted duck, wipe the duck inside and out with paper towels, rub all over with salt, place in a large bowl, and refrigerate for 2 to 3 days—remembering to turn the duck daily. Remove the duck from the refrigerator for 4 hours prior to cooking.

Preheat the oven to 425°F.

Dry the unchilled duck thoroughly. Season the inside of the duck with the shallot, and sprinkle all over the outside with thyme, sage, and fennel. Secure the legs, wings, and neck skin to the body.

Place the duck breast side up in a shallow roasting pan, just large enough to hold the duck, and cook in the middle of the oven for 15 minutes. Reduce the heat to 350°F. Turn the duck after 45 minutes, and cook for another 45 minutes.

Meanwhile, to make the white sauce, in a heavy saucepan heat the milk, cream, onion, and nutmeg over medium heat until it boils. Remove from the heat, and let sit for 15 minutes. Remove the onion from the sauce.

Melt the butter in the saucepan over low heat, and add the flour, mixing well with a wooden spoon to make a roux. Strain the milk into the roux, whisking well until thickened. Allow to cook for 4 minutes, stirring constantly. Season with the salt and pepper.

Remove the duck from the oven, and put the shallot and the onion in a blender, adding liquid as needed to help puree. Add the mixture to the hot sauce, cook for 5 minutes and strain into a sauceboat.

Cut the duck into portions, garnish with watercress, and serve it with the sauce on the side.

Serves 4.

Welsh Currant Teabread
BARA BRITH

Rosemary Anstey, a farmer's daughter married to a farmer's son, works a cattle farm in Monmouthshire. Like the farm, food is a family affair; the meals include fresh ingredients prepared and seasoned according to old family recipes. As Anstey tells it, "Too often family recipes get lost because new generations of children think they're too ordinary, so I hope to save them. For example, I often serve this famous Welsh teabread (literally means 'speckled bread') for afternoon tea."

4 ounces dark raisins
4 ounces golden raisins
2 ounces candied peel
5 ounces light brown sugar
1 1/4 cups strong hot tea
4 teaspoons dried yeast
1 cup whole milk, warmed
3 ounces unsalted butter
3 cups plain flour
1 teaspoon salt
1 large egg, beaten

*Delicious bread for
afternoon tea.*
Anne Parsons

Put the dark and golden raisins, candied peel, and sugar into a bowl. Pour the tea over top, and set aside, covered, overnight.

Preheat the oven to 375°F. Butter a 2-pound loaf pan.

Mix the yeast with the warm milk. Rub the butter into the flour and salt. Add the yeast and the egg to the flour mixture. Mix to a soft dough, knead well, and let rise in a warm place for 1 1/2 hours. Knead in the *drained* fruit and sugar. Pour into the loaf pan, *level* the surface, and let rise for 30 minutes.

Bake for 50 minutes, and cover top with foil during the last 15 minutes. Cool on a wire rack. To serve, slice thinly and *slather* with butter. Store in an airtight tin.

Makes a 2-pound loaf.

ADD YOUR OWN KITCHEN MEMORIES

First we eat, then we do everything else.
> —M.F.K. Fisher, author of *The Art of Eating*

Saving recipes, food anecdotes, photos, and stories about family get-togethers—kitchen memories—makes a precious gift for future generations, much like composing a family album brimming with snapshots and jotted notes. The following pages give you the chance to preserve your kitchen favorites by writing down your happy memories of shared meals, of favorite recipes, and of family members gathering in the kitchen to cook.

As you write, memories will likely spill forth and awaken other happy recollections. Best of all, by logging your thoughts and recording your family's best recipes, you can hand to future generations a treasured piece of family history, a gift that not only preserves traditions but also brings them to life. What a great legacy for children and grandchildren!

GLOSSARY

Amchor: Also known as *amchoor* or *amchur*, this product comes from grinding dried unripe mangoes to a fine powder; it adds an astringent sourness to many Indian dishes. Look for this in Indian markets.

Ashet (assiette): deep dish

Banana leaves: Many Asians wrap their foods prior to cooking in the large, pliable, and aromatic leaves of the banana plant. Most Asian stores sell frozen banana leaves; thaw and soften them before use by dipping them in very hot water. Wipe off any white spots.

Barberry: The edible berry of a perennial shrub, the barberry is bright red, somewhat acidic, and often used in condiments or in pies.

Cazuela: Earthenware cooking pot used extensively in Spanish cooking.

Collops: Another word for escallopes or scallops.

Galangal: This fragrant rhizome with its citrusy taste is an important seasoning for many Southeast Asian cooks.

Ginko nuts: The slightly bitter nuts from the maidenhair tree, ginkos are popular for use in many Japanese and Korean dishes, and may also be eaten as a snack.

Girdle: griddle or skillet

Kaffir limes: The leaves and rind of this Southeast Asian citrus tree are critical to the success of many traditional Thai dishes. The leaves are readily available frozen at Asian markets.

Knead: A technique used to mix and work dough. Kneading allows the gluten to stretch and expand so the dough holds the gas bubbles formed by the leavener. To knead, one uses the heels of the hand to press, turn, and fold the dough. Usual manual kneading takes about 15 minutes, depending on the dough, to make it smooth and elastic.

Lemongrass: Stalks of a grass used in many Southeast Asian cookpots, lemongrass imparts a delicate citrusy fragrance and flavor; it's best fresh, but is readily available frozen at Asian markets. Pound the thick stem ends to release its juices before slicing. Western lemons are not a substitute.

Mahlab: The ground kernel from a type of cherry, mahlab imparts a slightly bitter taste that enhances baked goods and pastries from Middle Eastern kitchens.

Orange flower water: Distilled from bitter-orange blossoms, this essence is popular in Western, European, and Middle Eastern kitchens as a flavor boost in savory dishes and baked goods.

Palm sugar: Palm sugar comes from the juice of either the palmyra or the sugar palm, and in many Asian countries, is a key sweetener. It is sold either as a thick paste or dried and shaped into discs or balls. To use the solid sugar, break off chunks and let it eventually dissolve, or crush the chunks into pieces.

Phyllo Dough: Paper-thin pastry dough used often in Greek and Middle Eastern recipes. Readily available in most supermarkets in the frozen foods sections. Follow package directions. Also spelled filo.

Quince: A yellow, applelike fruit from an Asian shrub, the quince has its place in Mediterranean and Asian kitchens, where it is treasured for its tart taste and high pectin content. Available in Western markets during the fall, the quince can be stored in the refrigerator for up to two months.

Rhizome: Also known as lesser galangal, this fingerlike cluster of roots is prized for its delicate gingery flavor and used in many Southeast Asian seafood dishes. It is available frozen in Asian markets.

Rice: Rice comes in a seemingly infinite variety, but the most common types include the fragrant long-grain Indian basmati rice; the equally fragrant long-grain Thai jasmine rice; long-grain polished white rice; short-grain white and brown rice with a high starch content favored by many Asian cooks; and the long-grain opaque sticky, or "sweet," rice favored by many Southeast Asians and which requires steaming over hot water because of its sticky quality. In much of the world, rice is eaten daily, often with every meal, so it is not surprising that many cultures have developed their own special way with rice. For example, the Persians have a complicated cooking and steaming process (see the "Iran" chapter for specific instructions) that produces a feathery cooked grain that seems to float.

Tamarind: Probably a native of Africa, the tamarind tree grows plentifully in tropical climates, and it has developed its culinary fans: the pods yield a pulpy fruit, which, when soaked in warm water to loosen the pulp from the seeds, yields a sweet-tart juice that Indians and Asian alike use in drinks, desserts, and curries, plus numerous other ways. Sold commercially as a slab needing soaking or as a concentrate needing diluting, tamarind is readily available in Asian and Indian markets. In season, tamarind pods are often sold fresh.

Turmeric: A relative of the ginger family, the turmeric tuber is an essential seasoning ingredient when dried and ground to a powder. Its brilliant yellow adds a distinctive color to curries and other dishes. Besides its use as a seasoning agent, turmeric is also valued for its medicinal properties.

Where to Shop Online

Asia Food: http://www.asiafood.org/
Asian Food Grocer: http://www.asianfoodgrocer.com/
The Cooking Post: www.cookingpost.com
Dean & Deluca: www.deananddeluca.com
Grocery Thai: http://grocerythai.com
Herbie's Spice: http://ozevillage.com.au/herbies/store/index.asp?product_
    id=215
Hoo Hing: http://www.hoohing.com/
Igourmet: http://www.igourmet.com/greekfood.asp
Indira: http://www.indirafood.com
iShopIndian: http://ishopindian.com/shop/
Jagaja: http://www.jagajagamall.com
Kalustyan's: www.kalustyans.com
Katagiri & Co., Inc.: www.katagiri.com
Little Armenia: http://www.littlearmenia.com/html/shop/food/
Mexican Foods: http://www.onlymexicanfoods.com
Penzeys Spices: www.penzeys.com
Rafal Spice Company: www.rafalspicecompany.com
Temple of Thai: http://www.templeofthai.com/
Thai Supermarket Online: http://importfood.com/
Whole Foods Market: www.wholefoods.com
Williams-Sonoma: www.williamssonoma.com

BIBLIOGRAPHY

GENERAL

Brillat-Savarin, John Anthelme. *Physiologue du Gout: Ou Meditations de Gastronomie Transcendante.* Paris, France: Sauteler et Cie, 1826.

Civitello, Linda. *Cuisine and Culture: A History of Food and People.* New Jersey: John Wiley & Sons, Inc., 2004.

Greeley, Alexandra. *Asian Grills.* New York, NY: Doubleday, 1993.

Greeley, Alexandra. *Asian Soups, Stew & Curries.* New York, NY: Macmillan, 1998.

Herbst, Sharon Tyler. *The New Food Lover's Companion.* 2nd ed. Hauppauge, NY: Barron's Educational Series, Inc., 1995.

Lo, Kenneth. *The Encyclopedia of Chinese Cooking.* New York, NY: Galahad Books, 1992.

Passmore, Jacki. *The Encyclopedia of Asian Food and Cooking.* New York, NY: Hearst Books, 1991.

Tannahill, Reay. *Food in History.* New York, NY: Three Rivers Press, 1989.

ARGENTINA

Eating the Argentinean Way: http://www.argentour.com/gente/food.html

A Guide to Argentinean Food for Visitors: La Falda: http://www.lafalda.com/food.htm

Global Destinations: http://www.globalgourmet.com/destinations/argentina/

Vazquez-Prego, Alberto. *Asi Cocinan los Argentinos* (*How Argentina Cooks*). Buenos Aires, Argentina: Editorial El Ateneo, 1979.

ARMENIA

Armenian Food: Fact, Fiction & Folklore: http://www.lulu.com/Armenia

European Centre for Modern Languages: http://www.ecml.at/html/armenian/html/traditions.html

The Detroit Women's Chapter of the Armenian General Benevolent Union. *Treasured Armenian Recipes*. New York, NY, 1949.

AUSTRIA

Epicurious: http://www.epicurious.com/features/going_global/austrian/intro

BOLIVIA

Bolivia Web: http://boliviaweb.com/

CAMBODIA

Asia Food: http://www.asiafood.org/elephantwalk.cfm

De Monteiro, Longtiene and Katherine Neustadt. *The Elephant Walk*

Cookbook. New York, NY: Houghton Mifflin Co., 1998.

CANADA

Virtual Villagers: http://frenchfood.about.com/od/frenchcanadian/French_Canadian_Cuisine_and_recipes.htm

CHINA

CCTV.com—Your Window on China and the World: http://www.cctv.com/english/TouchChina/ChineseCooking/History/20020512/100059.html

ENGLAND

English Heritage: http://www.english-heritage.org.uk/

The Internet Gateway to Yorkshire: http://www.yorkshirenet.co.uk/

FRANCE

Briard, Jacques. *The Megaliths of Brittany*. Luçon, France: Pollina, 1997.

Child, Julia, and Alex Prud'homme. *My Life in France*. New York, NY: Knopf, 2006.

Diner's Digest: http://www.cuisinenet.com/glossary/france.html

GREECE

About: Greek Food: http://greekfood.about.com/od/questionsanswers/f/ancientfood.htm

Cooking and Food: http://www.cooking-and-food.com/international-recipes/greek-cooking.php

About: Greek Food: http://greekfood.about.com/od/discovergreekfood/a/food_intro.htm

Sally's Place: http://www.sallys-place.com/food/ethnic_cusine/greece.htm

IRAN

Iranian Culture Information Center: http://persia.org/

IRELAND

The Quotations Page: http://en.wikipedia.org/wiki/Irish_cuisine

ITALY

Bianchi, Anne. *Italian Festival Food: Recipes and Traditions from Italy's Regional Country Food Fairs.* New York, NY: Macmillan, Inc., 1999.

JAPAN

Ask.com: http://www.japan-guide.com/e/e2035.html

Diner's Digest: http://www.cuisinenet.com/glossary/japan.html

MEXICO

MEXonline.com: http://www.mexonline.com/mexfood.htm

Sally's Place: http://www.sallys-place.com/food/ethnic_cusine/mexico.htm

Mexican Cuisine: mexico.udg.mx/cocina/ingles/ingles.html

MOROCCO

History of Morocco: http://www.mincom.gov.ma/english/generalities/history/history.html

POLAND

Poland-Online Info-Center: http://www.polandonline.com/

SCANDINAVIA/ICELAND

Wikipedia: The Free Encyclopedia: http://en.wikipedia.org/wiki/Scandinavia

SCOTLAND

Herman, Arthur. *How the Scots Invented the Modern World: The True Story of How Western Europe's Poorest Nation Created Our World and Everything in It.* New York, NY: Three Rivers Press, 2001.

McNeill, F. Marian. *The Scots Kitchen: Its Traditions and Lore with Old-Time Recipes.* Edinburgh, Scotland: Mercat Press, 2004.

SPAIN

Si, Spain: http://www.sispain.org/english/index.html

U.S.A.

Wertz Candies—Opera Fudge: http://www.wertzcandy.com/opera.asp

Food Timeline: Candy History Notes: www.foodtimeline.org/foodcandy.html

WALES

Whittle, Elisabeth. *A Guide to Ancient and Historic Wales: Glamorgan and Gwent.* London, England: HMSO, 1992.

European Commission: Agriculture and Food: http://ec.europa.eu/agriculture/foodqual/quali1_en.htm

RECIPE INDEX

About the Authors

Alexandra Greeley is the former food editor of *Vegetarian Times* and a well-established Washington, D.C., area food journalist and restaurant critic. Her work has been featured in *Gastronomica*, Gayot.com, *D.C. Examiner, Fine Cooking, Chili Pepper, On The Grill*, the *New York Times, Long Island Life*, the *Washington Post, Washingtonian* magazine, and *Newsday*. In addition to coauthoring the recent *Vegetarian Times Complete Cookbook*, she is the author of *Asian Soups, Stews & Curries; Asian Grills;* and *Good Enough to Eat*. She has written several mini Asian cookbooks for Periplus publishers in Singapore, written text and edited the recipes for a book/CD package entitled *Mexico!*, was a staff writer for Time-Life's cookbook series, *Great Meals in Minutes*, and was the food editor/writer for the *South China Morning Post* in Hong Kong. Ms. Greeley is a member of the culinary groups Les Dames d'Escoffier and the International Association of Culinary Professionals and is the co-leader of Slow Food Washington, D.C. She lives in Reston, Virginia.

Alexandra Greeley
Margo Moser

Anne Snape Parsons grew up in a large, close-knit family in Bothwellpark, Scotland. While literature and cultural pursuits were important, the core of her family's activities was food—food as the binding power in family and friendships, food as the intersection between generations, and food as the bridge between cultures.

Insatiably curious about traditions and cultures, Ms. Parsons has traveled extensively around the globe. During her trips, she spends most of her time with local people, eats regional foods, and visits their places of worship. Ms. Parsons has an MA in English Literature, is currently writing two cookbooks—*Seashore Suppers: Edible Reading from the Barefoot Book Clubs of the OBX* and *Cooking, Conversation, and Conviviality: A Year of Slow Eating Events*—and is researching material for a civil war journal. Ms. Parsons is the leader of the Slow Food Convivium of East North Carolina and a member of the International Association of Culinary Professionals and the Culinary Historians of Washington. She also writes travel articles and a monthly food column for *Tidewater Women* called "Around the Table," and food and people articles for the *North Beach Sun.*

Anne Snape Parsons
Brooke Mayo